TRANSNATIONAL BUSINESS AND CORPORATE CULTURE

Problems and Opportunities

edited by
STUART BRUCHEY
Allan Nevins Professor Emeritus
Columbia University

COPYRIGHT LAW AND COMPUTER PROGRAMS

The Role of Communication in Legal Structure

JISUK WOO

Routledge
Taylor & Francis Group
LONDON AND NEW YORK

First published 2000 by Garland Publishing, Inc.

2 Park Square, Milton Park, Abingdon, Oxon OX14 4RN
711 Third Avenue, New York, NY 10017, USA

Routledge is an imprint of the Taylor & Francis Group, an informa business

First issued in paperback 2016

Library of Congress Cataloging-in-Publication Data

Woo, Jisuk.
Copyright law and computer programs : the role of communication in legal structure / Jisuk Woo.
p. cm. — (Transnational business and culture)
Includes bibliographical references and index.
ISBN 0-8153-3471-0 (alk. paper)
1. Copyright—Computer programs—United States. 2. Copyright—Computer programs—Social aspects. 3. Copyright—Computer programs—Language. I. Title. II. Title: And computer programs. III. Series.

KF3024.C6 W66 1999
346.7304'82 21 —dc21

99-045885

ISBN 978-0-8153-3471-2 (hbk)
ISBN 978-1-138-96675-8 (pbk)

To my best friend and husband, Jae-Hyup

Contents

Part III Process of Structuration in Copyright Cases

Foreword

GENTLY, GENTLY, CATCH THE MONKEY. RUSH, AND CATCH THE AIR

Gently, gently, catch the monkey, is an admonition popular among the Wolof people of Senegal. The wisdom at the heart of this warning often escapes the researcher/theorist anxious to declare an early victory and claim the prize. As scholars and policymakers we ought not rush to judgement, if by our movement we scatter the clues that we might have put to good use had we taken a slower, more cautious route.

Critical observers of technological change have assumed that the nature of power and influence was so well known that its nature could be observed in every place and at any time. Size is equated with strength, yet, as with the monkey, in some spheres, it is quickness and speed that matter. Others, with mainstream economists in the lead, deny the existence of power in any form. They grant a mystical inherency to both markets and courts which they assume are continuously adjusted by an invisible, but beneficent hand. They assume the monkey will come to them if they wait long enough.

Jisuk Woo treads gently, but with determination through the tangles, webs, and snares that are the matted underbrush of intellectual property law. She is in pursuit of the relations between action and structure that shape the development of technology, markets, and the cultures of legitimate use. Intellectual property law has developed in such an apparently haphazard fashion because of the special nature of information. As a product of labor, a productive resource, and an intangible possession of great potential value, information confounds the rule of the market, and respects neither size nor speed. The difficulties involved in establishing and protecting rights and interests in information are multiplied in the case of computer software.

Modern economic theory recognizes the role of strategic actions taken in pursuit of private interests. Often these actions are anticompetitive in their impact as well as in their design. Competitors in search of market power dart back and forth between the barriers and vantage points afforded by copyright, patent, or trade secret regimes. A naive idealist model would argue that a natural, but ultimately efficient process guides the development of law and practice in these three related spheres. A more realistic strategic model would argue that each is shaped by the exercise of power. The challenge is to identify the variety of ways in which the exercise of power has shaped the laws, that influence the development of computer software.

Power shapes the law through both legislative and judicial paths. Critical observers have traditionally focused their attention on the ways in which policy actors, referred to as "special interests," have shaped the market through their influence on legislators. Policy scholars have largely ignored the ways in which these special interests shape the market through their activity within the courts. Jisuk Woo's study of the development of copyright law is among the first to apply the tools of critical social theory to decisionmaking within the courts.

Informed by Anthony Giddens's theory of structuration, Woo's analysis gives due consideration to the traditional characterization of actors in terms of their financial and material resources. Yet, her analysis reveals that it is their status as authors that represents the most important resource. This is a status that is realized almost entirely through rhetorical claims. Woo's analysis of legal arguments within the context of structural rules represents an important milestone in the application of social science methods to the study of legal procedure. Traditional legal scholarship, driven by the desire to make a case, rather than to find a path, calls our attention selectively to arguments that are consistent with a prior theory. Woo examines all the arguments that justify inclusion in the extended report of judicial action. It is this expanded scope of the social scientist's gaze, which includes characterizations and assessments of petitioner, defendant, and jurist, that allow Woo to determine which factors are most important in determining the outcome of individual cases, and through precedent, the cases which follow.

After reminding us that the rationale for copyright and other intellectual property regimes has historically presented the interests of authors as being derived from the more fundamental concerns about benefits to users, and to society more generally, Dr. Woo observes that the interests of users has been consistently marginalized because neither users, nor their advocates are participants in these cases.

As her former advisor, I am of course pleased to see that Dr. Woo has succeeded so admirably in revealing the nature of the changing relations of power and influence within this critical domain. I am confident that her approach will be applied carefully, and with great reward by scholars and policy makers in other areas of public policy.

January, 1999
Oscar H. Gandy, Jr.
Professor of Communication
Annenberg School for Communication
University of Pennsylvania

Preface

This book is about the relationships and struggles of the judicial parties that are actually manifested through communication, and the strategic communication of the parties that influences the structural environment of copyright law. It is a product of my endeavor over six years to explore the territory between law and communication and of my attempt to understand communication in law and law in communication through an interdisciplinary approach.

This book began as a doctoral dissertation. When I was looking for a topic for my research in 1992, I had only a vague idea that it would be somehow related to copyright policy in which I had taken an interest for quite a while. Regarding the specific area in copyright I chose computer software programs as my advisor Oscar Gandy suggested, because computer programs raise various difficult questions regarding copyright and examining the areas where clashes occur always helps to understand its fundamentals. But a difficulty arose when I decided to study copyright "law," especially case law as a crystalized form of copyright policy, which has great influence on future activities of stakeholders. How to approach the study of law as a social scientist was the difficult question I set out to answer. I realized that traditional methods in the field of communication that are used for news content analysis, media effects analysis, and policy analysis would certainly help, but they could not be used without a theoretical framework more suited to the analysis of law.

Reviewing the relevant legal literature added more confusion. Previous studies mostly considered law to be objective and neutral, and even those that took social structures and actors into account focused on economic and political factors. This book greatly benefited from critical legal movements that developed proliferating new discourses defined by economic analysis, critical legal studies, feminism, literature, race consciousness and postmodernism, which suggested different types of theoretical tools. But it was hard to imagine that adopting such "legal" research for my dissertation would yield informative and useful results in the field of social science, let alone would fulfill the requirements of the doctoral degree at the Annenberg School for Communication. Greater challenge lied in finding methodological assistance in terms of how to undertake empirical and systematic research. This meant that I had to devise an approach that had not been employed yet, but would provide more insight and understanding of law, or the legal process.

So the journey began. I examined social theories in an effort to find an appropriate framework to analyze case law and capture the dynamics of the decision-making process. Many theories have helped, but the theory of structuration by Anthony Giddens was the most helpful in formulating the theoretical underpinnings of this book for the reasons that will be discussed in the second and third chapters. This study is the first to apply the theory of structuration to analyze law empirically. For analytic and methodological refinement of the theory, I relied on news discourse analysis and other approaches developed in the field of communication.

But the challenge did not stop there. The more I read the court cases and applied the framework to the data, the more I felt uncertain about the results of my analysis and the conclusions I tried to draw from them. I consulted with a law professor and she provided me with many valuable insights, but it was clear that we had different views as to which areas are the significant areas requiring study. Moreover, it seemed that those in the two fields of study use different language and dialogue between the two is not only rather uncommon but also limited. This made me confused about the significance of this study itself, the so-called social scientific approach to the law. It was disturbing to realize that those who are in the tradition of law may not find this study understandable. I was also afraid that the possible lack of the understanding and appreciation of the study may not so much result from the different views on the same subject but from simple misunderstanding of the law or legal process on my part. It also made me recall one incident at a conference where a communication scholar was presenting a paper about some media-related law issue and there was a lawyer who spoke that he simply did not think that it was the "correct" reading of the case. It is the tendency of communication scholars to generally oppose the existence of any correct reading of a text, but still, I thought it would be necessary to at least understand what is the "correct" reading from the perspective of lawyers and legal scholars before being able to suggest any "alternative" reading.

Thus another journey of three years at law school began, to obtain some internal perspective. I had almost finished the dissertation when I started my first classes of torts and contracts in 1994. The analysis was completed, but I had left the writing of it until after the first year of law school ended, when I thought I would have a basic understanding of legal procedures and basic legal subjects. I completed writing the analysis part during the summer after the first year, and defended the dissertation in the fall. One year spent at law school did not make me a legal expert, but it certainly made me understand the procedural issues better and helped me become more familiar with legal terms. It also made me more confidant about the results of my analysis. If any lawyer or legal scholar challenges me, I thought, I would at least know what he or she is talking about.

Then I continued my study at law school, taking more classes in intellectual property law and information law. As is always said, law school education aspires to be not about teaching the law but about teaching "how to think like a lawyer." I spent more time at law school reading case laws and legal papers, and serving as a law clerk during summers. Whether this endeavor made me think like a lawyer, although it was my intention to have expertise in communications law or media law as a scholar not as a lawyer, may be reflected in this study, and remains to be seen. I came back to Korea in 1997 and have been doing research in the area of information/communication law and policy. It is in this process of a long journey of exploration this book has been written.

This book is a product of my attempt to see whether an interdisciplinary study integrating legal and social scientific approaches would yield fruitful understanding of the copyright law as a system. This attempt seems to have generated more challenges than accomplishments and raised more questions than answers. But it is my hope that this process of exploration, as well as my personal grapples in the fields of communication and law, is present in this study.

Acknowledgments

This book would not have existed without the support and assistance of numerous individuals. My training in the Department of Mass Communication at Yonsei University, at the Annenberg School for Communication at the University of Pennsylvania, and at the New York University School of Law provided me with the necessary intellectual foundation to carry out this research. Special thanks are due to Yonsei Professors Joung-Ho Choi, Joung-Woo Suh, In-Hwan Oh, Heong-Soo Park, Young-Suk Kim, and Sang-Hyun Kang who introduced me to the field of communication theories and information policy. At Annenberg, my advisor Oscar Gandy, Jr., supervised my dissertation from its inception, encouraged its interdisciplinary approach, and contributed many hours to the consideration of the issues presented there. I feel truly honored that such an innovative scholar of social theories and empirical studies in information technology has written the foreword for this book. Professor Zhongdan Pan was my teacher, mentor, and friend who believed in me even when I found it difficult to believe in myself. His constant encouragement, warmth, and humor have made the process of writing the dissertation and my life at Annenberg an enjoyable one. Professor George Gerbner participated in my intellectual development since my first days at Annenberg, and showed me how to be a challenging scholar and an ardent social activist who truly cares. I am also grateful to Professor Paul Messaris, my master's thesis advisor, whose perspective and encouragement were invaluable to me since my earliest courses at Annenberg. Professors Klaus Krippendorff, Charles Wright, Kathleen Jamieson, and Joseph Cappella also contributed to my intellectual growth with their perceptive guidance. At NYU, Professors Amy Adler, Yochai Benkler, and Diane Zimmerman helped broaden my perspective and develop legal mind.

The most significant personal outcome of this book has been the dear friends I have met. Interactions with fellow students at Annenberg were some of the most rewarding parts of my academic life. Through the years, Renee Wilcoxen, Kelly D'Apice, Yoshimi Nishino, Wendy Mansfield, Fatos Goksen, Shinichi Saito, Kent Goshorn, Pamela Inglesby, Bernadette Barker-Plummer and Eleanor Novek have been good friends who have helped me through and enriched my studies immeasurably. June Woong Rhee provided essential feedback and support for the development of this work. I also want to express my heartfelt appreciation to Annenberg security guards Captain James Rush, Kevin Lynch, and Frank Zinz for their support. Knowing that they were there, literally watching me go through all the ups and downs of the process, helped me remain sane during some of my darker moments. I'll always keep in mind their advice, "Stop running, Jisuk. Walk sometimes." Jun Han and many others helped me with gathering data for this research and the process of analysis. My thanks to all of them for their ideas, praise, criticism, commiseration, and friendship.

I was fortunate to have friends who gave me support in the last and most difficult stage of writing the dissertation while I was in law school. John Kim and many friends at NYU School of Law gave me constant encouragement to keep working on the project, with gentle reminders that the discipline of dissertation writing requires time in the library instead of in the streets of Village. I am most grateful for my dear friend Cecily Redhead whose enthusiasm for my dissertation sometimes surpassed my own. Thanks to her genuine friendship, the process of finishing the dissertation was filled with joy and laughter.

I am indebted to the reviewers and editors at Garland Publishing Inc., who provided thoughtful suggestions and expertise as I began the task of revision for publication. In particular, without Mr. Demon Zucca's reminders, the manuscript might still be sitting on my desk waiting to be finished. Many colleagues and friends at the Korea Information Society Development Institute helped me during the tense period of completing the final manuscript. My special thanks go to Kiho Yoon, Hun-Yeong Kwon, and Junmo Kang who shared interests in my work and provided constant emotional support. I also thank Professor Alec Gordon of the Hankuk University of Foreign Studies for his helpful comments.

Respectful appreciation is devoted to my parents Sung-Joo Woo and Yong-Min Kim and brother Young-Jae Woo whose love and support during the long process of my study abroad far exceeded my hopes. My brother's comments as a computer programmer helped me broaden my understanding of the practical implications of this project.

I dedicate this book to my long-time friend Jae-Hyup Lee who has become my husband during the process of writing it. Since we first met at the University of Pennsylvania as graduate students, he has been a devoted and trusted friend whose endless help and generosity provided an environment in which I could concentrate on studying and writing the dissertation without being overwhelmed by the burdens and worries of everyday life. Even after we went to different law schools, I could always count on his encouragement and intellectual support. In every difficult moment of my life, his firm belief in me as a person and as a scholar has been a guiding light. It is hard to imagine having been able to write this book without his special kind of love and friendship.

Jisuk Woo
Seoul, Korea

COPYRIGHT LAW AND COMPUTER PROGRAMS

The Role of Communication in Legal Structure

CHAPTER 1

Introduction

This book examines how judicial actors such as plaintiffs, defendants, and judges interact through their strategic communication activities, and how these activities influence the structural environment of copyright law. The focus is to explore how the structure of copyright law is reproduced and transformed by the processes in which actors with different resources interact. This book emphasizes the role of communication, as manifested in the interactions of judicial actors, in legal decision making processes.

The study of copyright law with regards to computer programs has not only a theoretical significance for the study of law and communication, but also a serious practical implication. In a constantly changing, information-based society, copyright law that controls the flow of information and information technology has particular importance. The roots of copyright as a legal statute may be traced to the proliferation of the book trade in Europe, coinciding with the advent of the printing press in the early 15th century (Bettig, 1992; Patterson and Lindberg, 1991). Of course, the concept of copyright had already existed before, but more out of concerns about the moral and natural rights of the authors rather than because of legal or economic considerations. For example, although the rights of authors were recognized in Greek culture and plagiarism was considered to be morally wrong in Roman law, there was no evidence that legal sanctions existed (Ploman and Hamilton, 1980). During the Middle Ages as well, plagiarism and the wrongful or incorrect attribution to an author was subject to society's ridicule but not a law suit.

The proliferation of the book trade in England led to the first copyright statute in the modern legal sense, the Statute of Queen Anne,[1] which was the result of the efforts of publishers, authors, and the State to legitimate their concerns and interests (Bettig, 1989; Ploman and Hamilton, 1980). This Statute, which made it legal for any person, not only the authors and publishers, to acquire copyright, was the direct ancestor of American copyright law as it served as the model for the Copyright Act of 1790, the first U.S. Copyright Statute (Patterson and Lindberg, 1991, p. 47). The U.S. Copyright Act was amended in 1909 and most recently in 1976, and the Act states that "Copyright protection subsists ... in original works of authorship fixed in tangible medium of expression ..."[2] However, despite this relatively specific provision, conceptual and implementational questions still remain, for example, because of the difficulty in distinguishing between ideas and expression with respect to determining what is original and what is not. Only in the processes in which courts apply the provisions to particular incidents does the meaning of the texts of the provisions become realized. Therefore, these court cases become important precedents in interpreting the law and they have a significant influence not only on the dispute situation of the concerned cases but also on problems of later situations. In addition, while courts deal with particular incidents involving two disputed parties and do not necessarily consider the broader context of policy-making in an explicit way, the decisions concerning the copyright protection of computer programs have an indirect influence on the software industry and users. The ways in which legal decisions are made have significant policy implications because they provide rules and guidelines for those involved with the development, the distribution, and the use of computer software.

Copyright law is closely related to the development of information technology. Among the various technological developments that have generated substantial changes in human lives and relationships in almost all societies, computers are credited with

---

[1] It is also known as the 1710 Copyright Act, and its full title is "An Act for the Encouragement of Learning and for Securing the Property of Copies of Books to the Rightful Owners Thereof."

[2] 17 U.S.C. sec. 102(a).

having transformed the way information is created, processed, transmitted, and provided to individuals and institutions (Office of Technology Assessment, 1990). Computer programs have become a valuable resource for the functioning of an information-based economy and the means to increase the exchange of information. Questions as to what kind of rights are given to whom with regard to computer software have significant economic and social implications, since the access to software plays an important role in increasing the sharing of information, which is believed to be a fundamental prerequisite for scientific and social progress.

Some special characteristics of computer programs pose a remarkable challenge to the existing regimes of copyright law. Traditional distinctions between various stages in the creation cannot be maintained: these programs are both writings, descriptions, and processes (Office of Technology Assessment, 1986). A somewhat related problem is that while copyright law has traditionally protected "literary" works, the functional rather than expressive aspects of computer programs are often considered to be their essence. Problem also arises as to whether the visual displays and functions that appear as a result of executing a computer program should be considered a computer program as well, and if so, what should be the relationship between these displays and functions and the program as codes. In addition, many computer programs are the product of intellectual team-work. The development of software programs can be characteristically incremental and cumulative, as developers commonly adopt software design elements by consulting examples in other programs (Samuelson, et. al., 1994). In this complex production process, it is not easy to find the original author.

Acknowledging this difficulty, some scholars have conducted normative analyses of the kind of legal protection that would be socially desirable for computer software and how it might best be accomplished, and have suggested that a new system for protecting the software such as *a sui generis* approach is necessary (see Samuelson, et. al., 1994). But most scholars and commentators in the U.S. have argued that existing laws can and should be applied to computer programs. Consequently, the U.S. Copyright Act was amended in 1979 to include computer programs as the subject matter of protection, and now it has become common to protect computer programs by copyright law. Indeed, program developers tend to rely on copyright protection rather than patent or other laws partly because of the relative easiness of being copyrighted.

However, a literature review of this important area of software copyright reveals a lack of systematic studies and a gap between what has been assumed or believed and what has been actually studied. Although legal scholars and decision-makers have shown great concern and interest in applying copyright law to computer programs, most debates concentrating on the issues of how existing copyright law should and may be applied to programs have not provided insight into the relationship between copyright law and information technology. Legal studies that have examined relevant cases have tended to analyze in detail one or two important cases, thus they do not amount to a systematic study of the processes by which copyright decisions are made. A recent notable contribution stems from various interdisciplinary approaches of literary and legal critics who have tried to understand the underlying values and mechanisms in copyright law (see Woodmansee and Jaszi, 1994; Sherman and Strowel, 1994). Although these studies provide some insights into the elements of copyright law in relation to computer software, systematic studies on the processes of software copyright decision-making have been scarce. Studies that examine the mechanisms by which the copyright law with regards to computer software has been established and transformed are almost non-existent. Also the factors that influence the judges' decision-making regarding the software copyright law have not been systematically identified. This poses a serious problem in that various approaches to understanding the mechanisms by which software copyright law is shaped remain untested. Consequently, questions as to whether there has been change in the structure of copyright law in relation to the development of the new information technology, and if so, what was the main factor of the change, remain yet to be answered.

Thus, I analyze decisions and arguments of all the U.S. federal cases regarding the copyright protection of computer programs that were held between 1987 and 1993 in order to derive a conceptual framework that helps us capture the variety of factors shaping copyright law and the relationship between those factors. In this book I conceptualize copyright case law as a system, and explore how the structure of the system is reproduced and changed. This book also distinguishes itself from other approaches in that it conceptualizes the interactions among the judicial actors as the original focus of the mechanism, by which copyright law is established and transformed. Even some critical legal scholars that have paid attention to the judicial actors' interactions focused on the areas related to human rights such as gender, race, or religion, or antitrust areas, which are easily considered to be subject to political and social influences. Consequently, it remains to be explored whether their arguments and conclusions also apply to other areas of law such as economic or industry laws, especially those related to technological matters, which are often assumed to be more "neutral" areas of law. Thus, particular significance lies in examining computer software copyright law, which is often regarded as one of the areas that are least likely to be influenced by judicial actors' interactions and socio-political factors and most likely to be strictly subject to legal and statutory intepretations.

Study of the copyright rules and discourses regarding computer software in particular helps to understand the interactions among the actors and institutional rules also because the rules in this area are relatively less-grounded and are still evolving. The enacted law is constantly being reinterpreted by individual decisions made in the courts. The laws and practices of the copyright system, as those of any legal system, reflect the relationships among the stakeholders and the tensions among the interests and values that copyright law tries to protect. At the same time, the laws and practices also generate and reinforce these relationships and tensions. The underlying relationships and competing interests and values can be best understood by conceptualizing interactions between knowledgeable legal actors and institutions as the forces influencing the copyright decisions. The interactions of the actors in the legal decision-making processes are basically made through legal arguments. Thus interactions through communicative activities in particular become a crucial nexus providing an understanding of the decision-making process in this study. The focus of the book is on how different stakeholders with differing resources use the rules and resources in legal arguments, which influence the structuring of the information environment of the copyright system. How, in the process of actors' communicative interactions, the rules and resources themselves are reproduced and transformed is the main concern of this study. Examining copyright decisions and arguments pertaining to computer software should not only enhance our understanding of the role of strategic communication in legal decision-making processes but also should provide a context for evaluating these decisions.

The next chapter is an analysis of theoretical frameworks that help us to inquire into the processes by which the copyright law is shaped. The theoretical perspectives that are discussed include: Critical Legal Studies that emphasize the role of actors in legal processes; instrumentalist and structuralist theories that focus on influential factors on social reproduction and change; and the theory of structuration formulated by Anthony Giddens that reconciles the relationship between actors and structures. The conceptual framework used in this book is proposed at the end of this chapter.

In the third chapter, the conceptual framework proposed in the second chapter is applied to the copyright system of computer programs. The critical concepts of the framework are defined and discussed in relation to the copyright decision-making process. In order to derive useful frames to analyze legal arguments, this chapter examines some of the approaches which aim to understand the copyright principles and to recognize the social, political, and economic underpinnings that have contributed to the shaping of the copyright concept and system. The main research questions are proposed at the end of the chapter.

Chapter four describes the methods used in gathering data, instrumenting variables, and analyzing the data. The next three chapters present the results of the analyses. Chapter five offers descriptive analyses of the nature of cases and other variables. Chapter six analyses the relationships between the legal actors, issues, and court decisions. Chapter seven analyzes the legal actors' use of rules and resources as they are reflected in their legal arguments. The findings of these analyzses identify the ways in which structural rules of the copyright system are created, reproduced, and transformed.

Chapter 8 combines the analyzes presented in the previous three chapters to examine the interactions among the actors, their use of structural rules and resources, and the copyright decisions. The process of structuration in the copyright arguments and decisions is illustrated in this chapter. Also, the relationships, interests, and values that are reflected, generated, transformed, and reinforced in this process are discussed.

The final chapter discusses the theoretical and policy implications of the findings of the study presented in this book. It focuses on discussing the role of communication in the reproduction and transformation of legal structure.

Part I

Copyright System as Legal Structure

CHAPTER 2

Law as a Process of Structuration

Any study that examines a certain kind of law, copyright law in this case, presupposes a particular perspective or approach to law. This chapter sets out the theoretical underpinnings of the book. Traditional legal studies have tended not to be interested in the relationship between law and other dimensions in a society. Although law's potential or actual effects have been a source of concern for some sociological studies of law, the complexity of the relationship between law and other social phenomena is yet to be fully investigated. Concerned with unraveling this complexity as it is reflected in court decision-making processes, I attempt to explore the various strands of legal and social thought and studies with the aim of finding the most suitable approach to deal with copyright law in this book.

This chapter reviews the literature relating to five related themes. It starts with comparing different legal approaches to the legal decision-making process, with a special focus on the liberal legal formalism and critical legal studies (CLS). I will also describe different sociological approaches to the mechanism of power and the role of law in the mechanism. Then in order to discuss how social structures and social actors may play a role in the legal decision-making process, I will review social theories about social structure and actors, with a particular emphasis on the tension between the structuralist and the instrumentalist strands. Next I offer a detailed discussion of Giddens' theory of structuration, which attempts to reconcile this tension. Based on this theory I will propose the analytical framework used in this book. The importance of the aspect of communication, with respect to the legal arguments made by knowledgeable legal actors, is emphasized here. Finally discussed will be how the scheme of news discourse analysis drawn from the perspective of constructivism may help the examination of legal arguments.

APPROACHES TO LEGAL SYSTEMS AND LEGAL DECISION-MAKING PROCESS

There are various streams in the field of legal scholarship that characterize legal systems and legal decision making process. I will discuss two roughly broad streams: Liberal legal formalism, which dominates mainstream law and practice, and critical legal studies, which is a new current in contemporary legal theory. The doctrine of legal formalism posits that law is a body of intelligible and impersonal purposes, policies, and principles that form a "gapless" system of rules from which legal reasoning and subsequent decisions are derived (Unger, 1983, p. 1). These decisions are assumed to come after 'objective' hearings where evidence is presented according to certain rules, and thus 'truth' ultimately emerges. Influenced by the doctrine of objectivism, Liberal legal scholarship views law as an apolitical realm for the exercise of power relationships.

Liberal legal scholarship, therefore, is based on the belief that legal systems, decisions and arguments are natural, neutral, apolitical, rational and objective. Consequently, political, social, and economic factors which might influence the decision-making process, and the implications of the decisions have not received much attention by liberal legal scholars. In particular, legal decisions involving new technology such as computer programs are more easily argued and perceived to be "value-free," "technical" decisions.

The assumption that legal decisions and arguments are value-free or objective is problematic in many ways. Legal decisions are made by human beings who are inseparable from their social surroundings and cultural backgrounds. Also, legal arguments are made through language, which is created and used by humans in the context of the social and historical structures. In this context, language and procedures using language cannot be value-free, and legal arguments and decisions based on the language and the procedures are made within the social structure and value system.

This issue has been raised by scholars of critical legal studies. CLS scholars generally believe that any kind of human reality is socially constructed. The perspective of the social construction of reality posits that aspects of human social life such as "rights" are always socially constructed, contingent, and context-bound, instead of being natural or universal (Streeter, 1990, p. 4). CLS scholars point out that law is a form of human activity, a practice carried out by people (Olsen, 1990, p. 208). For example, the very fact of a judge's humanity brings ineradicable subjectivity to a legal system (Boyle, 1985, p. 692). According to CLS scholars, the activities of lawyers and judges are embedded in social structure, and not objective procedures that stand above social reality and power relations (Streeter, p. 4). In the same vein, Bettig (1989) analyzed the Betamax case on home recording rights and VCRs and found that the formal rules that judges are supposed to follow in reaching decisions in particular areas of litigation are biased toward the protection of private property. He points out that not only are the judges themselves biased toward the protection of private property rights, but so are the formal rules that they are required to apply (p. 190). However, the selection of particular rules and different interpretations of the rules were not examined in this study.

CLS scholars also argue that it is impossible to separate law from politics not only because of the judge's subjectivity, but also of the impossibility of constructing a set of rules that could be applied in a neutral or objective manner (Boyle, 1985, p. 692). They are also critical of the notion that law is principled, which is based upon the belief that law consists of a few rules and principles and that these general rules provide a principled basis for deciding individual cases (Olsen, 1990, p. 208). According to CLS scholars, law is actually made up of an agglomeration of specific rules and some general standards, and the rules are too specific, definite, and contextualized to count as principles, and the standards are too vague and indeterminate to decide cases (Olsen, 1990, pp. 208-209). Therefore, law is not abstract and principled but rather personalized and contextualized (Olsen, 1990, pp. 208-209).

This non-principled nature of law directly contradicts the assumption that, given a certain set of legal rules and a certain legally defined situation, a properly trained judge or lawyer, within certain boundaries, can use his or her expertise in legal language and reasoning to arrive at, or at least approximate, the correct interpretation (Streeter, 1990, p.46). CLS rejects this idealized model of law by stressing the inconsistency in the application of legal doctrine, evidenced by the wide range of choices and outcomes that are possible in any particular case.

This indeterminacy parallels the linguistic and literary premise that the meaning of words is not fixed by their referent, rather signs are arbitrary and conventional (Streeter, 1990, p. 47). Applied to the legal decision-making process, just as there is no immutable language standard or logic that determines the "correctness" of grammatical structures, there is no fixed, objective logic that can determine the correctness of a legal decision (Cohen, 1935; Streeter, 1990, p. 47). As legal modes of interpretation change over time, what was once considered a correct legal decision is now considered incorrect, and vice versa, it could be argued that law is fundamentally indeterminate (Streeter, 1990, p. 47). Hence the law enacted by the Congress is interpreted by the judiciary in individual cases and is constantly reinterpreted and redefined, and, it follows logically that different interpretations can be possibly made from a single law (Patterson and Lindberg, 1991, p. 3). Detailed textual analyses of laws and legal judgments conducted by CLS scholars show that opposite interpretations are equally valid within the logic of legal reasoning (Streeter, 1990, p. 46-47).

Accordingly, if legal decisions are closely interconnected with social structures and social actors' understandings and perceptions, it follows logically that attention should be given to the mechanisms through which the legal decisions may be influenced by social structures and actors. Although CLS has provided important insight, specific attempts or empirical studies to identify these mechanisms have been scarce. Now I review some theories and studies that have dealt with the role of law in the mechanism of power within the legal discipline.

SOCIOLOGICAL APPROACHES TO THE ROLE OF LAW IN THE MECHANISM OF POWER

Different strands of thought have suggested various ways of examining the role of law in the mechanism of power. Here I will review how the approaches of pluralism, structuralism, post-structuralism, and post-modernism have contributed to our understanding of the role of law in the mechanism of power, and examine the issues and questions that remain unanswered by these approaches. A few scholars' arguments in each approach will be discussed in detail.

Pluralism assumes that multiple forces of power co-exist in a society, and pluralistic accounts of power focus on defining the relative power or relative influence of different institutions and groups. Legal institutions are considered one of multiple forces of power, thus pluralist scholars examine how much power legal institutions have in comparison with other forces or entities, or identify the conditions under which legal institutions exert relative influence. For example, Dahl (1957) examines the role of the Supreme Court of the United States and demonstrated how the Court is not only a legal institution but a political institution in which controversial questions of national policy are decided. Drawing our attention to the ways in which the Supreme Court justices are appointed by the presidents, he expects that the Court is least likely to be successful in blocking a determined and persistent lawmaking majority on a major policy and most likely to succeed against a "weak" majority which is dead, transient, fragile, or weakly united upon a policy of subordinate importance.

Against the seemingly prevalent view that the Court stands as a protection of minorities against tyranny by majorities, Dahl tests the hypothesis that the Supreme Court is shield and buckler for minorities against national majorities. In the absence of relatively direct information of the national majority, he employed an indirect test by looking at the 86 provisions-of federal law that have been declared unconstitutional which were initially passed by majorities of those voting in the Senate and in the House and had the president's formal approval. Thus, he took a lawmaking majority as equivalent to a national majority.

Dahl's first argument is that Congress and the president generally succeeded in overcoming a hostile Court on major policy issues, which is supported by the finding that cases involving major legislative policy were propelled to the Court much more rapidly than cases involving minor policy. He also points out that although the Court seemed never to have succeeded in holding out indefinitely, in a very small number of important cases it has delayed the application of policy up to as much as 25 years. Therefore, he argues, the belief that the Court upheld minorities against national majorities is not supported by evidence because lawmaking majorities have had their way. Dahl concludes that except for short-lived transitional periods when the old alliance is disintegrating and the new one is struggling to take control of political institutions, the Supreme Court is inevitably a part of the dominant national alliance, and as an element in the political leadership of the dominant alliance, the Court supports the major policies of the alliance. Therefore, he contends, the Court by itself is almost powerless to affect the course of national policy.

This conclusion does not mean that Dahl considers the Supreme Court is an insignificant institution in American politics. Rather, he argues that the Supreme Court is not simply an agent of the alliance, but an essential part of the political leadership and possesses some bases of power of its own, which is the unique legitimacy attributed to its interpretations of the Constitution. According to Dahl, the role of the Court is to operate to confer legitimacy, not simply on the particular and parochial policies of the dominant political alliance, but upon the basic patterns of behavior required for the operation of a democracy. In that sense, Dahl contends, the process in which the Court makes policy decisions at the national level is neither minority rule nor majority rule but minorities rule, where an aggregation of minorities achieves policies opposed by another aggregation.

Considering the Supreme Court as a legitimacy-conferring institution, Dahl seems to suggest that the relative power the Supreme Court can generate against other forces such as the presidents and the Congress merely depends on situations that render the other forces independent and strong or dependent and weak. The question then still remains as to how power is exercised and where the force of power lies. Dahl also suggests that different groups struggle to achieve their policy goals and these procedures themselves are legitimized by the Supreme Court. But he does not explain where the potential power of different minority groups fits in this mechanism and what exactly influences the decision-making process.

Casper (1976) criticizes Dahl's analysis and argues that the Supreme Court participates more significantly in national policy-making than Dahl suggests. Casper's criticism is mainly based on the ways in which Dahl selects and treats his evidence. For example, Casper points out that Dahl's decision to consider lawmaking majorities as a measure of national majorities is troublesome, and that Dahl considers only cases in which federal legislation has been declared unconstitutional, thereby eliminating other types of activities such as statutory construction and federal constitutional issues arising out of state and local legislation or practice. Casper also contends that considering the decisiveness dimension only for cases occurring within four years of enactment leaves more than half the cases Dahl discovered falling into a category in which under his coding rules it is not possible to conclude that the Court (or the lawmaking majority) has been influential.

The question here is whether there is any reason to believe that this omission of data has any "systematic" impact upon Dahl's conclusion drawn from his evidence. Because Casper does not seem to clearly demonstrate in which direction Dahl's conclusion might have been different from the other data, his argument that the Supreme Court is more actively involved in the policy-making process is less based on his own analysis of data than on the illustrations of some (not all) of the omitted cases. Casper's criticism and arguments themselves might be valid, and he adds different dimensions regarding the role of the Supreme Court as a political institution, including providing access to participants, placing issues on the agenda of public opinion, mobilizing resources and building institutions, etc. But this does not seem to invalidate the analysis and conclusion of Dahl. Dahl and Casper just differently define the conception of policy making and the role of the Court in it. In addition, while Casper is right in arguing that the policy-making process involves more than producing outcomes that prevail, he does not provide any evidence that supports his conclusion that interests that lack resources for effective influence in legislative, executive, or administrative arenas find the legal system an attractive spot in which to attempt to influence public policy and succeed in it.

Dahl and Casper generates different conclusions about the role of the Supreme Court in the American political process, especially its role in preserving and enhancing minority group interests. Dahl attempts to define the relative influence of the Supreme Court and the Congress and concludes that the influence of the Supreme Court is not as great as is usually believed, whereas Casper argues that the role of the Supreme Court encompasses more activities but the role just appears to be relatively small when one ignores the fact that no institution is capable of having the decisive role. While they are involved with the seemingly half-full versus half-empty cup arguments, both assume the existence of different entities as potential forces of power, whether they are legal institutions, interest groups, the government, etc. But questions remain to be answered as to the mechanism of power: What is it that makes the Court or any institution an important part of the policy-making process? How to identify the crucial participants in the policy-development process? What are the conditions that make for the success or failure of interest groups in their struggle to influence policy-making process? Instead of answering these questions, pluralist scholars focus more on the fact that different groups and institutions attain a balance and the fact that the Supreme Court participates in a consensus. Moreover, the application of the pluralistic approach can be limited to a society where power is relatively evenly distributed. The basic premise that interest groups would contest to influence policy-making processes and that this struggle is a main force influencing a society does not apply when it comes to countries where powerful states govern the policy making process and the participation of interest groups or different institutions is seriously limited. Next I will discuss a perspective that focuses on the limited autonomy of agents due to the structural constraints.

Structuralism focuses on the structural constraints of the system and tries to explain why the structures reinforce class domination and inequalities. Some scholars seek to explain how the capitalist class is consciously able to protect and extend its interests through the exercise of power in private and public institutions. Miliband argues that judges are "by no means, and cannot be, independent of the multitude of influence, notably class origin, education, class situation and professional tendency . . . (1969, p. 138)." He adds that judicial elites are drawn mainly from the upper and middle layers of society. He goes on to emphasize the common professional legal background of most judges as a profession that produces individuals "whose ideological dispositions are traditionally cast in a highly conservative mold" (p. 138). According to Miliband, these ideological influences both at the conscious and unconscious levels enter the process of legal decision-making and produce results accordingly.

But most structuralists are skeptical about focusing on human agency, especially at the level of consciousness. Thus structuralist accounts tend to move away from a focus on the wishes of the individuals who make up the ruling class, and toward a focus on the objective structural interests of that class. Poulantzas' (1969) criticism of Miliband's focus on social relations as opposed to objective structures stems from this context. Poulantzas criticizes Miliband's focus on the social origin of members of the ruling class and their participation because the relation between the bourgeois class and the State is an objective relation. Thus if the function of the State in a determinate social formation and the interests of the dominant class in this formation, it is by the reason of the system itself. Therefore, Poulantzas sees the relations between the ruling class and the State as the effect rather than the cause of the objective structures, and opposes the focus on social actors and their motivations of conduct as a mechanism of power.

Poulantzas also argues that Miliband has difficulties in comprehending social classes and the State as "objective structures," and their relations as an "objective system of regular connections." For example, he argues, Miliband considers managers one among the distinct economic elites composing the ruling class. According to Poulantzas, the class position of managers, their place in production and their relationship to the ownership of the means of production needs to be considered because the ownership of economic property is the only genuine economic power. In that sense, considering managers one of the elites suggests that he assumes a "plurality of elites."

In response to Poulantzas' critique, Miliband (1970) warns against "structural super-determinism," and cautions that an exclusive stress on "objective relations" makes impossible a truly realistic consideration of the dialectical relationship between the State and the system. Miliband first affirms that he does believe that governments and bureaucracy, irrespective of social origin, class situation and even ideological dispositions, are subject to the structural constraints of the system. Then he questions whether the structural constraints of the system would be so absolutely compelling as to turn those who run the state into the merest functionaries and excutants of policies imposed upon them by "the system." Miliband draws our attention to how the state elite is involved in a far more complex relationship with the system and with the society as a whole. And he raises the important point that the structural super-determinism is politically dangerous because it suggests that if the state elite is totally imprisoned in objective structures, it follows that who rules the state, i.e., constitutionalists or Fascists, makes no real difference.

Both Poulantzas and Miliband view legal institutions as ideological institutions, although Poulantzas considers ideological institutions a part of the State while for Miliband they are outside of the State. As structural analysis emphasizes the determination of structures by the logic of capital, when the theoretical approaches of structuralism are applied to the study of law and legal institutions, law is seen as evolving out of the logic of capitalism and hence ultimately economy as determinant and the legal system as an output. There can be different accounts of the process by which the economic substructure determines the ideological superstructure of the law, but all tend to stress the one-way nature of the relationship: economy determines law rather than vice versa.

The deterministic aspect of structuralism has been criticized by many scholars including Miliband himself. The structuralist approach to the law might only switch the determining power away from the individual wills of capitalists towards the structural requisites of capitalism, and so does not solve the deficiency of considering multiple social forces. Particular forms and functions of the structures seem to be neither precisely determined nor inevitable. This approach focuses on the structural partial reflection of a dialectical interaction between human agency and social structures.

There have been numerous theoretical attempts to consider the interdependency of structure and agency. For example, Foucault (1980) shifts our attention from the economic analysis of power to knowledge and disciplines as the mechanism of power. Post-structuralist accounts of power, including Foucault's, come from the acknowledgment that in order to explain what is the structure, we have to posture some "agency" to whom the knowledge of structural constraint will be useful.

The post-structural approach reflects a switch of inquiry from structural determinants to a social creation process. An important aspect of post-structural theories is that they explicitly acknowledge the importance of the processes by which individuals in society and social structures interact, while structural constraints remain the focus of study. Consequently, the post-structural analysis of power and law explores the constraining nature of the structures of everyday life which, in a legal context, are embedded in legal decisions, in standard legal arguments, or in the assumptions upon which legal discourse is based. For example, Foucault considers that power is neither given, nor exchanged, nor even recovered, but rather exercised, and that it only exists in action. He notes regarding the importance of local research:

> "It is not that these global theories have not provided, nor continue to provide in a fairly consistent fashion, useful tools for local research.... but I believe these tools have only been provided on the condition that the theoretical utility of these discourses was in some sense put in abeyance, or at least curtailed, divided, overthrown, theatricalised, or what you will. In each case, the attempt to think in terms of a totality has proved to be hindrance to research.
>
> So the main point to be gleaned from these events of the last fifteen years, their predominant feature, is the local character of criticism. . . I believe that what this essentially local character of criticism indicates in reality is an autonomous non-centralized kind of theoretical production, one, that is to say, whose validity is not dependent on the approval of the established regimes of thought." (1980, pp. 80-81)

Foucault suggests that there have been two schemes for the analysis of power. The contract-oppression schema, which is the juridical one, and the domination-repression or war-repression schema for which the pertinent opposition is not between the legitimate and illegitimate, as in the first schema, but between struggle and submission. Pointing out that juridical or liberal conceptions of political power and the Marxist conception all imply an economism in the theory of power, he questions whether the analysis of power, or indeed of powers, is to be deduced in one way or another from the economy. Also, he does not think that the mechanisms of repression, that is the hostile engagement of forces, help us much to understand the mechanism of power.

Foucault then suggests a new type of power, non-sovereign power, which is more dependent upon bodies and is one of the great inventions of bourgeois society: disciplinary power. He argues that the discourse of disciplines has nothing in common with that of law, rule, or sovereign will, but is a natural rule, a norm. The code that comes to be defined is not that of law but that of normalization. And this is why subjugated knowledges play an important role in the exercise of power, knowledges which are concerned with a historical knowledge of struggles, a whole set of knowledges that have been disqualified as inadequate or insufficiently elaborated, particular, local, regional knowledge as opposed to general or scientific knowledge.

Therefore, although Foucault argues that the discourse of disciplines has nothing in common with that of law, he points out that the disciplinary form of power and the principle of sovereignty, which is an ideology of right, are intertwined. His arguments may be used to interpret the role law or legal rules play in exerting power to the extent that discourse regarding legal rules and rights have normalizing effects in everyday life. Because the decisions and arguments made in courts suggest to a society which behavior is considered acceptable and which is not, thus should be punished, law performs an important role on the ways in which power is exercised by disciplinary discourse.

The postmodern conception of law focuses on bringing to the fore the complexity of social reality; whilst at the same time it attempts to demonstrate that this complexity is not chaotic but is the determinate result of processes of social construction. Santos (1987) demonstrates that relations between law and social reality are similar to those between maps and spatial reality. According to him, law creates the reality that fits in its application, and this creation operates according to certain rules, such as those of scale, projection, and symbolization. Describing these different kinds of law and reality, Santos emphasizes the notion of interlegality. His notion of interlegality can be considered a new kind of legal pluralism, but not one in which different legal orders are conceived as separate coexisting in the same political space. Rather his approach emphasizes the conception of different legal spaces that are superimposed and mixed in our minds as much as in our actions as well as in the dull routine of eventless everyday life.

The notion of interlegality thus refers to complex relations between customary law and state law using different scales, between the geocentric legality of the nation-state and the new egocentric legality of international private particularism, and between the legality characterized by formal and abstract terms and that characterized by figurative and informal terms. Such a conception of legal pluralism and interlegality calls for complex analytical tools. According to Santos, the fragmentation of legality is not chaotic, but is a social construction built according to the rules of scale, projection, and symbolization, which is not a neutral process. Law is thus viewed as a network of legal orders. The potential of the mechanism of power in Santo's arguments lies in the fact that scale, projection, and symbolization are not neutral procedures, because the choice made within each of them promote the expression of certain types of interests and disputes and suppress that of others. Therefore, power represents social and physical reality chosen for its capacity to create those phenomena that maximize the conditions for the reproduction of power. The distortion and concealment of reality is thus a presupposition of the exercise of power.

Adler (1990) also examines the relation between law and reality in her review of postmodern art and the obscenity law. She demonstrates how a legal rule that is established based on one kind of social reality can be no longer a coherent standard in the face of the change of social reality. Adler shows that because Miller's new test to distinguish sexually explicit art from obscenity, that protects such art only if it demonstrates "serious . . . artistic . . . value," evaluates contemporary art by the very standard which art seeks to defy. She argues that the reason is because the test was drafted at a radical turning point in the history of art, and the new art that has arisen since Miller has rendered standards such as "serious artistic value" obsolete, and because this new art—postmodern art—rebels against the demand that a work of art be serious, or that it have any traditional "value" at all.

Adler argues that defining art by the artist's intentions is not adequate because postmodernism ridicules the notion of sincerity, that defining art by the art world acceptance would chill the work of unpopular and unrecognized artists, and that we cannot depend on a trier of fact who would know art when he sees it because many contemporary artists are so estranged from lay notions of what constitutes "art." Demonstrating the difficulty in defining obscenity, and even defining "art," Adler warns us that any attempt to define obscenity will result in leaving some art unprotected, which might be the art we most care to protect.

Postmodern approaches to law introduce the complexity of the relation between law and reality and demonstrate the discrepancies that often result in between the law and the reality that it attempts to regulate. Postmodernists consider this discrepancy to be a result of a non-neutral process of the social construction of reality, which has implications in the ways in which power is exercised. However, it is not clear how a certain reality is chosen over the other ones, and to what extent agents can influence the ways in which the reality is constructed, e.g., to what extent and how postmodern artists can influence how the obscenity law perceives and understands the reality of contemporary art. Clearly defining the role of agents in the process of constructing social reality would help postmodern accounts of law to provide more insight into questions regarding what is the mechanism of the reproduction of existing structures and where lies the potential for a structural change.

STRUCTURE VERSUS AGENCY IN SOCIAL THEORIES

Critical scholars from various traditions of social theories have examined the mechanisms through which legal decisions may be influenced by social structures and actors, although copyright has not been an issue of particular interest to these scholars. Also, many social theories have dealt with the relationship between social structures and actors, although they have rarely been applied to explain the legal decision-making processes. Most of these approaches can be placed into two broad categories: structuralism and instrumentalism (also called subjectivism). Instrumentalism tends to emphasize human agency at the level of consciousness while structuralism stresses unconscious, structural determinations. These approaches are not mutually exclusive, but may rather represent different levels of analysis and emphasis. Both structuralism and instrumentalism each by itself is a partial intellectual reflection of a dialectical interaction between human agency and social structures. Among the various attempts to deal with this nexus, Giddens's theory of structuration is adopted here as a useful framework with which to approach the legal decision-making process and its relationship to social structure and agency.

The instrumentalist approach rejects both formalism and objectivism, upon which modern legal thought is based. The instrumentalist perspective sees the struggle of agency and the ruling class to maintain their power as a main force of influencing the social structure. An instrumental approach to the role of law in capitalist society begins by identifying the class background or social status of the judicial elite. It is argued that judges themselves are "by no means, and cannot be, independent of the multitude of influence, notably class origin, education, class situation and professional tendency, . . . (Miliband, 1969, p. 138)." The judicial elite are drawn mainly from the upper and middle layers of society, and share the common law school experiences and professional legal background as a profession that produce individuals whose ideological dispositions are highly conservative (Miliband, 1969, p. 138; Kairys, 1982, p. 5). These ideological influences enter the process of legal decision-making and produce results that are not random (Bettig, 1989, p. 188). Thus instrumentalist approachs attempt to explore the ways in which the law is neither separate from nor above politics, economics, culture, values, or the particular ideological dispositions of judges (Kairys, 1982, p. 17). They also emphasize the influence of social and political factors on judges, both at the conscious and unconscious levels.

However, this instrumentalist view of the law has been criticized by many scholars. It is very hard to imagine so many individuals accurately perceiving their long-term self-interest and acting accordingly to institutionalize it as law, and always having the intended consequences (Boyle, 1985). A more general criticism centers around the argument that the instrumentalist view tends to de-emphasize the other aspects of the legal system. The recognition of this deficiency provides the impetus for the second standard position in critical legal thought. This is the move away from a focus on the wishes of the individuals who make up the ruling class and toward a focus on the objective structural interests of that class (Miliband, 1969).

As has already been discussed, the theoretical approaches of structuralism have been applied in the study of law and legal institutions. The structuralist picture of law generally has two tiers, a determining substructure and a determined superstructure. Structuralism tries to explain why social structures reinforce class domination and inequalities. Structuralist analysis sees the law as evolving out of the logic of capitalism, and hence emphasizes particularly the determination of structures by the logic of capital (Boyle, 1985, p. 722). This view sees the economy as determinant and the legal system as an output. There are different accounts of the process by which the economic substructure determines the ideological superstructure of the law, morals, religion, and aesthetics, but all tend to stress the one-way nature of the relationship: economy determines law rather than vice versa (Boyle, 1985, pp. 722-723). On the other hand, Poulantzas (1969) sees the relations between the ruling class and the State as the effect rather than the cause of the objective structures, and opposes focusing on social actors and their motivations of conduct as a mechanism of power. If the structuralist approach is applied to the study of law, the structural aspects of the law would be the focus of the examination, as legal rules and structures would not be considered a result of legal actors' interactions, but as a factor that influences legal actors.

The structuralist account of law may be criticized as both being too deterministic and objectivistic. One important problem with structuralism is related to its assumption of "objective" legal structures and the "objective" legal principles. But as discussed earlier, the ideas of the subject and the structure as the object are both socially produced categories, and both ideas come from the social world. It becomes meaningless then to imagine that there is an objective set of historical laws that act on the subjects of those laws (Boyle, 1985, p. 759). In addition, even if we assume the existence of a structure as an object, the structure is ultimately a distillation of our experience of social life (pp. 759-760).

Gordon (1982) makes a similar point. He asserts that critical inquiries into the objective determinants of social reality are meaningless, precisely because it is social reality, that is, a reality constructed by subjects, and not by structures (1982, p. 287). Gordon goes on to argue that "what we experience as 'social reality' is something that we ourselves are constantly constructing. . . (p. 287)." His argument, however, is also vulnerable to another criticism stating that it merely switches the privilege from the structuralist strand of hidden economic determinism to the subjectivist strand of hidden personal choice (Boyle, 1985, p. 776). In that sense, a social theory created by any combination of the two strands becomes unstable.

The structuralist approach to the law is also vulnerable to another criticism that it simply switches the determining power away from the individual wills towards the structural requisites of economic determinism, so is not able to solve the deficiency of considering multiple social forces. The particular forms and functions of the structures are neither precisely determined nor inevitable because human beings create and recreate these structures (Bettig, 1989, p. 196). However, the interdependency of the structuralist and instrumentalist accounts is recognized by some CLS scholars. Boyle, for example, illustrates that in order to explain what is the structure, we have to posture some "agency" to whom the knowledge of structural constraint will be useful. Similarly, to describe the instrumentalist strand, we have to rely on the vision of breaking through a dominant structure. Therefore, each strand both contradicts and relies on the other (Boyle, 1985, pp. 743-744).

A tension between the instrumentalist and the structuralist strands has long existed in critical legal thought. Many scholars from various scholarly perspectives have tried to resolve this tension between structure and actors. As a response, a "relatively autonomous" account of the law has been suggested, which leaves room for the dialectical interaction between multiple sets of structures, and for the possibility of historically informed subjects. But the critical theories of law discussed so far in this chapter, whether of the instrumentalist, of structural determinist, or of relatively autonomous varieties, are all vulnerable to the criticism of giving emphasis to one or the other of the elements, while disregarding the interactive processes among them. It has also been suggested that we should try to expose the constraining quality of the structures of everyday life, which are embedded in legal decisions, in standard arguments, or in the assumptions upon which legal discussion is based (Boyle, 1985, p. 743). In this case, "structure" is applied in a broader sense to mean a focus on beliefs, ideas, or economic forces that supposedly have their own internal logic, and that somehow organize, explain, or are reflected in the subjective experiences of those who are influenced by them (Boyle, 1985, p. 742).

In order to deal with this tension, the shift from structural or subjectivist determinism to a social creation process becomes necessary. The "processes" by which individuals in a society and social structures interact to maintain or change social relations are emphasized by some scholars. They suggest local theory or analysis that is not based on large-scale ideologies, but looks for practice in the most routine and ordinary interactions of daily life (Boyle, 1985; Gordon, 1982). Foucault (1979; 1980) also notes the importance of local research arguing that power only exists in action and that power is exercised by disciplinary discourse of everyday life. Anthony Giddens's theory of structuration reflects his rigorous attempt to embrace this notion of routine interactions in order to reconcile the structuralist and instrumentalist perspectives of social theory (1979; 1984). The theory of structuration, which is consistent with the premise of this book that the reality (including the legal reality) is symbolically and socially created rather than objective and concrete, provides a useful framework to understand the interactions between social actors and structures. Since the theory of structuration is the original basis of the conceptual framework of this book, this theory is now discussed in detail.

THEORY OF STRUCTURATION: REPRODUCTION AND CHANGE OF STRUCTURE

Giddens notes that all structuralist theory fails to conceptualize structure as being actively produced and reproduced by reflexive human agents. The integration of structuralism and instrumentalism is attempted through the conceptualization of structure. Giddens emphasizes the concept of the "duality of structure," which is arguably the most important concept of his structuration theory. According to Giddens, structures are analyzed as dualities: They are both the medium and the outcome of social interaction. Structures act not only to constrain social action, but also to make social action possible by providing the paths for appropriate behavior. Giddens's theory, therefore, is different from the structuralist view, not only in terms of its emphasis on social action, but also in its explicit argument that structural elements "enable" as well as constrain social action. He argues social structures, or social systems be envisioned not as frameworks outside of and constraining social action, but as a product of social action, enabling as well as limiting it. This is what he means by the "duality of structure."

In order to understand this concept better, we need to examine the meaning of "structure" in Giddens's theory. Structures consist of the structural rules and structural resources people use in interaction. Structural rules are a form of practical knowledge of "how to do something" rather than how something ought to be done, which has been accepted and taken-for-granted by actors through previous interactions. Structural resources mean allocative and authoritative factors that can be used by actors to understand and employ the structural rules. Giddens argues that the parameters of structures are continually re-created in the daily routines of social life:

> "By duality of structure, I mean the essential recursiveness of social life, as constituted in social practices: structure is both medium and outcome of the reproduction of practices. Structure enters simultaneously into the constitution of the agent and social practices, and 'exists" in the generating moments of this constitution (1984, p.5)"

Therefore, structuration is the production and reproduction of social systems through the application of generative rules and resources. Giddens emphasizes the importance of recognizing the role of antecedent frameworks of meaning in the recursive creation of social reality (pp. 25-28). The systems of deeply layered structures explain the "framework" of the organization, for example, a copyright law system, while people creating and recreating structures form the patterns of interaction. The importance of individuals in the structuration process needs to be underscored since they are carriers and creators of the rules and structures. Thus structuration is grounded in individual interactions that, over time and space, constitute institutions. A central concern of structuration theory, therefore, is the identification of the conditions that govern the continuity, or transformation, of structures, and thus the reproduction and change of systems.

In Giddens's theory, stress is placed on social behavior and more specifically on the purposiveness of individuals in situated practice. Thus the knowledgeability and directedness of social agents is underscored. Three levels of social awareness—unconscious, practical, and discursive—are considered in the general theme of re-creating the social fabric across time and space (Giddens, 1984, pp. 5-14). Unconscious levels of social awareness have a psychological sense of requiring a basic security or needs system. Practical consciousness refers to that level of knowledge or awareness whereby daily social life is constituted and reconstituted across time and space. Discursive consciousness presumes the ability to give a coherent account of the social rules that govern one's situation and action.

Since action involves power in the sense of transformative capacity, the major issue is the power dimension inherent in the ability of an individual to create his or her own reality (Giddens, 1984, p. 15). Power is defined as the ability to achieve outcomes: it "presumes structures of domination whereby the power flows smoothly in the process of social reproduction" (Giddens, 1984, p. 257). Power is exercised and realized through two types of social resources, allocative and authoritative (Giddens, 1984, p. 16). Allocative resources are of a material nature, while authoritative resources tend to be associated with control over persons. Power, generated through control of such resources, results in the continual reconstitution of social domination: "Structures of domination involve asymmetries of resources employed in the sustaining of power relations in and between systems of interaction" (Giddens, 1979, p.93). But Giddens also recognizes that power relations are always two-way, in that even the most dependent actors have some resources with which to influence the activities of their superiors (1984, p.16). Giddens' notion of the relationship between resources and the structure of domination suggests that differences in the resources of the legal actors may result in different levels of their discursive ability to make arguments in a court, which in turn may influence the court's decisions.

Social change itself, consequently, cannot be based on structural or dialectical models (Giddens, 1984, pp. 227-256). Rather, a social system is both maintained and modified in every social act. The subtle but powerful movement of change is contained by that component of the duality of structure that precedes and frames social action, which in itself is the product of antecedent social practice and is both the intended and unintended consequences of such activity. Change is also influenced by the motivations of knowledgeable social actors who seek to control the feedback that helps further define and reconstitute the system. Also, unintended consequences are an important outcome of this interaction of dominant and inferior agents, which Giddens calls the "dialectic of control." Both intended and unintended consequences serve to influence perceptions of social reality and social forms, to modify future structures—rules and resources, and figure as a component in social change (Giddens, 1984, p. 288-97).

Giddens's theory of structuration offers a conceptual framework for understanding the process of power and dominance presumed in the process, although it does not explicitly address the legal decision-making process. This book applies these concepts of the structuration theory to copyright law, and views the process of legal decision-making as that of reproducing and transforming the structure by knowledgeable actors who use the precedent structural framework. In other words, this book attempts to unravel the process of structuration as reflected in the legal decision-making process regarding copyright law.

COMMUNICATION IN THE PROCESS OF STRUCTURATION

The concepts regarding the structuration process discussed above serve to illuminate social processes, and especially in the present case the process of legal decision making on copyright. A central concern of structuration theory is the identification of the conditions that govern the reproduction or transformation of structures. In the routinization of everyday life many aspects of social systems develop a transparency, a "taken-for-grantedness," that commands their habitual reconstitution, but militates against their conscious manipulation (Giddens, 1984). Alternatively, some components are apparent and understood and thereby open to attempts at control. Each component plays a role in affecting social or political interaction, and such interaction in turn reconstitutes those different forms. Since actors tend not to see such structures as easily changeable, their "taken-for-granted" nature provides the lever for their continual social regeneration.

Thus, study of the copyright decision-making process will benefit from the analysis of both the transparent and the apparent components of the structure of the copyright system and the examination of how this structure is reproduced. In order to carry out this examination, differing levels of analysis are needed. The examination of the reproduction of the structure starts with the analysis of the pre-existing structural rules and resources that are used as assumptions of authority and legitimacy, which frame interactions among legal actors. I will identify the rules and resources that constrain and enable legal actors vis-a-vis issues of the copyright protection of computer software. I will also examine how these rules and resources change over time.

The second level of analysis assesses the allocative resources of the knowledgeable actors, which can be used to employ these rules and resources. In the case of copyright law decision-making, the actors comprise judges, plaintiffs, and defendants. Thus I will analyze the resources available to various actors, how such resources are used, and how there might be "asymmetries of autonomy and dependence" among knowledgeable actors (1984, p.289).

The symmetries or asymmetries of actors' resources are expected to be reflected in the ways in which they employ those rules and resources in making interpretive schemes and norms. Therefore, the third level of analysis attempts to discover how the rules and resources defined in the first analysis are used in interpretive and normative arguments regarding the copyright protection of computer software. I will analyze the ways in which the structural rules and resources as well as allocative resources shape the communicative interactions of actors.

Based on these analyses, I will examine the relationship between the level of actors' allocative resources and court decisions. In addition, I will analyze the relationship between the use of rules and resources and court decisions. Decisions made by judges become intended and unintended consequences of the activities of knowledgeable actors which again form conditions for further action, although these consequences may not be acknowledged by actors. How the decisions and arguments accepted as legitimate contribute to reproducing recursive structure consisting of rules and resources will be also examined by conducting these analyses. The analyses that are conducted across time allow us to learn when and how changes in the structure may occur.

This book explores how resources and other structured properties of the copyright legal system are drawn upon and reproduced by knowledgeable actors in the course of communicative interactions, and how these communicative interactions relate to the judges' decision-making processes. In this way, the patterns of maintenance and transformation of rules and resources relevant to the ways in which knowledgeable actors make arguments are examined. The interplay between the legal structure related to copyright and the actors' use of the structural frameworks, which again forms the structure for further action, is significant in determining how the relationships of domination are sustained. This book, through its findings, attempts to provide an insight into the processes in which power and dominance are practiced through communication in the copyright decision-making process.

NEWS DISCOURSE APPROACH TO LEGAL ARGUMENTS: TYPIFICATION AND OBJECTIFICATION

A central notion of this book is the process of communication activities in legal decision-making. A conceptual framework and analytic methods of examining news discourse that have been developed and refined in the field of communication provide a fruitful means of examining the role of legal arguments in the decision-making process. Thus I will discuss two central concepts of the news discourse analysis that are directly related to the process of structuration: typification and objectification.

The analogy that can be made between the perspectives used in the legal scholarship and in the study of news is striking. There are two broad theoretical perspectives that guide studies on news stories: One is the research on news bias and objectivity and another is the research on news framing in the construction of news discourse. The study of objectivity and bias and Liberal legal formalism both fall under the doctrine of objectivism, in which value-free and fixed accounts of reality are assumed to be possible. The news discourse approach and Critical Legal Studies, on the other hand, share the premise of constructivism, which assumes that the meanings of language are not fixed but are arbitrary and conventional. Both accept the notion that reality is seen not as a given set of facts or rules, but is the result of particular way of constructing reality (Hall, 1982).

The notion of journalistic objectivity consists of two dimensions: "factuality" and "balance or impartiality" (McManus, 1991). The latter means giving fair and equal treatment to opposing camps and requires that reports include both positive and negative value judgments (McManus, 1991; Hacket, 1984). The notion of factuality suggests that news reporting is a mirror of reality, and therefore that the journalist's mission is to find truth and disseminate it (Hacket, 1984). The two components of factuality and impartiality are incompatible at an epistemological level. The notion of balance assumes a relativist position in which bias is avoided by juxtaposing competing, incompatible, and equally valid world views, while the goal of factuality implies a non-relativist affirmation of the ultimate "knowability" of the truth. It logically follows that news content that can be regarded as "balanced" reporting is not necessarily a "reflection of reality" (Hacket, 1984).

In addition to their incompatibility, the assumption that a plurality of viewpoints approximates truth is also problematic. The attempts of networks to balance news stories are partly a response to government fairness rules and to the concerns of affiliate stations (Epstein, 1974). Also, the journalist's attempt to present conflicting truth-claims is one of several "strategic rituals," through which news workers protect themselves from such occupational hazards as missed deadlines, libel suits, and superiors' reprimands (Tuchman, 1972). Since journalists often depend upon legitimized institutions for "objective" facts and information, media professionalism and the cannons of objectivity, ironically become an unarticulated commitment to the established order.

Another assumption of objectivity is the notion of "factual reality." This notion assumes that facts can be separated from opinion or value judgments, that journalists can be fully detached observers of the external world, and that a neutral transmission of an event through the media is possible. But since language cannot function on its own to transmit the meaning presumably inherent in news events, neutral and value-free news is impossible. Even those who advocate journalistic objectivity acknowledge that it is impossible for journalists to stay value-free in reporting social events because no account is independent of the perceiver (McManus, 1991).

If no observation or presentation of observation via a text can be value-free, it follows logically that the news media unavoidably structure their representations of social and political events in ways which are not pre-given in themselves, nor is this representation necessarily the "distortion" of the real. Thus, news media are inevitably involved in a process of meaning construction. The premise that social reality is constructed actively is reflected in analyses of the role of mass media frames in shaping public discourse and in reproducing a dominant culture (Tuchman, 1978; Gitlin, 1979; Gamson, 1988). It is suggested that through the process of ideology as a system of coding reality, journalists tend to serve as a support for the reproduction of a dominant ideological discursive field (Hall, 1982).

Constructivism makes interpretive processes central and stresses the interpretive scheme which plays a decisive role in the construction of meaning of everyday life (Berger and Luckman, 1967). In this perspective, discourses have been defined as "historically specific, socially situated, signifying practices" (Fraser, 1992). In discourse analysis, a news text is viewed as a system of organized signs and of symbolic devices that may interact with audience members in the construction of meaning. Assuming that these signs and symbolic devices are not put together randomly, but are involved with some kind of persuasion, discourse analyses pay attention to the basically ideological nature of the media reconstruction of reality, as a form of reproduction of the dominant forces and ideologies in society.

Drawing on these premises, scholars of news discourse analysis consider discourse as a process rather than as a text product, and understand the news discourse as a process of meaning construction. The act of making news is considered an act of constructing reality, and the news itself is socially constructed (Tuchman, 1978). Van Dijk (1988) also approaches news as a type of discourse and a form of interaction, and views media discourse as a form of social and institutional practice. In short, news discourse analysis is concerned with the interplay between the interpretive processes of actors and the structural elements in a society, which relates to the ideological processes of news discourse. The primary contribution of the scholars in this area is their attempt to link the social and cognitive dimensions of the news construction process. The central concepts of the news discourse process involving the news text production and comprehension are typification and objectification.

The notion of typification relates to the social coordination of time and space in human activities. Drawing on the concept of frames (or script, schemata, constructs, etc.) as a concept related to human cognition, 'framing' is viewed as an act of providing the ordering of activities and meanings. Berger and Luckman (1967) observe that the reality of everyday life contains typificatory schemes in terms of which others are apprehended and dealt with in face-to-face encounters. In face-to-face situations, the typificatory schemes of two people enter into an ongoing negotiation. They argue that social structure is the sum total of these typifications and of the recurrent patterns of interaction established by means of typifications. Goffman (1974) also notes that the frameworks that are implied when people recognize a particular event render what would otherwise be a meaningless aspect into something meaningful. He argues that people tend to perceive events in terms of primary frameworks, and the type of framework they employ provides a way of a description to which it is applied.

Tuchman (1978) applies this notion of frameworks or typificatory schemes to the news production process. Her notion of typification refers to a classification in which relevant characteristics are central to the solution of practical tasks or problems at hand, and are constituted and grounded in everyday activity. She points out that by reducing all phenomena to known classifications, newsworkers are allowed to manage the unexpected and produce a fixed amount of news (independent of what really happens) within the constraints of deadlines or budget limitations. Owing to these typifications, the occurrences of the everyday world can be subjected to routine processing and dissemination. These classificatory schemes also channel the newsworkers' perceptions of everyday world and guide decisions on what is newsworthy. Therefore, the news typifications become part of the reporter's professional stock of knowledge-at-hand, and the use of typification is a necessary, routinized, organizational device that helps to produce news.

Typification and classificatory schemes can be elements that influence, and are influenced by the internal structures of news texts. Hall (1982) makes a similar argument that, since meaning does not depend on "how things are" but on "how things are signified," the internal structures rather than content will be important. According to him, particular discursive formulations would be ideological, not because of the manifest bias or distortions of their surface contents, but because they are generated out of, or are transformations based on, a limited ideological matrix or set.

Tuchman's (1978) concept of typifications is also rather content-free. She argues that typifications of kinds of news draw upon the "way" occurrences happen, not upon "what" is happening, although some sort of occurrences are likely to happen one way.

Gamson (1983; 1988), in his examination of the mechanisms by which frames in the news text relate to public opinion, also argues that journalists' working norms and practices, including journalists' routine relationship with official sponsors and with other journalists, play an important role in the production of an issue culture, since they influence the organization of signature elements in the newsmaking processes. He emphasizes that the idea elements in an issue culture are not separated, but are organized and grouped into interpretive packages. He calls this package an "interpretive" package to relate it to human cognitive processing. These interpretive packages are produced in a complex process involving an interaction between sources and journalists.

These packages are divided into two parts: one deals with the pattern organizing (framing) nature of the issue culture, and the other with reasoning and justifications for positions. Framing devices are metaphors, exemplars, catchphrases, depictions, and visual images. The reasoning devices are roots, consequences, and appeals to principle. Using these elements, Gamson provides a sophisticated framework with which to analyze framing devices, called a signature matrix. His categorization of a pattern organizing nature and a reasoning/justifying nature of framing is related to Giddens's (1984) notion of interpretive schemes and normative schemes as modalities of communication. Normative elements and codes of signification are the two feature of structural rules. According to Giddens, interpretive schemes are the modes of typification incorporated within actors' stocks of knowledge, applied reflexively in the sustaining of structuration. Thus typification and objectification are parallel concepts to Giddens's notion of signification and legitimation.

Typification is a concept that is employed to relate the cognitive schemes of newsmakers and the internal structure of the news text. Typification is a routinized framework or scheme through which newsmakers understand phenomena in the world and process other source materials. Therefore, typifications work not only as constraints but also as enablements to newsmakers. These cognitive schemes, and the notion of newsworthiness defined through the schemes, are being constantly redefined by newsmakers and influenced by the structure of the news text itself.

The notion of typification provides another important point in relation to the notion of objectification. The typified categories are often presented as objective categories, not as constructed or changeable ones (Tuchman, 1978). If objectified, typifications are more likely to be used by newsworkers and taken for granted by them and the audience. Presenting the typificatory schemes as objectively real elements is a legitimation process (Berger and Luckman, 1966). The "taken-for-grantedness" is also recognized by Giddens (1984). According to him, many aspects of social systems develop a transparency, a taken-for-grantedness. Since actors tend not to see such structures as greatly malleable, their taken-for-grated nature provides the lever for their social regeneration.

In order to routinize their work and at the same time obtain legitimacy and credibility, newsmakers try to provide facts and legitimate sources (Tuchman, 1978). Thus, the facticity used by newsmakers not only creates an illusion of objectivity and credibility, but also ultimately legitimates the status quo. The rules requiring and identifying proper sources, and identifying and gathering facts are embedded in socially structured understandings of the everyday world and its institutions (Tuchman, 1988). Therefore, despite the fact that questions of "what are the facts," "what are the relevant facts," "who are the legitimate sources" are all socially and ideologically defined and constructed, the selective use of sources and facts can serve to legitimate the sources themselves and the ideologies from which definitions are drawn. Therefore, ideology or social meanings are crystallized into common sense knowledge, which is considered natural, taken for granted, and thereby legitimated and reproduced.

Many scholars stress how institutions including the media objectify social meanings. Social meanings, constituted in social interactions, are transformed into institutional and organizational rules and procedures that may be invoked as resources to justify actions. Through these processes in which social meanings are redefined and legitimated, the "processes" in which the meanings are constructed themselves are also defined and legitimated (Tuchman, 1978; Berger and Luckman, 1966).

In this process, the "facts" taken for granted by members of a society become resources to be invoked for the accomplishment of action (Tuchman, 1978). The facts and sources that have been socially constructed gain legitimacy and facticity, thus serve as resources in the reproduction of social structures. Therefore, socially, these resources are unequally distributed, and individuals have different access to and ability to use the resources (Berger and Luckman, 1966; Tuchman, 1978). This implies that some people have a greater ability to reproduce social meanings and construct social reality. Therefore, a power dimension is inherent in the ability of an individual to create his or her own reality (Giddens, 1984). Power is exercised and realized through resources—allocative and authoritative—and since the typified schemes and facts become resources, structural rules and resources are reproduced.

The above discussions have tried to unify the various scholarly approaches to news discourse into a coherent framework through the notions of typification and objectification. News discourse is a process of meaning construction in which the interplay between cognitive frameworks and textual structures plays a central role. Newsmakers employ typified schemes (frameworks) in the course of their daily activities to routinely negotiate the production of news. These typificatory schemes which enable and constrain this process involve the cognitive processes of the actors. The process of typification relates to the structure of text as a discursive product. By being objectified, typifications gain legitimacy and credibility. The objectified typificatory schemes become structural rules and resources that people will use in future interactions. Therefore, the schemes are a medium through which news discourse process occurs and at the same time become an outcome of the process. In this way, the parameters of structures are continually re-created in the daily routines of social life. In addition, the resources are not equally distributed and power is exercised through the use of these rules and resources to construct social meanings.

The application of this framework to the legal discourse generates a two-fold contribution: one relates to the larger conceptual framework, and the other to the discourse analysis devices suggested. Considering the legal decision-making process as a meaning-construction process involving signification and legitimation practices, the framework discussed above provides a helpful conceptualization of the legal decision-making process. In legal decision-making process, meanings are mediated by the legal arguments of the actors (judges, plaintiffs, and defendants) within the enablements and constraints of routines related to the judiciary and larger social structures and ideologies. Therefore, in analyzing legal discourse, the rules and resources of the legal actions that frame the interactions among legal actors are essential. Also institutional rules or typified categories in the law system need to be identified.

The structure of the legal decision-making system is constructed by legal rules and facts—the structural rules—and human and allocative resources that actors have. The actors employ these rules and resources in generating the court opinions and decisions, and the decisions are transformed into objective facts. Here the legal rules and facts are objectified and become themselves resources for legal actors. Through this process of gaining facticity and objectivity, both the court decisions and opinions as a discursive product, and the sources and facts used in the decisions are legitimized. In this way, the structural rules and resources are reproduced in the legal discourse. Therefore, identifying relevant legal rules and facts and the resources that actors have provides an entry point for the study of legal argumentation and decision-making.

Conceptualizing legal arguments and the decision-making process as a form of discourse provides a particular insight, in that it suggests the importance of analyzing the structures of discourse texts in their relationship to cognitive schemes. Through these cognitive schemes that involve the codes of typifications and objectifications (interpretive schemes and normative schemes in Giddens's sense), the arguments made by plaintiffs and defendants may shape the frames and options and thus influence the judges' opinions.

Regarding the specific devices of analyzing the structures of arguments, Gamson's (1983; 1989) categorization of exemplars and metaphors as framing devices, and roots, consequences, and appeals to principle as reasoning devices is particularly relevant to legal argumentation. Metaphors are used as an explicit device to signify a certain understanding of the issue, by providing an association between the metaphor and the principle subject. Exemplars are the real events of the past or present which are used to frame the principle subject. In legal argumentation, precedent cases and opinions are essential elements that are often suggested as authorities to support actors' arguments. Although all of these are "real" events or cases, the choices of the relevant cases and proper interpretations of the opinions are not usually definitive. The use of metaphor also involves choices of relevant objects or events, and can be particularly powerful when used to present a new subject or event. Thus these choices necessarily involve some social and ideological judgmental processes. Therefore, the use of metaphors and exemplars is another process of social construction of meaning, and also serves to reproduce the existing structure. The representation of possible causes and consequences, and justification through the moral appeals to some general principles (in this case, statutes, precedents, etc.) are also frequently used in legal discourse. The precedent as exemplars and as appeals to principles are often used because they are considered as the "facts" and the "rules" in the legal decision-making process. And the decisions made in this way with the use of facts, sources and norms will gain facticity and objectivity, and become another "facts" which are authoritative resources for later decisions. The kind of sources and facts that are more likely to be used and legitimized in terms of expert testimony, the precedent, etc., may illustrate how a legal system is maintained and changed.

Gamson (1988) also emphasizes that there is ample room for disagreement within the overall frame, which can be interpreted in different ways. This is why he constructed a matrix containing the "core frame" and the "core position" separately, arguing that frames should not be confused with positions for or against some specific policy measure. In the analysis of legal argumentation, therefore, not only should the presence or absence of certain legal theories be considered, but also the interpretations of the theories and their relevance to the theories presented by plaintiffs and defendants needs to be examined.

As noted before, news typifications are considered part of the reporter's professional stock of knowledge-at-hand (Tuchman, 1987). Being a professional reporter capable of coping with idiosyncratic occurrences means being able to use typifications to invoke appropriate reportorial techniques. In a similar way, being a professional lawyer means being able to use typifications (legal rules and facts) to invoke appropriate legal technique. This point underscores the importance of the lawyers' ability to find out relevant rules (legal theories) and factual evidence and authorities to support the theories, which may help to frame the discourse in a way that is more likely to give advantage to their clients.

Therefore, these typifications and the practical ability to employ them become rules and resources which enable them to work effectively, and at the same time, constrain them, by providing the frame for categorizing and evaluating events.

Related to this, Gamson's (1983) notion of sponsor activities can be particularly relevant to the case of legal discourse, since it deals with more intentional and strategic arguments. He argues that certain framing packages frequently have sponsors interested in promoting their careers. He suggests that usually organizations employ professional specialists to prepare materials. The importance of the use of legal expertise as a resource to influence the framing of the issue is illustrated here again. Organizations engaged in court cases can be an another example of "signifying agents" who are actively engaged in the production of meaning (Snow and Benford, 1988).

The framework of discourse analysis provides a dynamic model of legal decision-making processes which involve the interactions between structures and actors, and between their social and cognitive dimensions. Examining legal argumentation in terms of a legal discourse will help understand how legal actors work within these structural rules employing their resources, and at the same time, redefine and reproduce the structures. Through the interpretive processes among the actors, between actors and textual structures, and between textual structures and larger structural frameworks, a legal system is reconstructed. Thus a central focus of this book is to examine the legal discourse regarding the copyright protection of computer software programs. It has been suggested that the potential of change as well as of reproduction is also contained in the duality of structure which are the product of antecedent practices (Giddens, 1988). As Hall (1980) also implies, the possibility of the transformation of the system may be also found in the change related to classificatory schemes, in other words, the use of structural rules and resources. In this book, I will examine the ways in which these rules and resources enable and constrain actors in the system who try to obtain their objectives through their communicative activities—their arguments. The main concern is how, in doing so, the legal actors produce and reproduce those rules and resources in the legal system, which in itself is the intended and unintended product of antecedent social practice, and thereby reproduce the enablements and constraints that are implicit in social and economic power relationships.

CHAPER 3

Structural Rules and Resources in Copyright System

The previous chapter provided the theoretical underpinnings of this book and proposed an analytical framework in which the theory of structuration is applied to legal decision-making processes. In this chapter, I place the conceptual framework in the area of copyright law regarding computer software programs. The key concepts of the framework in the context of copyright protection of computer programs are defined in terms of structure (rules and resources) and agency (the arguments of actors who employ structural rules and resources). In order to understand the structural rules of the copyright system, various approaches to analyze the history of copyright law and its origins and modern principles will be examined. Through a critical examination of theses different approaches, I will draw a more detailed framework of analyzing legal arguments in this book. A series of research questions are developed at the end.

LEGAL RULES AND FACTUAL EVIDENCE AS STRUCTURAL RULES OF THE COPYRIGHT SYSTEM

The conceptualization of the structure of the copyright system requires identifying the institutional orders of the legal system that frame the interactions among legal actors. As noted before, the institutional orders refer to the "rules and resources." The concept of "rules" as an element of the structure in the structuration theory is not the same as the conventional meaning of "rules," which some of the scholars who will be cited in this chapter also use. Rules, for Giddens, mean not followable prescriptions but a form of practical knowledge of "how to do something" rather than how something ought to or must be done (Cohen, 1987, p. 27). In order to avoid possible confusion, rules as an element of structure will be referred to as "structural rules" in this book, whereas particular rules to be applied in legal decision-making will be referred to as "legal rules."

Conrey and O'Barr (1990) point out that the law is rule-oriented, in theory, if not always in practice. A thought process learned by law students involves finding the facts, selecting the proper legal rules, and then applying these rules to the facts to produce a result (Conrey and O'Barr, 1990, p. 59-60). In all stages of legal decision-making, argument is central, whether in a written or oral form. The structure of the argument is typically a complex blend of legal theory and factual statements to justify the theory (Majone, 1989, pp. 10-11). In order to make any interactions in courts meaningful, actors should act within this framework of legal rules and facts. Thus this book conceptualizes "legal rules" and "facts" (or legal theory and evidence) as the two important elements that constitute the institutional orders of the legal decision-making system.

Legal rules are illustrated as an essential element of the legal structure in the study of Conrey and O'Barr, which examined the ways in which ordinary people relate to the American legal system. Conrey and O'Barr find a striking difference between the approaches of lay people and legal professionals to the resolution of everyday problems. They categorize litigants of informal courts as "rule-oriented" and "relational." Relational litigants were found to focus heavily on status and social relationships, believing that the law is empowered to assign rewards and punishments according to broad notions of social need and entitlement. Rule-oriented litigants interpret disputes in terms of rules and principles that apply irrespective of social status, seeing the law as a system of precise rules for assessing responsibility, and rejecting as irrelevant everything not circumscribed within these rules (Conrey and O'Barr, 1990, pp. 58-59). Therefore, the "rules" mentioned by Conrey and O'Barr more precisely mean "legal" rules as opposed to "structural" rules.

Conrey and O'Barr focus also on a fundamental division between those who view the law as an enabling mechanism and those who view it as an instrument of limitation. Among litigants, those with an ideology of enablement tend to be those with a philosophy of social governance that is characterized as relational. Thus they seek to apportion rights and responsibilities according to need and social worth rather than rules of law. However, Conrey and O'Barr argue, the "official" ideology of the legal system is the ideology of limitation. The law in the framework of the official ideology is limited to dealing with violations of specific rules of narrow applicability. Moreover, far from seeking out wrongs to rights, the legal system responds only to claims that are framed in appropriate terms. Litigants who share this ideology, or are able to come to terms with it, enjoy obvious practical advantages in dealing with the system (p. 163-164). The rule-oriented accounts contain few "extraneous" facts, but instead concentrate on the issues that the court is likely to deem relevant to the case. Conrey and O'Barr argue that, since the law is (legal) rule-oriented, these rule-oriented accounts engage better than relational ones with the logic of the law and the agenda of the courts.

In addition to legal rules, "facts" are another element comprising the institutional order of the legal system. Facts are examined first in order to find appropriate legal rules. The emphasis on the facts upon which actors interact is well known in legal scholarship. Wren and Wren (1986) in their book on legal research point out the role facts play in actual lawyering and suggest ways to gather and analyze facts for legal researchers. They suggest people, tangible evidence, books, periodicals, reports, expert witnesses, etc., as sources of pertinent information (Wren and Wren, 1986, pp. 29-31). Patterson and Lindberg (1991) also note the role of facts, especially regarding copyright decisions. According to them, in enacting copyright legislation, Congress starts with the intellectual property clause of the Constitution. In deciding copyright cases, however, a judge starts with the facts of a single case and then goes back to the Copyright Act.

Facts play a critical role in legal decision-making through their relationship with the rules they support. Rules become significant determinants in decision making when they are considered appropriate for the particular case and for the particular facts in the case. If it is decided that there is insufficient factual evidence, the rules are not considered applicable. Therefore, it is important that rules are chosen for their relevance to the facts and are supported by appropriate precedent decisions and opinions. In this sense, it is important to point out that a specific combination of rules and facts, rather than certain rules or facts themselves, may constitute the structural rules at a given time for a given case.

A combination of legal rules and facts is used by actors in providing "interpretive schemes and norms" in Giddens's terms. Interpretive schemes are the modes of typification incorporated within the actors' stocks of knowledge, applied reflexively in the sustaining of communication (Giddens, 1984, p. 29). Their interpretive scheme would influence judges' and other actors' understanding of the problem and copyright issues by providing factual evidence. Normative accounts of interaction always center upon relations between the rights and obligations 'expected' of those participating in a range of interaction contexts (p. 30). Thus a legal theory that actors choose should provide them with the normative grounds according to which their activities or arguments can be 'justified' (p. 30).

Actors act within this framework of legal rules and facts, in which they make use of their knowledge in such a way as to render their interchange meaningful (Giddens, 1984, p. 331). By invoking the institutional order in this way, they contribute to reproducing it. Moreover, in reproducing it they also reproduce its "facticity" as a source of structural constraint (Giddens, 1984, p. 331). How this framework consisting of legal rules and facts is related to the nature of stakeholders and their arguments will be discussed later in this chapter.

An important point related to the role of "facts" in the legal system involves the following interrelated processes: the arguments of legal actors are framed within the framework of facts; decisions are influenced by the relevant factual evidence; and once a decision is made, the decision and opinion become "facts," which are "accepted-as-real" in future cases. As Giddens suggests, the structural rule becomes both the medium and the outcome of actions. Precedent court decisions and opinions are regarded as "authorities," sometimes mandatorily and other times optionally, and they provide a basis for future decisions. In their study on the effects of the expert testimony on some court decisions about school segregation, Chesler, Sanders, and Kalmuss (1988) interviewed one social scientist whose remarks keenly illustrate the importance of precedent decisions:

> I remember in one case I was talking with the judge from the witness box, and questioning some of the testimony in Brown (v. Board of Education of Topeka I) . He asked me, "Are you questioning the facts of Brown?" And I said "Yes," and he said, "Well, that's not admissible for you to be doing that." So it kind of stymies a person. The evidence in Brown argues that desegregation will change attitudes, increase self-esteem, and improve school performance, when in fact that doesn't happen. We know that it doesn't happen. But there's a difficulty in making that point with the judge. (1988, pp. 43-44)

Thus the court decisions which have become facts often overrule "socially-accepted-facts."

Precedent court decisions and arguments become important structural rules that enable and constrain the legal cases in the future. Consequently, each case in different time periods has different structural rules. The nature of decisions in related former cases and the extent to which those decisions are differentially cited in other cases will consist of structural rules for future cases.

JUDICIAL ACTORS AND THEIR RESOURCES

The main stakeholders in the debates regarding software programs can be categorized in many ways. According to the Office of Technology Assessment, software stakeholders include software creators, software users, large and small commercial software developers, computer hardware manufacturers, educators, students, academic and other software and computer science researchers, etc. (1992, p. 9). In a broader categorization, the actors in the copyright system regarding computer software programs consist of judges and stakeholders including software users (private, corporate, or government), software creators (individuals or organizations; small or large firms), and software distributors.

In the cases related to the copyright protection of computer programs, however, the parties involved in the litigations do not usually include members of the public as end users of programs. Rather, most consumers of software programs tend to be large firms which use the software for their own businesses, or other immediate consumers who are retailers distributing the products through licensing agreement. Therefore, the involved parties in copyright cases usually consist of software developers who own their copyright at the same time, developers who are not copyright holders, and copyright holders who are not developers, or non-developers and non-copyright holders but retailers or other sellers.

The nature of the legal actors itself can become an important resource in their communicative activities. The controversy along the lines of "large firm vs. small developer" can have significant implications in how copyright decisions are made. For example, when a legal actor effectively presents himself as a developer who contributes to important innovation in the software industry, the actor may gain a sense of legitimacy in making his arguments, and thus be in a strong position to obtain a judge's sympathy. In that sense, the nature of the actor can be considered a status resource.

Conrey and O'Barr try to link the (legal) rule-orientation of the legal system to the notion of hegemony. According to them, this rule-orientation could be characterized as an acquired skill, so the mastery of rule-orientation helps the dominant class to maintain its authority, since members of the other classes have little opportunity to acquire the skill. They also point out that this system of control is both subtle and particularly effective because rule-oriented decision making has an appearance of strict neutrality (p. 80).

Attorneys try to choose the rules that the court would most likely use in its opinion and the authority that supports the rules. Thus the mastery of the institutional orders of the legal system then becomes a resource for legal actors to meet their ends in courts. Approaches of resource-mobilization and resource-dependency help us understand the relationship between the resources that organizations acquire and their organizational activities. Basic arguments of resource-dependency models basically suggest that the ability to adapt organizational practice to the demands of resource acquisition ultimately means the difference between organizational survival or death (Pfepper, 1972; Aldrich, 1979). Resource mobilization is the process by which the organization gains control over resources that it previously did not control (Knoke and Wood, 1981). The perspective of the resource-mobilization model is similar to that of the resource-dependency model, although it gives relatively more emphasis on the process rather than the structure. The organizational capacity to act in terms of their ability to monitor and gather relevant information influences the degree to which they can meet their organizational interests (Lauman and Knoke, 1987).

Resources are broadly defined as any means or facilities potentially controllable by an organization that can be used in adaptations between the organization and its environment (Knoke and Wood, 1981). A variety of items may serve as mobilizing resources. Many scholars demonstrate various essential elements of sustaining organized activity: funds, personnel, information, and products or services (Aldrich, 1979), money and authority (Benson, 1975), money, information, legitimacy, and power (Parsons, 1966), specialized expertise, personnel, funds, good connections, and authority (Lauman and Knoke, 1987).

The types of resources an organization can bring to bear in attempting to meet its objectives differ depending upon the type of the organization and the type of the environment the organization attempts to influence. In the case of the legal decision making process, importance should be given to the organization's ability to gather relevant information and communicate effectively using the information. Since certain legal rules and facts may become important structural rules in which the actors should interact, mobilizing resources is the factor that helps the organizations to use persuasive legal theory and to gather and use relevant factual information. In that sense, the resources suggested by Chesler, Sanders, and Kalmuss (1988) are also useful.

Chesler, Sanders, and Kalmuss examined how social movement organizations mobilize legal resources as a strategy to influence judges' understandings of the causes and effects of problems and decisions. The legal resources included "people willing to go to court, attorneys with legal knowledge of and ability in constitutional litigation, a legal theory which would cause courts to grant the relief sought, facts to support the application of that theory in a specific situation, witnesses to present those facts, and enough money to support all of these people in their efforts and to pay the costs of litigation" (p. 15). Although this is a quite useful and comprehensive account of possible factors that may influence the legal decisions, the factors are of different dimensions and stages. This book conceptualizes as human and allocative resources people willing to go to court, attorneys with legal knowledge and ability, witnesses to present the facts, and money. However, the precedent arguments and decisions that include legal theories supported by facts are conceptualized as structural rules of the legal decision-making system. I will discuss in detail possible resources such as specialized attorneys, judges' characteristics, scientific experts, money, and precedent court arguments and decisions.

Although all legal actors presumably have considerable knowledge of the institutional orders of the court system, they may have differing degrees of ability to use legal theory or provide factual evidence more persuasively. In order to choose a legal theory that would cause courts to reach a decision sought by the organization, and to communicate effectively based upon the theory, attorneys with legal knowledge of and ability in constitutional litigation are also important. Because copyright, especially the copyright of computer programs, is a specialized area, full-time specialized lawyers working on behalf of the organization may become important resources.

Factual accounts can be provided by the parties, witnesses, and experts. In a legal system, recruiting and preparing experts are a essential part of a plaintiff's mobilization strategy (Chesler, Sanders, and Kalmuss, 1988, p. 89). It is a feature of the American legal system that evidence is almost always introduced by a witness. As a result, parties to litigation must find and mobilize individuals willing to testify about facts and ideas in court (Chesler, Sanders, and Kalmuss , 1988, p. 62). Chesler, Sanders, and Kalmuss also find that the use of social science and expert testimony altered judges' general understanding of the causes of school segregation and this altered understanding affected the way judges interpreted evidence of violation, the nature and scope of the remedy, and the procedures used by the judges to construct a remedy, although there have been limits according to the judicial capacity and the movement organizations themselves (p. 203, pp. 233-234).

Expert testimony can be even more significant in the area of computer programs, which is one of the newer areas of debate. Since the copyright protection of computer programs involves technical and scientific matters that judges and other actors do not always find familiar, testimony of experts is often necessary and determining. In addition, when there is no objective way of checking the conclusions of analysis, the credibility of the expert also becomes important (Majone, 1989, p. 4).

The characteristics of the judge may become another important resource. Since the judge's understanding of the issues and implications can have important intervening effects on decision making, his ideological orientation may play an important role. As discussed in the case of journalists as agents, the judges' ideological inclination may influence the ways in which they understand issues and events. Various studies on the relationship between the judges' characteristics and their voting behavior have suggested that political orientation of judges may influence the decision-making process especially regarding economic and moral issues (Nagel, 1961; Ulmer, 1962; Glick and Emmert, 1986). Although it is difficult to assess the political and ideological orientation of each judge, investigation into the administration under which the judges were appointed could provide some indication of what their orientation is likely to be.

The judges' ideological orientation may relate to decision making in software copyright cases in two contradictory ways. It is possible that Republican judges are more willing to decide in favor of providing copyright protection as it preserves the status quo and thus benefits large corporations. Democratic judges may favor limiting the scope of copyright protection if that is considered to enhance the public interest. On the other hand, it is also possible that Democratic judges are more willing to decide in favor of broadening copyright protection, as they are supposed to be more willing to intervene to help small businesses in the industry. If that is the case, it seems that the relationship between the judges' characteristics and their decisions may depend on the situation of the software industry, i.e., how monopolized or centralized it is. This is a question that may be best answered through data analysis.

Recruiting and preparing specialized lawyers, experts, and preparing for court cases can all be costly. Thus enough money to support all these people and procedures is also an important mobilizing resource. Although it is not always the case, large firms usually have a relative advantage on these financial matters over small firms or individuals. It can be expected that the size of an organization may have a relationship to its ability to acquire mobilizing resources. It seems that the legal and financial resources partly inferred by the size of the firms give important characteristics to the stakeholders in the copyright decisions in relation to computer programs. The human and allocative resources can be assessed in terms of the size of the firm and the expertise of the legal counsel. This book examines how the legal and financial resources of the stakeholders may have implications on the current copyright decision-making process.

LEGAL ARGUMENTS

The structural rules and resources discussed above serve as constraints and enablements originating from the actors' capabilities and the givenness of the environment. Within the framework of structural rules and resources actors interact in order to meet their objectives. The essential processes of their interactions occur through their communication activities in the legal decision-making system, since arguments are central in all stages of the decision-making process. The arguments composed of legal theories and factual evidence are the result of strategic efforts of the participants, and can influence the understanding of what copyright is, what the problem is, and what the causes and effects of the problem are.

As argued before, in order to make effective and persuasive arguments, legal actors must be able to use typifications (combinations of legal rules, factual evidence, and authorities to support the theories) to frame the discourse in a way that is more likely to give advantage to their parties. How these typifications become "taken-for-granted" structural rules through the legal actors' communicative interactions, and how in this process, the typified structures gain objectivity and legitimacy, will be examined in a later chapter.

The arguments thus center around the statement of legal principles and rules supported by factual evidence. The legal rules are usually drawn from documented laws such as the Constitution, statutes, or precedent court decisions. Therefore, in theory, for example, the purpose of these rules, theories, doctrines is to "balance the exclusive right of copyright owners against the public's interest in the dissemination of information affecting areas of universal concern, such as art, science, and industry" (*Wainsright Secs. Inc. v. Wall Street Transcript Corp.*). But in reality, the Constitution, statutes, or legal principles and rules are subject to more than one reading (Wren and Wren, 1983, p. 83). Rules are "interpreted," sometimes through claims to reveal the original intent of the Founding Fathers or the legislature. The very attempt to add clarity, precision, and meaning to legislative words by the courts inevitably puts the courts in the role of adding dimensions to those words (Patterson and Lindberg, 1991). In the copyright law of computer programs, the ambiguity of statutes is even larger because the matters to which legislators responded to when they enacted the early copyright statutes would not have included written computer programs. Therefore, copyright-related legal theories can be interpreted in different ways by legal actors seeking different objectives.

In order to define various frames in the copyright discourse, this study categorizes the types of arguments in relation to the copyright protection principles and legal theories. This categorization does not necessarily allow any expectation about whether a certain principle or theory would benefit the plaintiff or the defendant; it only provides a framework for the legal actors to approach the copyright issues and for other actors in the court to understand the issues. The use of particular theories, not others, and interpretations of the theories in a certain way, not in another way, also provides frames with which people make sense of the copyright issues related to the court cases.

The concepts of "frames" and "framing" have been developed by Goffman (1974) and elaborated by communication scholars, especially in studies of interpersonal communication and media content (Edelman, 1988; Gitlin, 1980). Frames are organizing devices that individuals or organizations use to impose meaning on issues. The concept of framing rejects the proposition that there can be a single possible meaning that a text can offer or that a text can be understood by everyone in the same way. Rather, the structural and lexical features of the text will have an influence of "constructing some of the limits and parameters within which decodings will operate" (Hall, 1980, p. 135). Therefore, "some degree of reciprocity" seems to exist between frames in the arguments and the frames with which actors understand the issues (van Dijk, 1989; Hall, 1980). But this reciprocity does not suggest that there is a "necessary correspondence" between a set of structural and lexical features of a text and its meanings, since meanings result from actors' active interpretations of the text by linking the textual features to their knowledge and experiences (Hall, 1980). These frames are neither mutually exclusive nor exhaustive. All of these frames may be equally valid, but they provide a different insight of the trend in copyright law and the underlying values that are protected and reinforced by the copyright law.

The frames should be defined in a way that they could suggest socially embedded values that become constraints and enablements in the copyright discourse in relation to computer programs. These social values may be discerned by principles that lead to rules of action in concrete copyright cases. A great number of scholars have attempted to understand and define the principles and rules at work in the copyright system, employing historic, economic, literary, legal or interdisciplinary approaches. These approaches are neither mutually exclusive nor contradictory with each other (rather, they seem to be interrelated), but differ in terms of which kind of tension or conflicts of interests in the copyright law they focus on. In order to derive a useful framework to understand values implicit in copyright law regarding computer software, I will discuss different ways of categorizing legal arguments in detail in the next section.

Many of the critical historical analyses focus on demonstrating how the process of shaping copyright laws deprived or minimized the author's rights while the publishers were granted exclusive rights in the works created by the authors. Another frame that is commonly considered pertains to policy implications and consequences on the market. Some of policy-oriented arguments focus on the tension between the public access to the intellectual work and the author's rights to the work. This tension can be captured as a tension between authors and users or a tension between the public interest and private proprietary rights. A marketplace theme can be understood as an economic version of focusing on the tension between the public access and the author's rights or between innovation and control. The most recent trend in the comments on copyright law regards the distinction between authorship and the work as a product of the author's skills and effort. This frame focuses on the tension between the authorship (especially the Romantic notion of author-genius) and the work that is alienated from the author. Some scholars argue that the underlying tension of this distinction between work and authorship represents a conflict between individual autonomy and collectivism. There now follows a discussion of the arguments of scholars who have employed each frame.

Authors versus Copyright-Holders

Many historians have demonstrated how the power relations among the authors, publishers, and the State, which they use to legitimize their own interests, contribute to the shaping of copyright law. Patterson and Lindberg (1991) noted that because copyright was originally the product of a new communications technology (the printing press), and copyright issues now extend to include products of other new communications technology (the computer), the early history of copyright has a particular contemporary relevance. Bettig (1992) argues that copyright evolved as a legal concept during the period of the Renaissance, coinciding with the growth of industrialization and the rise of capitalism in Western Europe. According to him, the roots of copyright as a legal statute can be traced to the proliferation of the book trade in Europe, concomitant with the advent of printing in the early part of the fifteenth century.

Although some legal scholars posit that nascent forms of copyright had already existed as early as ancient Graeco-Roman times, and were observed by Western societies throughout the Middle Ages (Ploman and Hamilton, 1980; Stewart, 1983), the copyright that existed during these times emerged more out of concerns about the moral or natural rights of the authors of intellectual and creative works rather than out of economic or political considerations (Aziz, 1990). According to Ploman and Hamilton, the rights of authors had already been recognized in classical Greek culture, in the Talmudic principles of ancient Jewish law, and in the Roman publishing system (1980, p. 5-8). For example, in Talmudic law, reporters who orally passed on principles of law from one generation to another were very careful not to express such principles without mentioning the author. Analyses of authors' rights in Roman law indicate that plagiarism was recognized as morally wrong, but there was no direct evidence that legal sanctions existed (Ploman and Hamilton, 1980). Therefore, the copyright laws of early Rome and Greece placed its emphasis on the "moral rights" of the authors rather than economic rights (Stewart, 1983). Also, plagiarism was viewed as morally wrong in the Jewish culture, and the principle of rightful attribution to an author was a major concern of the Jewish prophets.

During the Middle Ages the religious institutions, particularly the monasteries, are said to have primarily participated in the preservation and development of intellectual works. The monks functioned as copyists, scholars, and authors, but very few works during this period reveal the name of the author. Authorship was not considered a right of a monk as an individual, but was attributed to the monastery as a moral person (Ploman and Hamilton, 1980, p. 8). Plagiarism and the wrongful or incorrect attribution to an author were subject to society's ridicule but not a law suit (Stewart, 1983, p. 15). Historians argue that this emphasis given to moral rights changed when the legal concept of copyright emerged with technological developments.

The technology of printing by movable type rendered copying manuscripts much easier and faster. Printing enhanced the spread of literary activities as much as it inspired new thought and the spread of new knowledge (Eisenstein, 1983). The proliferation of the printing press and the book trade brought about two major concerns: printers, who also functioned as bookbinders and publishers, soon had to face competition from those printing unauthorized copies of the books; and the State perceived the free dissemination of ideas as threatening to the status quo (Ploman and Hamilton, 1980).

The mechanism adopted for organizing and controlling the printing trade was to grant a publisher of a specific work individual privileges which contained a prohibition preventing anyone other than the beneficiary to sell the privileged work. Hence, the granting of rights and privileges came out of the political and economic considerations of the censorship of printed matter, and the protection of the interests of entrepreneurs involved in the printing and publishing activities. Therefore, Ploman and Hamilton (1980) argues, functions of the privileges had little to do with the protection of the author and his or her rights.

The first country to adopt a copyright statute in the modern sense was England. The Stationer's Company, consisting of members of the book trade—printers, bookbinders and booksellers, held a monopoly over printing and publishing in England. The Stationers' Company originally used copyright to regulate trade by protecting works published by one member from piracy. The Star Chamber Decrees of 1586 and 1637 and a series of licensing acts granted exclusive privileges to the Company. Bettig (1990) argues that all of these acts protected the economic rights of Company members, but there was no reference to the protection of authors' rights regarding their creative works in these acts. Stewart also indicates that "though the economic rights of the merchant class of printers and publishers were made explicit and protected by the system of royal patronage and the by-laws of the Stationers' Company, the rights of authors in their creative works per se were not contained in or formalized by the licensing acts or any one of the Star Chamber Decrees" (1983, p. 21).

By the end of the 17th century, writing became one of the ways of making a living, and was gradually becoming an individual pursuit for personal recognition. Authors and printers began to articulate the notion of "natural rights" in creative and intellectual works. Some scholars argue that the concept of the author's intellectual property right was being defined by scholars like John Locke (Ploman and Hamilton, 1980, p. 13). In the second of his 'Two Treatises of Government' (1947), Locke articulated the conception of "natural rights" within the notion of common law property by extending his labor theory of value (Ploman and Hamilton, 1980, p. 13). However, for Locke this natural right to property did not belong to servants and wage laborers who had to sell their labor to survive. Thus laborers alienated their natural right to own the products they produced when they contracted to labor for someone else (Bettig, 1989, p. 9). Rather, this notion of natural right was used by publishers to argue that, since authors had a natural right in their works as a result of their creative labor, the transfer of the right to copy to the publisher gave them a license in perpetuity to publish and profit from the work (Bettig, 1989, p. 9). Aziz notes that although the Lockean view of intellectual property rights which positions the author as the "natural owner of his or her works implicitly meant the shift of the ownership rights from the publisher to the author, it was used by publishers to secure perpetual ownership of the rights to multiply copies once authors surrendered their original manuscripts for printing in this time of the impending decline of the power of the Stationers' Company" (1989, p. 64-65). There seemed to be little question that authors should be paid for their manuscripts, but the payments from publishers were not based so much on legal as economic grounds (Ploman and Hamilton, 1980, p. 11-12).

It is suggested that this Lockean libertarian idea coupled with the abolishment of the Court of Star Chamber in 1641, the decreased regulatory power of the Stationers' Company after the English Civil War, and the rampant piracy in the aftermath of the House of Common's refusal to renew the Licensing Act, led the members of the publishing industry to begin to seek some form of statutory protection, and to argue for it in a petition to the House of Commons in 1707 (Bettig, 1989). The campaign for authors' rights was led by publishers because they perceived that when the statutory terms of copyright protection expired they would lose their monopoly privileges. The petitioners—the copyright holding publishers and printers, and the wholesalers tied to the monopoly, but no authors—finally secured legal protection in the "Act for the Encouragement of Learning and for Securing the Property of Copies of Books to the Rightful Owners Thereof (known as the 1710 Copyright Act or the Statute of Queen Anne)" (Bettig, 1989, p. 10).

The Statute codified not only the Stationers' copyright but also the author's right to copy. The Statute of Anne made it legal for any person, not only the authors and publishers, to acquire copyright. Thus, this statutory copyright was limited in time but broadened in terms of those who are eligible to own the right. On the other hand, as Ploman and Hamilton points out, the Act had the effect of benefiting publishers since the Act did not provide for "natural" right ownership to an author when the copyright was transferred to a publisher or passed into the public domain:

> "The Statute concerned the right to copy and no more. There was nothing in this Statute that touched upon the creative or moral rights of the author. The right protected was a "property" right. (1980, p. 13)"

The critical analysis of the history of the copyright law suggests that the legal notion of intellectual property supported the expansion of the realm of creative human activities that could be commoditized. It also suggests that copyright law facilitated the private appropriation of intellectual creativity, and legitimized the concentration of the ownership of literary and artistic works in the hands of publishers, a part of the emerging capitalist class (Bettig, 1990). In exchange for political loyalty, economic privileges were granted to printers and entrepreneurial booksellers. Through such patronage "property" ownership of literary and artistic works and their reproduction rights were highly concentrated in the hands of the publishers. This group, by virtue of their offer of a specialized entrepreneurial activity, justified claims to the perpetual right of property by articulating the idea of the creators' "natural" rights (Aziz, 1990, p. 60). First, the author's natural right was not recognized in copyright, but when it was recognized, it was used as a rationale by publishers for granting property rights to themselves.

The history of the British publishing industry and the development of copyright also demonstrates that copyright in a legal sense has emerged as an instrument through which certain groups and institutions—authors, publishers, and the State—legitimize their own interests. The incorporation of an author's right into copyright principles has obscured the separate interests of authors and publishers. Rather, in the realm of literary and artistic creativity, scholars argue that the actual creators of the copyrighted work lost control over their product and were separated from it when copyright protection became exclusive for the owners of the copyright—usually publishers with capital (Bettig, 1992). This was mostly due to the persuasive arguments of publishers articulating the rationale of granting the author's right for the publishers' own sake, which fit with the idea of the State organizing and controlling the information flow in society. Most of these provisions were contained in the United States' first federal Copyright Act of 1790, which replicated those of the English Statute of Anne.

The 1710 Statute of Anne is the direct ancestor of American copyright law: its full title identified the fundamental ideas (the encouragement of learning, copyright for authors, and limited times) of the copyright clause of the U.S. Constitution, and the statute itself clearly served as the model for the first U.S. copyright statute (Patterson and Lindberg, 1991, p. 47). Patterson and Lindberg (1991) argue that the history of copyright reveals that the copyright served to give economic rights to publishers, while the authors of the copyrighted work lost control over their work. They also claim that copyright for television and the computer today serves precisely the same function that copyright for the printing press served originally—to give entrepreneurs a monopoly over their products—with little regard to, or concern for, the authors who produce the product (p. 7). Responding to this claim, this book explores how the modern copyright arguments and decisions regarding computer software programs reflect this struggle between authors and publishers.

Public Interest versus Private Property Rights

The public/private contradiction has been considered by many scholars to be the fundamental conflict of purpose regarding copyright law. On the one hand, copyright aims to promote public disclosure and the dissemination of the information product. On the other hand, it seeks to confer on the creators the power to restrict or deny distribution of their works. This conflict is reflected in the tension between public benefit and private reward inscribed in the full title of the Statute of Anne of 1709: An Act for the Encouragement of Learning by vesting the Copies of printed Books in the author's or Purchasers of such Copies dying the Times therein mentioned."

In the U.S. Constitution, the purpose of copyright is stated in the intellectual property clause, which grants to Congress the power to enact copyright legislation:

> The Congress shall have power . . . to Promote the progress of Science and useful Arts, by securing for limited Times to Authors and Inventors the exclusive Right to their respective Writings and Discoveries (U.S. Consti. art. 1, §8, cl. 8.).

The keystone of copyright is thus the promotion of learning, and the protection of the author is given as an instrument for achieving this.

On the other hand, many critics point out that although the promotion of learning for the public interest still serves as a rationale for protecting economic rights, there is a gap between the purpose and the means through which to achieve this purpose in the modern U.S. copyright system. They question the basic assumption of the American copyright clause that granting rights to authors will bring some benefit to society by promoting learning. They argue that this assumption is not always supported in reality since protecting authors' economic rights itself does not necessarily promote learning. In that sense, a marketplace norm is an important concept that is related to policy implications as to the public benefit. Marketplace norms imply a theory of incentives: in securing opportunities for profits on the marketplace, copyright is supposed to provide maximum amount of information product available to society. Samuelson and others (1994), acknowledging this gap in the assumption of the authors' incentives and innovation especially in the area of computer software that has a critically functional aspect, advocate a market-oriented legal regime for the copyright protection of computer software.

Geller (1994) suggests that the marketplace norms have been elaborated against a background of enlightenment values, and argues that Anglo-American copyright laws, in the usual course of affairs, rely on marketplace norms while Continental European laws, when a case calls for a choice, favor authorship norms. According to him, although marketplace and authorship norms often lead to much the same results, in some hard cases, following one norm can lead to results inconsistent with those reached in following the other. By comparing the codified copyright clauses of the U.S. and French systems, and by comparing their philosophical origins of the copyright law, many scholars have argued that the French laws tend to place authors' rights (often their moral rights) on a more elevated basis than the Anglo-American copyright law (Goldstein, 1994). Interestingly, Geller himself pointed out the inadequacies of the framework of marketplace versus authorship norm as a conceptual tool for describing copyright, and tried to provide alternative ways to thinking about copyright law. Another scholar Ginsburg (1994) also refuted the notion of the incompatibility of French and Anglo-American copyright laws through an examination of the regimes of literary copyright in Revolutionary France and America. However, the conceptions of French copyright law as author-oriented and of Anglo-American copyright law as society-oriented or market-oriented still seem to be a prevalent view.

The analysis of legal arguments based on this frame of public interest versus private rights, or that of marketplace versus authorship rights, will examine how often the policy concerns are the focus of legal arguments, and in what ways those concerns are expressed in those arguments, i.e., whether they involve public interest concerns, present the speculation or provide data on actual consequences on the actors or on the market, merely restate the policy concern without any basis, or use the encouragement of author's creativity as the only rationale.

Authorship versus Work

Some scholars have suggested that the formulation of the public/private contradiction may not accurately capture the true essence of the fundamental conflict of interests that underlies copyright (see Jaszi, 1994). It is partly because the public/private distinction is not a concrete entity but a construct, of which meanings change according to situations. Accordingly, some scholars suggest the examination of the different meaning of the public/private constructs. On the other hand, other scholars suggest a formulation of the work versus authorship as a more useful framework to understand the copyright system.

The work versus authorship frame is drawn from a series of critical arguments regarding the Romantic notion of authorship. This Romantic notion considers that "genuine" authorship is "originary," in the sense that it results not in a variation, an imitation, or an adaptation, and certainly not in a mere reproduction, but in an utterly new, unique, "original" work which may be said to be the property of its creator and to merit the law's protection (Woodmansee and Jaszi, 1994). In "What Is an Author?" Foucault (1979) posed questions about the causes and consequences of the persistent, over-determined power of the author construct. Locating the emergence of the "author" in the cultural context of the eighteenth century, he called our attention to neither neutral nor inevitable, but culturally laden concept of "authorship," which he argued represented means to the end of constraining the "proliferation of meaning." Scholars who examine the construction of authorship note that the Romantic ideas about creativity and individual authorship (which do not encompass comparative manifestations of creativity) remain in the realm of copyright. The powerful notion of the authorship and the possibility of its change were also an underlying concern for Kaplan (1967), when he pointed out the emergence of new kind of intellectual work, which "is now being made by teams, a practice apt to continue and grow." He argued that such collaboration may diffuse and diminish emotions of original discovery and exclusive ownership that is prevalent in copyright law.

The arguments that the ideology of individual creativity is praised in copyright law are seemingly contrary to the other scholars' claim that the right of authors was not recognized in copyright or only used as a rationale by publishers for granting property rights to themselves. However, these two strands of arguments actually agree in acknowledging that the shaping of the copyright law is influenced by interactions of stakeholders. Their conclusions seem to be contradictory in terms of their focus: the former focusing on the conflict between publishers and authors that resulted in furthering unequal power relations between them, and the latter focusing on the construction of the author as the bearer of special legal rights and cultural privileges which carries consequences for the ways in which power and wealth are distributed.

Jaszi (1991), in his "Toward a Theory of Copyright: The Metamorphoses of Authorship," illustrates how the authorship construct has been mobilized in legal discourse, especially in its relationship to the concept of the "work" alienated from its author. According to him, the authorship construct has been constantly modified but remains as the central notion in copyright, reflecting the contradiction between the collectivism of the marketplace and the prerogatives of the autonomous individual. He argues that the inherent instability of the "authorship" construct renders "work" the vehicle for a significant expansion of copyright protections. The "work" was the commodity form or the objectification of the "author's" labor, and the publisher was able to realize the surplus value of that labor. Thus the "work" displaced the "author" as the central idea of copyright law, minimizing the threat to free exchange posed by the notion of an intimate link between the author and her productions, which Jaszi calls the strategic suppression of the "author." On the other hand, the maturation of the "work" as a legal concept increased the leverage of publishers and other purchasers of "authors"' rights.

One example of the arguments in which the focus is on the work rather than on its author is the objective test of copyrightability for derivative works. According to Jaszi, the nature of any creative investment in the variations is, as a practical matter, simply irrelevant to the outcome, save in one respect: the variations must be traceable to a human actor; they cannot arise from mere mechanical mishaps. In this sense, he argues, "authorship" still matters. In substance, the opinion marginalizes and trivializes "authorship"; but in form, it continues to acknowledge the centrality of the concept by transforming itself into the "minimalist" and "democratized" vision of authorship. Another example illustrating how the notion of authorship interacts with the notion of the work involves the ownership or authorship dispute of the program. Jaszi argues that the individualistic Romantic vision of "authorship" is central to the conceptualization of the so-called "work-for-hire" doctrine. On the one hand, when a work is deemed to have been made "for-hire," that alienation of creative workers from the products of their labor is formally and legally complete: the "author" of the "work" is the person on whose behalf the "work" was made, not the individual who created it. On the other hand, the employers' claims are rationalized in terms of the Romantic conception of "authorship" with its concomitant values of "originality" and "inspiration."

The work versus authorship frame and Jaszi's interpretive scheme of analyzing the construct of authorship provide an analytical framework by which we can examine the underlying values in the copyright arguments and decisions regarding computer software, and how the values sustain or change through the process of arguments over time.

From the above review of some approaches to describing and understanding the shaping of copyright law, several important concepts emerge: the author, the work, the public interest, and marketplace. One important concept that is missing is the notion of use. The use of programs by purchasers as end users is only implicitly included in the discussion of the public interest and marketplace. In addition, the notion of the use of the underlying program by a potential developer of another program is important and complicated, and this is not considered explicitly in the above approaches. As Samuelson and others (1994) note, many programs on the market are composites of programs, each of which could exist separately because there is no material difference between a "task" and a "sub-task." Therefore, innovation in software development is typically incremental and largely cumulative. By adopting available software design elements either wholesale or to a new context, programs contribute to and benefit from a cumulative innovation process. These characteristics of computer programs, when acknowledged as distinguishable from other works of authorship, could be used as a basis to hold different decisions in infringement cases according to the nature of the defendant's use of the underlying program. Examining how the courts combine this issue of the nature of use with the various constructs of authorship will illustrate the ways in which the copyright law balances the different values underlying those concepts.

Therefore, the key concepts employed in this book in analyzing legal arguments are authorship, work, and use. The concepts of authorship and work can be divided into those of the plaintiff and those of the defendant, when necessary for analysis. The concept of use includes the use by the defendant, the use of the public as end users of the program, and the marketplace that determines the potential use of the program. While all the legal arguments are categorized in terms of these frames, many of them also contain identifiable legal rules or theories such as the originality rule or the fair use doctrine that are commonly used in copyright law. The description of each legal rule and its possible interpretations will be provided when the findings of the analysis are presented in later chapters. The legal theories are neither mutually exclusive nor are an exhaustive set of possible legal theories, but these theories are the rationales often suggested as a reason or means to implement copyright. All of these theories claim to serve the purpose of copyright, and all of them are valid on their own in regards to the copyright protection of computer programs. At the same time, all of these theories are subject to different interpretations. An argument using one doctrine can be used as an argument either in favor of or in opposition to extending copyright protection. Thus, the ways in which these theories are presented differently by different stakeholders in their arguments can have significant implications on how the copyright law is actually implemented, and on who receives the benefit and who receives the detriment.

The categorization of the frames and legal theories itself is not necessarily related to any result regarding whether a certain frame or theory would benefit the plaintiff or the defendant. Instead, the use of the frames and rules provides a framework for approaching the copyright issues. How the frames and rules are interpreted by the plaintiffs and defendants, how these different frames and theories function in relation to resources of the actors, and how the structural rules are reproduced and mobilized through the process of communicative interactions, are the main concern of this book.

RESEARCH QUESTIONS

In this section, I will summarize previous discussions with the aim of formulating a set of specific research questions in order to examine the process in which copyright stakeholders regarding computer programs use their strategic efforts to influence court decisions in their arguments, rationale, and interpretations. By examining the ways in which judges accept and reject the plaintiff's and defendant's use and interpretation of legal frames and theories, this book will explore the processes in which the structural rules and resources are reproduced and mobilized through actors' discursive interactions.

The structure of the legal decision-making system is constructed according to structural rules—legal rules and facts—and the human and allocative resources that the actors have. This book examines the ways in which these rules and resources work as enablements and constraints on the actors in the copyright system who try to obtain their objectives through their communicative activities, that is via their arguments. How, in doing so, the legal actors produce and reproduce those rules and resources in the copyright system, and thereby reproduce the enablements and constraints that are implicit in social and economic power relationships, is the critical concern of this study. Thus I will first examine the structural environment of legal rules, interpretations, or copyright decisions over time. It is important to identify the ways in which social meanings are embedded and transformed into the frames, legal rules, and interpretations. This analysis of legal arguments is combined with an examination of how human and allocative resources of legal actors relate to the ways in which they make legal arguments. I will explore how the two factors – the resources of actors and structural environment — may interactively relate to the ways in which the parties make arguments. I will then examine how the relationship between the resources of legal actors and court decisions can be explained with reference to the relationship between these resources and the ways in which legal actors make arguments using legal rules and facts.

This book tries to identify the conditions under which certain arguments using certain rules and facts are accepted or rejected by judges. In this process, the typified rules and facts become objectified when the court decisions and opinions once decided become the rules and facts in future cases. Therefore, examining these conditions helps us to explore the processes in which structural rules are reproduced and transformed, and thus social meanings embedded in the structure are reproduced and transformed.

Answering the following set of research questions will contribute to revealing the mechanisms by which the copyright system is shaped and reproduced through legal arguments. The questions start with the descriptive analyses of the important factors of the study. Then the relationships between the court decisions and possible explanatory variables such as the nature and resources of legal actors, judges' characteristics, or the nature of the case in terms of the programs are analytically questioned. Then questions regarding analyses of legal arguments follow. For the purpose of comparison, legal arguments are analyzed according to the issues involved in the cases. Regarding each issue, I will analyze the legal arguments made by the actors including the use of frames, legal theories, and their interpretations. The changes in legal arguments according to the time frame are also discussed. This book attempts to provide an important understanding of the ways in which the difference in the resources of actors are reflected in their arguments, through which a certain structure of power and dominance is maintained and transformed.

1 What are the general legal characteristics of the cases and the legal actors?

1.1 What are the distributions of the state and the circuit where the cases were held, the procedural status of the cases, the judges' characteristics, the major topic of the cases, the subject matter of the dispute, the kind of program developed by the defendant, if any, and the decisions of the cases? Have the general characteristics of the cases changed over time?

2. What are the nature of the actors?
2.1 How is the nature of the actors (in terms of whether they are software developers, copyright holders, both developers and copyright holders, distributors, or users) distributed? Is there any change over time?
2.2 What is the nature of the cases derived from the nature of the actors (such as developer versus developer, developer versus copyright holder, copyright holder versus copyright holder, etc.)? Is there any change over time?

3 How are the human and allocative resources measured and distributed?
3.1 How are the human and allocative resources, measured in terms of whether the party is an individual or a firm, distributed?
3.2 How are the human and allocative resources, measured in terms of the size of the organization, distributed among legal actors?
3.3 How does the nature of the actors relate to their human and allocative resources?

4 What are the factors that may influence the court decisions?
4.1 How do the general characteristics of the cases relate to the court decisions?
4.2 How do the nature of actors relate to the court decisions?
4.3 How do the human and allocative resources relate to the court decisions?

5 How can the legal arguments be characterized?
5.1 What are the identifiable frames of the legal arguments?
5.2 What are the legal theories that are used by the plaintiffs, defendants, and judges?

5.3 What are the different ways of interpreting the theories and arguments?
5.4 What are the possible social meanings embedded in the frames, legal theories, and interpretations?
5.5 What are the typified legal rules and arguments that become the structural rules of the copyright cases pertaining to computer software?

6 What is the relationship between the actors and their legal arguments?
6.1 Are there any differences in the use of frames and legal theories between plaintiffs and defendants?
6.2 Are there any differences in the interpretations of the frame and legal theories between plaintiffs and defendants?
6.3 Are there any differences in the use of frames, legal theories and interpretations according to the nature of the actors (developer, copyright holder, both, neither)?
6.4 Are there any differences in the use of frames, legal theories and interpretations according to the nature of the cases indicated by a different combination of actors?

7 What is the relationship between legal arguments and the court decisions?
7.1 Is there a particular frame of arguments that is more likely to be accepted or rejected by judges?
7.2 Are there particular legal theories that are more likely to lead to certain kind of decisions?

8 What are the conditions under which certain arguments are accepted or rejected by judges? How are the conditions related to the ways in which the parties use their resources and structural rules?
8.1 What are the frames, legal theories or certain kinds of interpretations that are accepted or rejected by judges in arguments made in each issue of the cases?
8.2 Are there any differences in the judges' acceptance or rejection of frames, legal theories, and interpretations

according to the argument makers? In other words, does the relationship between the nature of the actors and the use of legal arguments explain the relationship between the actors and decisions? Does it also explain the relationship between the nature of cases and decisions?

8.3 What kind of social meanings can be inferred from the conditions in which certain arguments (and frames, theories and interpretations used in the arguments) are accepted and rejected?

9 Are there identifiable ways in which the structural rules are reproduced or transformed (thus social meanings transmitted in them are reproduced or transformed) through these communicative interactions?

These research questions try to examine how different actors with different resources make arguments in the framework of legal rules and facts and how their interactions through arguments influence decisions. To reiterate, this book attempts to provide an understanding of the ways in which the difference in the resources of actors are reflected in their arguments, through which the structure of power and dominance is maintained and transformed.

CHAPTER 4

The Process of Research

This chapter describes the methods that are employed in the study. First, I will introduce an overview of the research design and its major conceptual categories. Following this, I will present the data of the study. Then I will discuss the instrumentation of each conceptual variable. Finally I will present the ways in which the data are analyzed.

RESEARCH DESIGN

I utilize both quantitative and qualitative approaches to examine how the different rules and resources that legal actors employ function as enablements and constraints in their communicative activities, and how these communicative activities relate to the court decisions. Content analysis of legal arguments is conducted and then related to the analyses using the other variables of legal arguments, legal actors' resources, and court decisions.

First, I will assess the level of resources of each legal actor in the court cases regarding the copyright of computer software. Then I will identify the legal resources including the nature and status of legal actors and their financial ability. In addition, I will assess the structural environment by examining precedent decisions by the time each case was held and the use of legal rules and interpretations in previous cases. I will also explore how the structural environment has changed over time. This study involves three related areas of analyses: the relationship between actors' resources and copyright decisions; the relationship between copyright decisions and the use and interpretation of rules and facts in legal arguments; and the relationship between actors' resources and the use and interpretation of rules and facts in legal arguments.

Data Collection

I analyze all of the federal court cases regarding the copyright protection of computer software programs that were filed and published by 1993. All the cases were held at the level of District Court or Court of Appeals. A comprehensive list of the relevant cases was obtained by a series of procedures. The Lexis/Nexis database was used to generate the initial list. In the library of federal copyright cases in the Lexis database, two hundred and eight cases regarding computer software programs were found. I compared all of the 208 cases that were retrieved from the Lexis database with the previous list and read them to determine whether each case was directly related to copyright protection of computer software program. Those cases that are not directly related to the copyright infringement or copyrightability issues of computer software were excluded from the data. Such cases that only concern trade secret preemption issues, patent issues, monopolies, license agreements, fraud, copyright registration issues were excluded. Unpublished cases were not used as data because it was not possible to obtain relevant information to use in the analyses. In this way, one hundred and fifteen cases were selected as data of this study (the list is presented in the appendix).

I analyzed the full-text reports of all the cases. Actors' allocative resources were gathered using outside materials including many data sets. The reports of the cases that are basically the judges' opinions and rationales of the decisions indirectly reflect the arguments of the plaintiffs and defendants. Therefore, I could also assess arguments of the plaintiffs and defendants through the reports of the judges' opinions. I was concerned about the limitation of this study in that it relies on the judges' reports in analyzing the arguments of all the actors. Judges may accept or ignore certain arguments made by plaintiffs or defendants without explicitly mentioning them. In order to examine the degree of discrepancy between the parties' initial arguments and their arguments reflected in the court opinions, I drew a sample of 13 cases and obtained the briefs submitted by the counsels of the plaintiffs and defendants. In 7 of the 13 cases briefs of the both parties were obtained and in the remaining 6 cases, I could only obtain briefs of only 1 of the parties. I recorded each issue included in the briefs, with a special focus on the use of legal theories and compared it with the judges' opinions. Among the 29 identified arguments used by the parties, only 3 of them were missing in the judges' opinions. And all the three arguments that are missing were the ones of the winning parties, which suggest that the omitted issue was not likely to be critical in decision-making. Between the plaintiffs and the defendants, the issues and legal theories they used in the briefs tended to be the same. Even when one of the issues that was covered in one party's briefs was not included in the other party's brief, the other party always included that issue in their reply brief.

Probably due to the tendency that the two parties usually communicate before the actual trial, the issues and legal theories that are used by the parties tend to be the same eventually, even though the interpretations of theories or conclusions they draw from the issue tend to be contrasting. This confirms the importance of analyzing different ways of interpreting legal theories rather than focusing exclusively on the existence of the theories. And the judges are found to be very likely to examine in their opinions all the issues that were initiated by the parties in their opinions. This is consistent with the arguments of Conrey and O'Barr as well as other critical legal scholars and feminists that legal decision makers, especially those in the adversarial U.S. system, choose among contending voices, and the law cannot have a voice apart from the voices of the participants (1990, p. 169). In addition, the rejection of certain arguments and behaviors provides important guidance with which other actors, both involved in legal cases and involved in the creation, distribution, and consumption of software programs in a society, learn and understand the copyright system. As the judges' opinions and decisions that define precedent are what become influential in the process of copyright law, examining the court reports written by the judges will provide a valuable insight into the processes in which structural rules are reproduced and transformed through communicative interactions among the legal actors.

INSTRUMENTATION

I will discuss the methods of measurement in three subject areas: resources, decisions, and structural rules. As discussed before, legal resources include the nature and size of the firms. Legal arguments are analyzed in terms of the ways in which frames and legal theories are used, the legal theories are interpreted, and the precedent cases are provided to support the legal theories. The decisions and arguments in precedent cases as well as characteristics of judges constitute the structural environment.

Procedural Status of Cases

The cases are different in terms of the procedural status. There are cases that are decided on their merits, i.e., whether infringement has or has not occurred, after full trial dealing with all the contested facts. In this case, final judgment is made. On the other hand, summary judgment is appropriate "if there is no genuine issue as to any material fact and that the moving party is entitled to a judgment as a matter of law (Fed. R. Civ. P. 56(c))." Judges grant summary judgments when there are no relevant facts in dispute, but only different legal interpretations given by the parties to the facts, in which case the judge can decide without a trial (but summary judgments will only be affirmed if there are no facts in dispute).

Preliminary injunction is granted to temporarily enjoin the alleged infringer from copying, manufacturing, using, or distributing the original program. There are four factors of which satisfaction most courts require: (1) the plaintiff has a likelihood of success on the merits of his claim; (2) the plaintiff does not have an adequate remedy at law and it will suffer irreparable harm without the injunction; (3) this harm is greater than the injury the defendant will suffer it the injunction is granted; and (4) the injunction will not harm the public interest. Other courts require that the plaintiff show either irreparable harm and likelihood of success, or irreparable harm and the existence of serious questions going to the merits and balance of hardship. Which exact combination of the above factors is used in the case depends on the judge and the court, while judges usually require some kind of variation of the four factors. Judges tend to claim that none of the four factors are definitive, although there are some judges who explicitly weigh the factors differently. In order to examine how these factors are considered in the arguments and decisions, arguments in the preliminary injunction cases will be analyzed separately.

Arguments regarding the likelihood of success on the merits in preliminary injunction cases have similar structure and considerations to the arguments on the merits in final judgments and summary judgment cases. The only difference is that the judges in preliminary injunction cases decide on the basis of only the "reasonable likelihood" of the success on the merits, whereas the judges full trials decide on the actual merits. Therefore, the arguments around the merits will be analyzed in all the cases.

Subject Matter

A computer program in the Copyright Act of 1980 is defined as a "set of statements or instructions to be used directly or indirectly in a computer in order to bring about a certain result." There are many ways to categorize computer programs. First, they can be classified according to form, having either literal elements or non-literal elements. Literal elements are divided into object code and source. A program in object code form, called machine language, can be directly executed by the computer. Because machine language consists of a series of binary numbers, programs in object code form are difficult for programmers to work with directly (Gage, 1987, p. 868). Thus programmers use higher level computer languages based on English words or symbols. Programs written in higher languages are called source code programs and must be converted into an object code before the computer can execute the program. Non-literal elements include the structure, sequence, and/or organization, screen display, user interface, and function or purpose.

Second, programs can be categorized by function, either as application programs or operating system programs. Application programs allow the computer user to accomplish specific tasks such as using spread sheets, playing games, or editing text. In contrast, operating system programs direct the computer to carry out steps that allow the user to operate the computer and run application programs. Videogame programs are included in the data and are considered a separate category in this study.

And third, computer programs are classified according to their embodiment, that is the memory device on which a program is stored. Computer programs are commonly stored on either magnetic disks or silicon chips. Within magnetic disks, a program is recorded on the face of a rotating disk and can be modified or copied relatively easily. While disks containing programs are generally kept outside the computer until needed, silicon chips are built into the computer. Within tiny silicon chips, a program is stored in integrated circuits and cannot be modified without substantial effort.

The computer programs considered in these legal cases are classified according to their form, function, and embodiment. In every case there is an original computer program of which the movant claims copyright ownership, and which the movant claims to be infringed by the program developed or used by the other party. The subject matter of each case is categorized according to the following dimensions: whether the original program is an operating system program, an application program, or a game program; whether the main issue of the cases is the literal (object code or source code) or non-literal elements (user interfaces, screen display, or structure, sequence and organization) of the original program; and whether the original program is embodied in silicon chips or in magnetic disks.

There can be other computer programs than the original programs which are developed or used by the defendant. In copyrightability cases, there is usually no other program involved, as the claims of the challengers of the copyright validity focus on the issue that the original program should not be copyrighted or its copyright is not valid. All the classifications that are made to the original program are applied to the other programs in the cases as well, i.e., what kind of characteristic the other programs have in relation to the original program. For example, whether the other program has the same function, but is written in different language, whether the other program is an application program that works on the original operating system program, whether the other program is a device to alter features of the original program, etc., will be examined.

Nature of Parties Involved in the Case

The parties involved in the cases consist of the plaintiffs and the defendants. Usually the plaintiffs initiate the case alleging that the defendants infringed the copyright of the plaintiff's program. However, in some cases, the plaintiff initiates the case as a response to the accusation of defendant that the plaintiff infringed the copyright of the defendant's program. The cases in which defendants become movants and vice versa are very rare (10 out of 115 cases). Therefore, for the purpose of analysis, this study categorizes the movant of the case as the plaintiff and the alleged infringer (in infringement cases) or the challenger of the copyright validity (in copyrightability cases) as the defendant.

The nature of the actors will be first examined according to the involvement of each actor with the original program, i.e., the developer of the original program who is not the copyright holder, the copyright holder of the program who is not a developer, the developer and copyright holder of the program, and neither (retailers, importers, etc.). In a case that a defendant is not involved with the original program in any way, it is important to examine whether he or she is associated with other kinds of programs or not. Thus, whether an actor is a developer or a copyright holder of any other programs will be also examined.

Judges' Characteristics

The judge's characteristics such as ideological orientation, age, and education may be an important factor of the structural environment that may have some intervening influence on the decision-making process. Some studies focusing on civil rights cases or antitrust cases show that decisions may be predicted according to the judges' ideological orientation. As discussed earlier, the judges' ideological orientation may play a role in the case of the copyright protection of computer software in two contradictory ways according to the market situation and the judges' view on the best way to enhance the public interest. Therefore, the examination of the relationship between the judges' characteristics and their decision-making in this area remains to be exploratory.

In order to find an accurate indication of their ideological orientation, I searched survey or data that provide information on the nature and the degree of ideological orientation of each judge.

Information on the party affiliation of a substantial number of judges was not available because many of the judges did not report their party affiliation in these sources. Therefore, alternatively, I assessed the administration under which the judges were appointed, since it can offer a relatively reliable indication of the judges' resources in terms of their ideological orientation. Information on the appointed year, age of the judges, and education was also found in the American Bench—Judges of the Nation and BNA's Directory of State & Federal Courts, Judges, & Clerks.

Time Periods

This study does not assume one clear classification according to time change. However, due to the number of cases, dissecting the 16 year periods into a smaller category is sometimes needed for the sake of analysis. In that case, the 16 years were divided into 5 periods, each of which has a 3 year period, except for the third period which is four years long. Thus, the first period is from 1978 to 1980, the second period from 1981 to 1983, the third period from 1984 to 1987, the fourth period from 1988-1990, and the fifth period from 1991 to 1993.

Decisions

The court decisions are first categorized as in favor of the plaintiff (movant) or of the defendant (alleged infringer in infringement cases and challenger in copyrightability cases). Next the analysis investigates whether the decision is that infringement occurred or that infringement did not occur in infringement cases, and that in favor of granting copyrightability or against granting copyrightability in copyrightability cases. The decisions are also categorized as "broadening the scope of copyright protection" or "narrowing the scope of copyright protection." In the preliminary injunction cases the decisions are also made as to whether the injunction was granted for the plaintiff or not. The decisions at the level of court of appeals additionally include the following categories: affirmed, reversed, and reversed and remanded. Judges in some cases sometimes ordered the cases to be "remanded" and send the cases back to the court at the lower level. In these cases, they are later combined with the "reversed" category.

Size of Firm

As noted before, large organizations usually have a relative advantage regarding financial matters over small firms or individuals. Since recruiting specialized lawyers, experts, and preparing for court cases can be all costly, the size of the firm is expected to relate to the ability of the firm to effectively use rules and resources in some of the cases.

It can be speculated that there are two ways in which the size of the firm may relate to legal arguments or decisions. First the financial ability to hire qualified attorneys and spend more money for litigation seems to be more directly related to the sales revenue. On the other hand, the perceived status of the firm can be either related to the number of employees or sales revenue. Therefore, two indices of the size of the firm are separately assessed and used in the analyses. Using Dialog Business Connection service including Dun's Market Identifiers in D&B database and the Computer Select database, I assessed the number of employees and the sales revenue for each company in the relevant cases.

It is important to note that the variables of the resources of legal actors such as the nature and size of the firm should be considered in relation to the opposing party in each case. A copyright holding firm of a middle size can be perceived in very different ways when it is defending against an individual developer and against a large non-developing corporation. Therefore, I create another variable to indicate a relative size of the firms in each case.

Legal Counsel

The ability to hire attorneys with legal knowledge and ability in litigation and expertise in the copyright law is an important legal resource. The names of the lawyers in the cases are identified in the reports of the decisions. The Martindale-Hubble Law Directory provides legal ability ratings on both lawyers and firm ratings on law firms. 'A' represents the rating from very high to preeminent, 'B'. from high to very high and 'C' from fair to high. The ratings of the law firms only consist of 'A' and 'B'. The ratings of the lawyers and the law firms they represent will be used to construct an index that indicates the ability and expertise of legal counsel. In the case the organization employs an in-house lawyer, the law firms for whom they worked previously will be identified.

Arguments

I analyze the arguments of the plaintiffs, defendants, and judges in court opinions in order to examine the actors' use of rules and resources in their communicative activities. The reports usually start with a description of the case including the issue of dispute, and the nature of the plaintiffs and defendants. The structure of legal arguments differs according to the judge. Usually judges respond to plaintiffs' and defendants' arguments even when they structure their arguments with their own analytical style. Since judges tend to articulate why they reject certain arguments made by a losing party rather than provide reasons why they accept certain arguments, judges' arguments mainly consist of the arguments that they are about to reject, followed by the judges' opinions on each point and issue.

The unit of analysis in relation to decision variables and actor variables is a case. For an analysis of arguments, however, I coded each argument in each case in order to include all the theories and issues dealt with in the case, because a case can have several different arguments. This usually does not pose any problem in analysis since the analysis of the arguments is conducted according to the issue of the case, regarding which each case tends to have one argument. Therefore, the unit of analysis in terms of the case and that in terms of the arguments remains the same in the detailed analysis of arguments conducted according to each case, unless the case has many arguments using the same frame and the same theory (some judges tend to write more when it's actually one argument). In this instance, the analysis of arguments employs each case as a unit of analysis by considering the arguments as one.

Arguments of legal actors are first coded according to whether the argument-maker is claiming: the subject matter is (or not) copyrightable, should (or not) be copyrighted; the copyright is (or not) valid; copying did (or not) occur; two programs are (or not) substantially similar; the copying does (or not) constitutes infringement; and the plaintiff (or the defendant) is the author. All of these arguments can be more broadly categorized as either broadening copyright protection or limiting copyright protection.

The contexts of these arguments are important in analyzing the legal arguments. In order to compare the plaintiff's and defendant's arguments and to examine the trend over time, arguments in the same category of issues should be compared. Thus the arguments are broadly categorized as copyrightability, ownership/authorship dispute, and infringement, and the analysis of frames and theories are conducted in each issue.

When the arguments are not initiated by judges, the judges' response to the arguments made by plaintiffs or defendants is coded as follows: accept the plaintiff's argument; accept the defendant's argument; reject the plaintiff's argument (implicitly accepting the defendant's argument; and reject the defendant's argument (implicitly accepting the plaintiff's argument). Since rejecting one party's argument usually means accepting the other party's argument in the court of adversarial system, all of the judges' arguments can be broadly categorized as in favor of the plaintiff and in favor of the defendant.

I also examine the reason for the rejection of the rules or the arguments about the rules made by plaintiffs or defendants: because the rule itself is not right or appropriate; on the basis of different interpretation of the rule; because the rule is not relevant to the case; because the rule is not applicable to the particular facts considered; due to insufficient factual evidence to support the rule; or due to the wrong use of the authority.

Most importantly, the legal arguments are categorized in terms of their primary frame, the existence of legal theories, the interpretation of the theories, and the provision of factual evidence and authorities to support the theories. As discussed in the previous chapter, frames of each of the legal arguments can be categorized as the author, the work, the use (by the defendant), the public interest, and market consequences. I will present examples of coding the arguments according to the frames.

Arguments that used the frame of the "plaintiff's work" are usually about whether computer programs are copyrightable as a subject matter or whether the copyright of the plaintiff's program is valid. For example, in *Uniden v. EFJ* (1985), EFJ, who manufactured and sold two-way radio systems, developed a software program, and Uniden developed and sold a compatible radio system. Uniden argued that EFJ's computer code is not copyrightable because a computer program is a "useful" work, but the judge held that a computer program is a "literary" work, thus copyrightable. These arguments were coded as having a frame of the plaintiff's work. Most of these arguments are made in the cases pertaining the copyrightability of the subject matter, and some of these arguments are also made in infringement cases where the defendants try to argue that the similarity between the two programs falls under the idea of the program rather than the expression of the program.

The frame of the "plaintiff's authorship" usually involves arguments on the originality of the program developed by the plaintiff. For example, in *Kramer v. Anrews*(1985), when Andrews and other defendants argued that the copyright of a video poker game 'Hi-Lo Double Up Joker Poker' developed by Kramer was invalid because it lacked originality, the judges argued that the standard for originality is minimal, enough if it is something "his own" and held that the copyright of the plaintiff's program was valid. These arguments are coded as having the frame of the "plaintiff's authorship." The arguments that use the frame of the plaintiff's authorship are usually made in the copyrightability cases, but in some infringement cases where the defendants try to challenge the validity of the plaintiff's copyright by challenging the originality of the program.

Many arguments focus on determining the substantial similarity between a program developed by the plaintiff and a program developed by the defendant. When the argument centered around finding the textual or functional similarity of the two programs, the argument was coded as having the frame of the "defendant's work." When the argument focused on the effort or expertise of the defendant in developing her program, the argument was coded as having the frame of the defendant's authorship. For example, in *Atari v. Williams* (1981), Williams who developed a game program 'Jawbreaker' argued that his idea came from Atari's 'PacMan,' but the expression of the idea through symbols and graphics was not similar to 'PacMan'. Employing some similarity tests, the judge held that 'Jawbreaker' did not infringe the copyright of 'PacMan' because Atari failed to show any possible confusion between the two games. These arguments were coded as having the frame of the defendant's work.

On the other hand, when Holiday Steel argued that they sought to create its own product through a laborious and expensive process in *NEC v. Holiday,* the judge held that a great effort to copy a work does not mean that a copier is not an infringer. Also, in *NEC v. Intel* (1986), when Intel argued that NEC must have copied its 8086 and 8088 microcodes because NEC's creator of the program was inexperienced, the judge disagreed by saying that he believed NEC's expert testimony that the NEC's creator did have expertise and talent as opposed to Intel's argument. These arguments that focused on how much the defendants contributed to the development of their own programs are coded as having the frame of the "defendant's authorship."

The arguments that have the frame of the "defendant's use" usually center around either fair use doctrine or the adaptation of the program. Modifications of programs were made valid under 17 U.S.C. §117, which permits the adaptation of the program for utilitarian purposes and for archival use. *In Allen-Myland, Inc. (AMI) v. IBM* (1990), AMI argued that their copying of the IBM's microcodes is permissible as it is an essential step in the owner's enhancement and used for archival use, and the judge held that these doctrines do not apply to AMI's copying. These arguments were coded as having the frame of the defendant's use of the program. Also, there are 4 factors required for fair use: the purpose of use, nature of the copyrighted work, amount and substantiality of the portion used from the copyrighted work, and the effect on the potential market. The arguments regarding fair use are usually coded as the ones having a frame of the defendant's use, unless one of the factors is considered a decisive one and discussed elaborately, in which case its frame is decided according to that particular factor. An analysis of how each of the 4 factors was considered is separately presented later.

Arguments that use the frame of "market consequences" usually focus on the impact of the defendant's program on the market or on the incentive to innovation. For example, in *Vault v. Quaid* (1988), Quaid manufactured a program called 'CopyWrite' with a segment of 'Ramkey' which allows a user to make copies of programs contained on floppy diskettes. Vault argued that because purchasers of 'CopyWrite' use them to make unauthorized copies, Vault lost customers of its program 'Prolok'. But the judges decided that while a purchaser of 'CopyWrite' violates the law, Quaid who developed the program does not. The plaintiff made an argument on the basis of the issue of market consequences and the judge rejected its argument implying that the market consequence is not an important factor to be considered. The plaintiff's and defendant's arguments were coded as having the frame of consequences.

The "public use" frame is not very common, as will be discussed later, but when the arguments focus on how the public may benefit from gaining more access to the programs or that the program was made available to the public, the arguments were coded as having the frame of public use/benefit.

In addition, plaintiffs, defendants, and judges often make arguments based on various legal theories such as originality, fixation requirement, idea versus expression, adaptation, fair use, first sale, etc. The theories are applied to the facts and sometimes interpreted in different ways by the courts and the judges. Even though certain theories tend to fall into a certain frame rather than the other, such as the originality theory usually falling into the frame of authorship, one theory does not necessarily match one particular frame. This is because parties in opposing interests can use the same theory to frame the arguments in their favor and the judges interpret or apply the theories differently according to the nature of the arguments and the nature of the cases. Therefore, I code legal theories and interpretations separately.

Sometimes the focus of the arguments is not definitively on one of these. For example, arguments regarding whether the plaintiff's work is in the public domain involve the nature of the plaintiff's work, but in relation to the others' potential use of the work. In this case, the decisive factor of the arguments, i.e., the factor on which the judge made her decision regarding that issue, is considered the frame of the argument.

The use of metaphor is particularly important. As the copyright law recently began to be applied to the area of computer programs, many actors in the legal cases use metaphors that create analogy between computer programs and other works that have been protected by copyright, such as literary works, artistic works, audiovisual works, graphic and pictorial works. Because the use of different metaphors may have importance influence on decision-making, I also code the use of metaphors.

Other elements that consist of legal arguments are the presentation of evidence and authorities. The ways in which judges require evidence and authorities, i.e., scientific or lay observer, are coded when relevant. I also code how the judges respond to the use of evidence and authorities.

ANALYSIS

I analyze the data obtained in three aspects. First, I conduct descriptive analyses of the important variables and their variances over time. The relationship between the court decisions and possible explanatory factors such as the level of resources, the nature of the case, the nature of actors, subject matter and topic of the case is examined by the analysis of variance and cross tabulations. Then I analyze the legal arguments to examine the use of frames and interpretations of legal theories and to identify the structural rules prevalent in copyright cases. The analysis of legal arguments includes the examination of how the actors' nature and resources relate to the ways in which legal theories and facts are used in legal arguments. Interpretive readings and cross tabulations are combined for this analysis. The important question here is to define the conditions under which the parties make arguments that are perceived as credible and convincing by the judges. Figure in Appendix I illustrates the interrelationships of the analyses that are conducted using the cases regarding the copyright protection of computer software programs. These analyses attempt to explore the mechanisms by which actors' resources and decisions relate to each other, by introducing the communicative activities of the actors as a critical intervening factor.

Part II

The Dynamics of Structural Change

CHAPTER 5

Computer Program Copyright Cases

I will now present the descriptive findings of the data analysis. The presentation of the findings of the study begins with this chapter that shows the general characteristics of the data of this study.

COURTS

Among one hundred and fifteen federal cases that dealt with the copyright protection of computer programs, 87 (76%) cases were held at the level of the District Court and 28 (24%) at the level of the Court of Appeals. In terms of the circuits in which the cases were held, 30 (26%) cases were held at the ninth circuit, 16 (14%) at the second circuit, 13 cases at the third circuit and seventh circuit, 11 at the fifth circuit, 9 cases at the fourth circuit, 6 at the tenth circuit, 5 at the first circuit, 4 at the 11th circuit, 3 at the sixth circuit, 2 at the eighth and thirteenth circuit, and 1 at the fourteenth circuit. The largest number of cases, 19 (17%), were held in the state of California, and 12 (10%) cases in the state of New York.

PROCEDURAL STATUS

The largest number of cases (41 cases, 36%) were decided on the preliminary injunction issue. Thirteen (11%) cases were summary judgment cases. Thirty-three (29%) cases were District Court level final judgment cases and 28 (24%) cases were appeals cases that made final judgment.

TOPIC OF THE CASE

The topic of the cases can be broadly categorized according to whether the issue in dispute was about copyrightability or infringement. Six (5%) cases were decided only on whether the program at issue was copyrightable or whether the copyright of the program(s) was valid. In these cases, infringement was not an issue. Seventy-five (65%) cases assumed the copyrightability of the program and were decided only regarding whether an infringement had occurred. Some of these cases do address the question of the copyrightability of the program but as a part of the discussion regarding the ownership of valid copyright or on the copyrightable expression related to the issue of infringement. In these cases, decisions involve only infringement and not copyrightability. Twenty-two (19%) cases were decided on both the issues of copyrightability and infringement. These cases have decision variables of both issues. There are 12 (10%) cases in which the primary focus of the arguments is authorship of the program and ownership of the copyright, but they also deal with infringement issue.

YEAR

There is a tendency that more cases are held in later time periods, although it is neither consistent nor linear. Meaningful temporal trends are found in relation to the ways in which arguments are made, and this will be discussed later. The first two cases regarding the copyright protection of computer software were decided in 1978, 1 in 1979, 1 in 1980, 10 in 1981, 11 in 1982, 7 in 1983, 3 in 1984, 4 in 1985, 5 in 1986, 7 in 1987, 8 in 1988, 11 in 1989, 12 in 1990, 13 in 1991, 17 in 1992, and 3 in 1993. According to the five time periods created in the previous chapter, there were 4 cases in the first period, 27 in the second, 19 in the third, 28 in the fourth, and 26 in the fifth.

SUBJECT MATTER

There are 17 (15%) cases in which operating system programs were the original programs in issue. In 65 (57%) cases, the original programs in issue were application programs and in 33 (29%) cases, they were video game programs. Twenty-six (23%) cases dealt with the literal elements of the program only, and 33 (29%) cases dealt with non-literal elements only. In 18 (16%) cases, both literal and non-literal elements were considered, and 38 (33%) cases did not distinguish between literal and non-literal elements. Among the 44 cases that dealt with literal elements, 1 case specifically considered the issue of only the object code, and 5 cases considered the issue of only the source code. The other 38 (33%) cases considered the object code and the source code together. Among the 52 cases that deal with non-literal elements, the focus of the most (32) cases was the screen display of application programs or the audiovisual display of video game programs, and 10 cases focused on the structure, sequence, and organization of the programs. Nine cases focused on user interfaces, and there was only 1 case that dealt with non-literal elements in general.

There is some difference in the subject matter according to different time periods. In the first period (1978-1980), all of the four cases dealt with application programs, but in the second period (1981-1983), the subject matter of the most (64%) cases was video game programs. During the last three periods (1984-1993), application programs were the subject matter of the most (69%) cases. Because the majority of cases dealing with video game programs focused on their audiovisual display, during the second period all of the non-literal elements considered were screen displays, while in the other periods they were more evenly distributed.

In the cases involving the issue of copyrightability alone, there was no other program involved because the program used by the other party is the same as the original program. In the cases involving the issue of infringement, however, there can be other programs. Among the cases involving other programs, 49 (43%) cases involved competing products, which achieve similar functions as the original program. There are 37 (32%) cases that can be also categorized as competing products, but have particular characteristics related to the underlying program. 29 of these programs have characteristics that may not disserve, if not benefit, the developer of the original program by providing more choices for the users: programs written in another kind of computer language (5 cases), programs that work on a different system (9 cases), programs that are used to enhance or update the underlying program (2 cases), programs that are made to be compatible with the underlying programs (9 cases), application programs that can work on the underlying operating system (2 cases), and an enhanced version of the underlying program (4 cases). Six of the competing products have characteristics that can clearly disserve the developer of the original user than other competing products in general: programs that are used as a device to alter the original program (4 cases), a program device to reproduce the original program (1 case), and a program device to de-effect the original program (1 case).

The reason why the programs other than the original program are categorized in this way is to examine whether the decision-making relates more to the characteristics that can benefit or harm the developers of the original program by providing more diverse products associated with underlying program in the market, or more to the possible involvement of the alleged infringer in any kind of developing activity. Programs that have the former characteristics are referred to as "add-on" software, which typically offers some enhanced functions to an existing program, either modifying the other program's behavior or supplementing it in some way (Samuelson and others, 1994). Samuelson and others (1994) indicate that although some courts allow the add-on software to be marketed due to its added pleasure for the users, a market-oriented approach to copyright will not excuse the developer of add-on software from infringement because the add-on software relies heavily on the value of the program by building on the underlying developer's research and development.

Therefore, examining the ways in which the courts deal with these computer programs that have clearly different characteristics will help us understand how the copyright law deals with the notion of users' choice or pleasure as opposed to the process of independent creation. If the programs with the characteristics that may benefit the users and possibly the developers of the underlying program are considered differently from the programs with the characteristics that can harm the original program, it suggests that issues from users of the infringing product are seriously considered in the decision-making process. However, if these programs that have two different kinds of characteristics but were created as a result of some developing activity are considered in a similar way in decision-making, it suggests that the degree to which an independent developing activity is involved in producing the allegedly infringing program is playing a critical role. Therefore, the important question in analysis using this variable is whether the courts deal with the programs with characteristics that are harmful to the underlying program more similarly to the other competing programs or to the cases in which no other programs were involved.

NATURE OF ACTORS

The plaintiffs of 7 (6%) cases are developers of the underlying program who do not have the copyright of the program, the plaintiffs of 77 (67%) cases are developers who are at the same time copyright holders of the program, and the plaintiffs of 30 (26%) cases are copyright holders who are not developers of the program. There is 1 case in which it was decided whether the plaintiff was a developer of the program. The plaintiffs can be also categorized as to whether or not they are developers of the program no matter whether they are copyright holders or not. The plaintiffs of 84 cases (73%) are developers and those of 30 cases (26%) are non-developing copyright holders.

Alleged infringers or challengers of copyright validity are more diverse than the plaintiffs. In terms of the relationship with the original program at issue, that is, the program of which copyrightability or infringement is at issue, the defendants of 2 (2%) cases are developers of the original program, and those of 2 (2%) cases are copyright holders of the original program at issue. Most of them are neither developers of the original program at issue nor copyright holders of the original program. However, they can be divided in terms of whether they are involved in developing other programs than the original program or whether they own the copyright of other programs. Defendants of 21 cases (18%) are neither developers nor copyright holders of any kinds of computer programs, but retailers, distributors, etc. Those of 67 cases (58%) are neither developers nor copyright holders of the original program at issue, but developers of other computer programs. Those of 8 cases (7%) were neither developers nor copyright holders of the original program at issue, but copyright holders of other computer programs, which the plaintiff alleges infringed the copyright of the original program. In 8 cases (7%), the copyright holders of the original program at issue had claims against the developers of the original program who did not own the copyright of the original program but developed other programs, which the plaintiffs claim infringed the copyright of the original program. In 6 cases it was being decided on who owns copyright of the program, so in these cases it was not clear who are developers. In 2 cases (2%) the developer of the program filed suits against a copyright registrar who denied granting registration for copyright of the program.

These diverse characteristics of the alleged infringers or challengers of the copyright validity can be broadly divided into two categories: 77 (67%) are developers of any kind of computer programs and 37 (32%) are non-developers of any computer programs.

The nature of actors shows some change over time. In the second time period there were more (64%) non-developing plaintiffs than developing plaintiffs, while in all the other periods most of the plaintiffs were developers (100% in the first period, 95% in the third, 81% in the fourth, and 79% in the fifth). This variation according to time seems to be related to the fact that in the second period many cases dealt with video game programs, which tend to involve more non-developing copyright holders.

The nature of the alleged infringers also varies over time. In the fourth period about half of the defendants are non-developers, while in the other periods more of them were developers (100% in the first period, 64% in the second, 68% in the third, and 79% in the fifth). In the second period, in which many plaintiffs were non-developers, more than half of the defendants were developers. This illustrates that video game cases that comprise of many cases in the second period tend to be the cases in which the defendants involved in some kind of developing activity in relation to the original program, of which copyright is owned by non-developing plaintiffs.

NATURE OF THE CASE

The nature of the cases can be drawn from the nature of actors. There are 4 cases in which developers of the original program filed suits against copyright holders of the program. In 3 cases copyright holders of the programs at issue filed suits against developers of the programs at issue. In 76 (66%) cases developers who are also copyright holders had claims against competitors. Among these 76 cases, 17 cases involved no other program than the original program, while in 59 cases programs other than the original program were involved. In 22 (19%) cases, copyright holders who are not developers filed suits against competitors. Among these, 3 cases involved only the original program while 19 cases involved other programs that are not the original programs. In 2 cases the developer of the program had claims for copyright against the copyright office registrar. In 6 cases the copyright holder of the program at issue sued the developer of the program, based on the infringement claim of other programs created by the developer. In 2 cases, the developer and copyright holder at the same time sued their clients. These are the only cases in the data that involve end-users of the program.

These cases can be categorized more generally. There are 59 (51%) cases in which developers of the original program had claims against developers of any kind of programs. In 24 (21%) cases, developers of the original programs had claims against non-developers who may or may not be copyright holders of any kind of programs. In 32 (28%) cases, non-developers claimed against developers of any kind of programs or non-developers.

There is another dimension along which these cases can be divided: the number of program(s) involved in the case. In every case, there is the original program of which the plaintiff claims the copyright. 28 (24%) cases involved only this original program. In the other 87 (76%) cases, other computer programs than the original program are involved, whether the programs are decided to be infringing the original program or not.

There is a difference in the nature of the cases according to the time period. In all the cases in the first period, 76% of the cases in the fifth period, and 63% in the third period, developers sued developers. In the second period, as expected, non-developers sued developers in 64% of the cases. In the fourth period, the nature of the cases was evenly distributed.

JUDGES' CHARACTERISTICS

Judges' characteristics that may have some relation to the ways in which they decide the copyright cases include their age, the presidents who appointed the judges, the year in which they were appointed, and the political party of the appointing presidents. Information about six of the judges was not available from any of the references that were used. For the purpose of analysis, even when a judge decided more than one case, she was counted as one judge each time she decided on a case.

The age of the judges at the time they decided the cases range from 45 to 90. 5 judges were in their forties, 15 in their fifties, 43 in their sixties, 32 in their seventies, and 14 were between the age of 80 and 90. The year in which the judges were appointed range between 1959 and 1992. Twenty judges were appointed between 1959 and 1970, 55 between 1971 and 1980, and 29 between 1981 and 1992.

There were 8 presidents who appointed the judges. Three judges were appointed by Eisenhower, 19 by Kennedy, 25 by Johnson, 46 by Nixon, 15 by Ford, 93 by Carter, 53 by Reagan, and 18 by Bush. Sixty-one judges were appointed by Republican presidents and 48 by Democratic presidents.

DECISIONS

The decisions relating to the study can be categorized in various ways. First they are categorized according to whether the plaintiff of the case won the case, or the defendants — the alleged infringer in infringement cases and the challenger in copyrightability cases — won the case. Among the 115 cases, the plaintiffs won 73 cases (64%) and the defendants won 42 cases (36%). When the decisions were divided broadly according to whether the decision was limiting the scope of copyright protection of computer software or expanding the scope, 43 cases (37%) limited the scope and 69 (60%) cases expanded the scope. Three cases (3%) were about who owns the authorship or ownership rights only, so they could not be categorized into either limiting or expanding the copyright scope.

According to the topic of the case, the cases may have decisions on copyrightability, infringement, or both copyrightability and infringement. Therefore, separate variables were made for the copyrightability decision and infringement decision. Among the 115 cases, 29 cases dealt with the issue of the copyrightability of the program. Twenty-six (90%) of the copyrightability cases were decided in favor of granting the copyright, while only 3 (10%) cases were decided against granting the copyright to the program. Among the 115 cases, 107 cases dealt with the infringement issue. Among these 107 cases, 65 cases (61%) decided that infringement occurred, while 42 (40%) decided that infringement did not occur. Therefore, it seems that a higher degree of consensus has been achieved in the courts on the issue of granting copyrightability to computer programs than on the issue of infringement, although more cases decided that infringement occurred than not.

Another dimension of the decisions was whether the case decided for or against the developer of the program or the copyright holder of the program. The plaintiffs of the cases consist of developers of the program, or developers and copyright holders at the same time, and copyright holders of the program who was not involved in any developing processes. One-hundred and eleven out of 115 cases involved the copyright holder of the program regardless of whether they were developers or not. Among these copyright holder-involved cases, 70 cases (63%) decided in favor of copyright holders, while 41 (36%) decided against copyright holders. There were 92 cases that involved developers of the program regardless of whether they were copyright holders of not. Fifty-nine cases (64%) decided in favor of developers and 33 (36%) decided against developers.

In summary, decisions pertaining to the cases regarding computer programs tended to be made in favor of granting copyright rather than against it, to find an infringement than not, in favor of developers than against them, in favor of copyright holders than against them, and in favor of developers than in favor of copyright holders when they are in dispute. Thus, the courts were generally in favor of expanding the scope of the copyright protection of computer programs, rather than of limiting the scope of copyright protection.

ACTORS' RESOURCES

One of the various measurements that indicate the level of resources is whether the actors are individuals or firms, or even multiple firms acting together for the litigation. The plaintiffs in 4 cases (4%) are individuals, in 3 (3%) cases are individuals who are affiliated to some firms (usually they own the companies), in 100 (87%) cases are firms, and in 8 (7%) cases are multiple firms. In the case of the defendants, there was 1 individual, 4 (4%) multiple individuals, 19 (17%) individuals who own the companies, 45 (40%) firms, 14 (12%) multiple firms, 30 (26%) firms with other individuals, and 2 (2%) copyright registrars. In a broad categorization, the plaintiffs in 7 (6%) cases were individuals and in 108 (99%) cases were firms, while the defendants in 26 (23%) cases were individuals and in 89 (77%) cases are firms.

The nature of the case can be also drawn from this categorization. The largest number (77%) of cases were between firms, and in 20 (17%) cases firms made claims against individuals. In 6 cases, the plaintiffs and the defendants were both individuals. There was only one case in which individuals filed against a firm.

In the case of firms their size can be measured by the amount of revenues and the number of employees. Despite the extensive use of various databases, obtaining this kind of data was extremely difficult. Thus, among the 108 cases in which the plaintiffs were firms, data regarding their size was obtained for 62 (57%) cases. Among the 89 cases in which the defendants were firms, data regarding their size was available for 58 (65%) cases. It is likely that there is a systematic difference between firms about which information was available at the time of data gathering and firms about which information was not available at the time of data gathering. However, it is difficult to imagine that any systematic bias operates for the plaintiffs and for the defendants. Also, because the analysis has been conducted in terms of the relative size between the parties in each case, only the cases in which there was data for both parties were considered in examining the relationship between actors' resources and court decisions.

In the 62 cases for which data was available, the plaintiffs were found to have greater revenues than the defendants, but this difference was not statistically significant because the variances were very large. Among the plaintiffs, the firms in 29 cases had revenues less than 100 million dollars, and in 33 cases more than 100 million dollars. Data for the defendants in 60 cases was available. Firms in 49 cases had revenues less than 100 million dollars and only in 11 cases more than 100 million. The average number of employers in the firms of the plaintiffs (9,246) was greater than that of the defendants (8,121). The average age of the firms of the plaintiffs (17 years) was also higher than that of the defendants (14 years).

As noted before, the level of resources only has a meaning when it is compared between the two parties involved in each case. Therefore, it is important to analyze only the cases for which the information on the both parties is available, although the problem of the lack of data is more compounded. In 88 cases in which both parties are firms, information on both parties was obtained for 31 cases. In 21 (68%) cases the revenues of the plaintiffs were greater than those of the defendants, and in 10 cases the opposite was the case.

In a similar vein, among the 44 cases for which information for both parties' numbers of employees are available, in 31 (70%) cases the plaintiffs had more employees, and in 11 cases the defendants had more employees. In 2 cases the number of employees was the same between the two parties. The age of the firms of the both parties was available in 30 cases. In 19 (63%) cases firms of the plaintiffs were older and in 10 cases those of the defendants were older. In one case the age of the firms was the same. Thus the available data suggest that in every aspect the plaintiffs had greater allocative and human resources than the defendants. Although the data only constitute 35% of the total data, there is no reason to suspect that the availability of information on the size of the firms is systematically different between the plaintiffs and the defendants.

The ratings of the legal counsels and the law firms turned out to be extremely homogeneous. Since almost all of the counsels and firms had 'A' ratings, the variance was not enough to make any comparison. It seems that all the parties sought to gain the first rate legal service as the stake involved in copyright cases pertaining to computer programs tends to be very high.

CHAPTER 6

Interplay of Actors, Resources, and Court Decisions

I will now review the analysis of the relationship between the various characteristics of cases and court decisions. The interaction of the actors' legal arguments with these characteristics of the cases will be discussed in the next chapter.

PROCEDURAL STATUS

Court decisions regarding infringement were made in a slightly different way according to the procedural status of the cases. In the summary judgment cases, more (7 out of 10) cases did not find any infringement, while in the other cases with the other procedural status, courts were more likely to find an infringement than not. This result can be attributed to the nature of the status. Because summary judgments can be given only when there are no genuine facts involved in the case, if it is found that there is any factual dispute, summary judgment cannot be given. The fact that the summary judgment was not granted does not mean that the opposing party won the case on the merits, but instead it means that the merits should be decided at trial.

TOPIC

The topic of the cases sharply relates to the court decisions. When the topic of the case was copyrightability, 25 (89%) out of 28 cases were decided in favor of granting copyrightability. In the infringement cases it was not as consistent. Sixty-one (62%) out of the remaining 98 cases were in favor of deciding that infringement has occurred, and 37 (38%) were against deciding that infringement had occurred. Some of these cases include both issues of copyrightability and infringement. In the cases that deal with the infringement issue only, the rulings were even more evenly decided. Thirty-five (47%) out of the 75 cases ruled that infringement has occurred, and 40 (53%) cases ruled that infringement has not occurred.

JUDGES' CHARACTERISTICS

In general, judges' characteristics were related to the decisions. Neither the age of the judges at the time of the decision-making nor the year in which they were appointed had any significant relationship to the way they made copyrightability or infringement decisions. Also, the appointing presidents and the political party of the appointing presidents did not influence the ways in which they made decisions in any significant way. Especially in copyrightability cases where decisions did not vary much, most of the judges decided in favor of granting the copyrightability of computer programs regardless of their appointing presidents. In infringement cases, slight differences were found among the judges. For example, the judges appointed by Eisenhower, Nixon, Ford, and Reagan found an infringement in about half of the cases over which they presided. The judges appointed by Kennedy and Bush were more likely to find an infringement and the judges appointed by Johnson and Carter were more likely to find that there was no infringement. This result seems to suggest only that in the copyright cases with regards to computer programs, individual differences among the judges may have played a larger role in decision making rather than their political orientation.

ALLOCATIVE AND HUMAN RESOURCES OF ACTORS

In examining whether the allocative and human resources of the actors relate to court decisions, there are different dimensions along which the level of resources can be measured. The first one is whether the actors are individuals or firms. When the plaintiffs were individuals, they were more likely to lose the case than when the plaintiffs were firms. On the other hand, when the defendants were individuals, they were more likely to win the case than when they were firms.

When both actors are firms, their resources are also measured by revenues, the number of employees, and the age of the firms. These three measures were not found to influence the decisions. Whether the decisions were made in favor of the plaintiffs or the defendants, the mean revenues, number of employees, and age of the firms were not significantly different. It is possible that the fact that the data on these variables are not complete contributes to this lack of relationship, but there is no reason to assume that the size of the firms about which the information was not available differs for the plaintiff and for the defendant. Tentatively, it can be concluded that the actors' allocative resources relate to the decision making more in terms of whether they were individuals or firms than in terms of the actual financial and human assets they possess. This conclusion suggests that it would be important to investigate the mechanisms by which the nature of the actors influences the decision-making process.

NATURE OF ACTORS

The decisions were not found to be influenced by the nature of the plaintiffs, that is, whether the plaintiffs were developers or not. However, it was found that the nature of the alleged infringers is significantly related to the decisions, while the nature of the challengers of the validity of copyright is not related to the decisions. No matter whether the defendants in copyrightability cases were developers or not, decisions tended to be made in favor of granti-ng copyrightability. On the other hand, in general, the defendants in infringement cases are more likely to lose the case than the plaintiffs of infringement cases. But when the alleged infringers were non-developers, they had only a 20% chance to win the case, but if they were developers of any kind of programs, they had a 45% of chance to win the case.

Therefore, it is concluded that the copyrightability decisions tend not to be influenced by the nature of actors, but the infringement decisions depend greatly on whether the alleged infringers have been involved in the developing activities in any way.

SUBJECT MATTER

First, it was found that the nature of the plaintiff's program in terms of whether it is an operating system program, an application program, or a video game program was not related to the decisions in any way. However, the nature of the other programs than the plaintiff's program involved in the case was clearly related to decision-making. These other programs are the ones that were created and/or used by the alleged infringers. In some cases they used the plaintiff's programs, but in other cases they developed other programs, which may have infringed the plaintiffs' original programs. Some of these newly developed products have particular characteristics in relation to the original program, as described in the previous chapter. Some of the characteristics may be reasonably expected to benefit the users and possibly the developers of the original program, while the other characteristics are clearly harmful to the developers of the original program because these programs help reproduce, de-effect, or alter the nature of the original program.

But the analysis shows that these two different kinds of characteristics did not result in different court decisions. When alleged infringers developed these programs, courts were less likely find that they infringed copyright than when the alleged infringers who developed no new programs or even developed competing programs without these particular characteristics. And this tendency was the same regardless of whether the characteristics of the other program may be beneficial or clearly harmful to the users and possibly the plaintiffs. For example, in *Vault v. Quaid* (1988), even though Quaid marketed a program that can be used to make unauthorized copies of other copyrighted software programs and Vault made an argument based on its consequences on the market of its own program, the judges decided that the Qauid program did not infringe on the copyright of Vault. On the contrary, when the defendant's software program can be considered "add-on" software which typically offers some enhanced functions to an existing program, the courts were split in their decisions and more likely to decide that there was an infringement than not. For example, in *Midway v. Artic* (1982), when Artic sold electronic devices intended to stimulate Midway's 'PacMan' and 'Galaxian,' as well as devices designed to be inserted into the Galaxian Game to speed up and otherwise alter the play of the game, the court decided that the Artic's game kits are infringing derivative works. But in *Galoob v. Nintendo* (1992) when Lewis Galoob marketed a video game accessory 'Game Genie,' which can be attached to a video game cartridge such as Nintendo products and allow the player temporarily alter certain attributes of the game, the court decided that the game accessory did not infringe on Galoob's copyright.

This result clearly suggests that the copyright decisions tend to consider the degree of involvement in the developing activity of the alleged infringers more seriously than the possible impacts of these other programs to the developers and users of the original program. In addition, this result is consistent with the finding that the nature of alleged infringers influences decisions. When the alleged infringers were developers of any programs, they were less likely to be found as infringers of the copyright than when they were non-developers of any programs. Thus it can be inferred again that copyright decisions in general tend to consider actors' involvement with developing activity very importantly.

REMAINING QUESTIONS

What do these findings about the relationship between the characteristics regarding the cases and court decisions mean? To summarize, the decisions were analyzed in relation to various factors of actors' resources. First it was found that the characteristics of judges such as age, educational background, and ideological inclination did not have any relationship with how a decision was made. For example, the decisions did not vary according to the president who appointed the judge, nor to whether the president was a Republican or a Democrat.

As a factor indicating the allocative resources of the actors, whether the party was an individual or a firm was first examined. There were no cases in which both parties were individuals. When the plaintiff was an individual and the defendant was a firm or firms, the defendant was more likely to win the case as was expected. But when the plaintiff was a firm or firms and the defendant was an individual, the defendant was more likely to win the case. When both parties were firms, the size of the firms measured by the sales revenue and the number of employees was assessed. No matter how the size of the firms was measured, it was not related to the court decisions in any way. That is, the financial ability of a firm did not help the firm to win the software copyright case. This result is in direct contrast with other studies and the expectation made by resource dependency theory. Rather, resources seem to be related to the decisions through the issue of whether the party was an individual or a firm. Examining the nature of the parties in another way shows that the decisions tended to be made in favor of individual-defendants because an individual-defendant was more likely to be a developer of the program than a firm-defendant.

It was found that whether the party was a developer or not is the most important factor that relates to decision making. This factor did not make a difference in copyrightability cases, probably because 90% of the cases were decided in favor of one party. But in infringement cases, while a defendant who was not a developer of the program won the case in only 20% of the cases, a defendant who was a developer won the case in 45% of the cases. On the other hand, whether the party was a copyright holder did not make any difference in decision making.

In conclusion, among the various factors, some that have traditionally been acknowledged to have an influence in other areas of law, such as the judges' political or educational characteristics and the financial resources of the parties, were not found to relate to the decisions regarding computer programs. The only factor that was found to influence the courts' decisions is the nature of the actors in terms of whether they were developers. The courts seem to be most concerned with the independent developing activity of the actors. This result is contrary to the argument that copyright law has transferred rights to the copyright holders while depriving the authors of their rights. To reconcile this seeming paradox, analyzing legal arguments in detail to understand the mechanisms by which copyright decisions are made becomes necessary.

CHAPTER 7

Use of Structural Rules and Resources in Legal Arguments

The analysis of legal arguments begins with the description of the general frames and theories used by the legal actors. Based on the approaches that have been discussed in the third chapter, I analyze the 261 argument-units with reference to the frame of the public interest versus private reward, and then with reference to the frame of authorship, work, and use. For the sake of comparison between frames and time periods, detailed analysis of legal arguments is conducted according to each issue of the copyright cases. By examining the parties' arguments and the judges' responses in earlier cases, I will identify important structural rules that have been established. I will also examine how the legal actors use these structural rules in relation to their resources in their arguments, and how the judges respond to the ways in which the parties use their communicative resources in their legal arguments. The reproduction and possible change of structural rules that occur through this process is explored as well.

GENERAL FRAMES

Analyzing the form of the argument-units shows that the judges' arguments in court opinions are usually (219 out of 261 arguments) made as a response to one or both of the parties' arguments. The judges' arguments were most frequently made in a way that responds to the defendants' arguments. In 145 (52%) out of 261 arguments, judges identified what the defendants' arguments were, but did not identify the plaintiffs' arguments. In 38 of the arguments, judges indicated the characteristics of both the plaintiffs' and defendants' arguments. In 36 arguments the judges only identified what the plaintiffs' arguments were, but did not identify the defendants' arguments. Judges did not explicitly identify any of the parties' arguments but presented their own analyses in 42 (16%) arguments.

The judges' arguments tended to be made in favor of broadening the scope of copyright protection (74%) than limiting the scope (26%). In order to examine the general trend of the arguments and use of frames over time, the time periods developed in the previous chapter were used. Even though the original time periods consisted of 5 categories with 3-4 years in each period, because the first period has only 4 arguments, I combined the first and second periods for analysis. As a result, the first period (1978-1983) has 69 arguments, the second period (1984-1986) 45 arguments, the third period (1987-1990) 68 arguments, and the fourth period (1991-1993) 79 arguments. The trend of broadening the scope of copyright protection was somewhat more clear in the first two time periods (81% and 84% for broadening the scope) than in the last two time periods (70% and 74%).

The issue that was dealt with most frequently in the arguments was that of copyrightability. In 58 (22%) arguments in the copyrightability cases, judges dealt with the question of whether the computer software or any element of it is copyrightable as a subject matter or the plaintiff's copyright in the original program is valid. They also asked the same question in infringement cases but in slightly different contexts. In order to decide on the infringement case, the court should first decide whether the plaintiff owns a valid copyright in the program involved in the case. Thus, another 27 (10%) of the judges' arguments regarding the question of copyrightability were made in this context. Once the ownership is established, the court should decide whether the defendant copied the plaintiff's program, which can also be inferred by showing access and substantial similarity. Except for one case access was not a matter of dispute. 54 (21%) arguments were made in the context of the substantial similarity issue. In this context, judges ask the question regarding the validity of copyright again, in order to define whether the copied portion of the program was a copyrightable expression or not. 39 (15%) arguments of the judges were made in this context. Altogether, the copyrightability question was asked in 120 (46%) of the 261 arguments and was a recurring theme in almost all of the cases. Finally, if it is found that copying has occurred and the copied portion was the copyrightable expression, the court should decide whether the copying constitutes infringement or not. 72 (28%) arguments were made in this context of copying as infringement. A question that was less frequently asked but carries a great significance in copyright law is about the authorship/ownership dispute. 17 arguments (7%) centered around this issue.

There is a high association between what the plaintiffs and the defendants argued and what the judges argued, naturally because many of the judges' arguments were made as a response to the disputing parties. Among the 70 arguments of the plaintiffs that were explicitly mentioned by judges, 20 (29%) of them were about copying as infringement, 19 (27%) 21 about the substantial similarity, 15 (21%) about copyrightable expression, 8 (11%) about ownership/authorship dispute, and 7 (10%) about copyrightability. The distribution of the defendants' arguments is similar to that of the plaintiffs', except that more arguments regarding the copyrightability issue were considered by the judges. Among the 184 arguments of the defendants that were mentioned by the judges in court opinions, 51 (28%) were about copyrightability, 49 (27%) were about infringement, 26 (14%) were about substantial similarity and copyrightable expression respectively, 19 (10%) about the validity of ownership, and 12 (7%) about authorship/ownership dispute.

When the judges responded to the other actors' arguments, most frequently judges discussed about how and why they rejected the parties' arguments, more so with the defendants' arguments. Among the 219 arguments in which judges were responding to the parties, 163 (74%) of them were rejecting the defendants' arguments while 44 (20%) of them were rejecting the plaintiffs' arguments. In these arguments judges explicitly or implicitly accepted the other party's arguments. Not so frequently judges only presented arguments that accepted a party's argument while not explicitly rejecting any arguments. In only 5 (2%) arguments judges indicated that they were agreeing to the plaintiffs' arguments and in 7 (3%) arguments judges indicated they were agreeing to the defendants' arguments. In summary, judges tended to agree, explicitly or implicitly, with the plaintiffs more frequently (167 arguments) than with the defendants (52 arguments).

Narrowly constructed frames are identified as follows: the nature of the work (made by the plaintiffs or the defendants), the authorship (creation process of the plaintiffs or the defendants), the nature of the use (use by the defendant, market consequences, and the public use and benefit). The frame that was most frequently used by the judges was that of the nature of work (62%, 162 arguments) followed by the frame of use (22%, 57 arguments) and the frame of authorship (16%, 42 arguments). The frame of work and the frame of authorship can be further divided in terms of whose work and whose authorship was being argued about. The nature of the plaintiff's work was more frequently considered (100 arguments) than the nature of the defendant's work (62 arguments). Similarly, the authorship issue of the plaintiff was more frequently considered (27 arguments) than the authorship issue of the defendant (17 arguments). The frame of use also can be further divided in terms of its focus: the use of the defendants (36 arguments), the public use (14), and market consequences (7).

The frames used by the defendant were similar to those of the judges while the plaintiffs' use of frames was slightly different. The defendants used the frame of work most frequently (58% of the arguments), followed by the frame of use (25%) and the frame of authorship (18%). The plaintiffs also used the frame of work (61%) most frequently, but they used the frame of authorship (23%) more often than the frame of use (16%).

I also examined if there is any difference in the frame of arguments when the judges were explicitly responding to the parties and when the judges did not clearly mention the parties' arguments. When the judges used their own arguments, they tended to use the frame of work even more frequently (81%) as opposed to the frame of authorship (5%) than when they were explicitly responding to the parties (58% for work and 20% for authorship). Also, when they used their own arguments, their arguments tended to have frames of the defendant's work/authorship (67%) more than frames of the plaintiff's work/authorship (31%), while when they were responding, the use of these two frames was more evenly distributed. Therefore, the most frequently used frame when the judges used their own arguments only was the nature of the defendant's work (52%), while the most frequently used frame when the judges were responding to the others' arguments was the frame of the plaintiff's work (37%). Also, the judges' arguments employing the frame of the public interest or market consequences were usually made when they were responding to the other parties (20 arguments). These frames were used only once when judges were making their own arguments.

The judges' use of frames also differed according to the kind of their arguments in terms of the scope of copyright protection. When the judges' arguments were in favor of expanding the scope of copyright protection, they were more likely to be using the frame of the nature of the plaintiff's work/authorship (52%). But when the judges' arguments were in favor of limiting the scope of protection, they were most likely to use the frame of the nature of the defendant's work/authorship (57%). Using the frame of work versus that of authorship did not make a clear difference in the judges' arguments in terms of the scope of protection.

In general, the arguments of the first 2 time periods focused more on the nature of the work (80% in the first period and 76% in the second period), while the arguments of the last 2 periods were more evenly distributed in terms of the use of frames. In the third period, 31 (46%) arguments made by the judges used the frame of work, 23 (34%) arguments used the frame of use (including public interest and marketplace frames), and 14 (21%) used the frame of authorship. In the fourth period, 42 (53%) used the frame of work, 21 (27%) used the frame of use, and 16 (20%) used the frame of authorship.

In a similar fashion, the judges' arguments also focused on the plaintiffs' work/authorship more frequently (64%) than on the defendants' work/authorship (28%) in the first time period. But as time went by, the arguments tended to include the frame of the defendants' work or authorship more frequently (28% in the first period, then 47%, 53%, and 48%).

These changes over time in the use of frames, from the frame of work toward that of use and from that of the plaintiff's toward that of the defendant's, seem to result partly from a change in the issues considered in the cases over time. In the first time period, most of the arguments were about the issue of copyrightability (61%). However, in later time periods the copyrightability arguments decreased (49% in the second period, 34% in the third period, 39% in the fourth period). At the same time, the arguments dealing with the issues of substantial similarity and copying as infringement tended to increase (36% in the first period, 47% in the second period, 59% in the third period, and 51% in the fourth period).

The use of frames differed according to the issue. When the issue was the authorship/ownership dispute, all the 17 arguments used the frame of authorship. When the issue was copyrightability (including those in copyrightability cases and in infringement cases), most of the arguments (97 arguments, 82%) had a frame of work, and only some arguments (18 arguments, 16%) had a frame of authorship. Among the 97 arguments that used a frame of work, 94 of them focused on the plaintiffs' work, while only 3 focused on the defendants' work. When the issue was substantial similarity, most of the arguments also used a frame of work (49 arguments, 91%), but among the 49 arguments, 46 focused on the defendants' work while only 3 focused on the plaintiffs' work. When the issue was copying as infringement, the most frequent frame was that of use (54 arguments, 75%).

As the issue of the cases relates to the use of frames, it is important to analyze legal arguments separately according to the issue of the cases in detail. While the focus of the detailed analysis is how the concepts of work and authorship interact with each other and are mobilized, and how these two concepts operate in conjunction with the concept of use that appears later, the frame of use includes the use of the public interest and market consequences as well. Therefore, a separate framework of analysis is needed to examine the question of how the concept of the public interest versus private proprietary rights plays a role in copyright cases, and how the marketplace norm and rationale relate to the concept of enhancing public benefit through the encouragement of innovation. Thus, before the analysis that used the frames of work, authorship, and use is conducted, the legal arguments are analyzed in terms of how the public interest or marketplace considerations are dealt with in copyright cases with regards to computer software programs.

PUBLIC INTEREST VERSUS PRIVATE PROPERTY RIGHTS

Contrary to the premise that the fundamental principle of the copyright regime concerns the public interest, the public interest is a theme that hardly becomes a basis for decision in copyright cases regarding computer programs. In the arguments that decided on the merits and the arguments in summary judgment cases, the public interest or policy considerations were only occasionally argued as a rationale for a decision. Even in the preliminary injunction cases of which four basic requirements included the public interest factor, this factor was often ignored in decisionmaking or was merely restated in the arguments without any further discussion. The considerations of the public interest and marketplace in the arguments that decided on the merits and in the arguments in preliminary injunction cases are separately analyzed.

Final Judgment and Summary Judgment Cases

The arguments employing the concept of public policy or the public interest are found to be rare in the copyright cases with regards to computer programs. The judges in only 8 cases among the 115 cases explicitly used the notion of public policy as a rationale for supporting their arguments and decisions on the merits. There were 3 different kinds of policy considerations: the intent of the Congress, the public benefit, and the consequences for innovation or competition. There was no significant relationship between the use of policy considerations and the nature of the actors or cases. But arguments regarding these policy considerations were usually made in the context of certain frames, such as the nature of the plaintiff's work and the use of the plaintiff's program, and these frames turned out to be an important factor that interacts with the policy considerations.

Among the 8 cases, 2 cases were about whether to grant copyrightability, and the remaining 6 were about finding an infringement. In the 2 copyrightability cases, the judges used the intention of the Congress as a policy argument. In ruling whether the computer software on the ROM was a "copy" or copyrightable, the judges stated that the intention of the Congress is to copyright computer programs (*Tandy v. Personal Micro Computers*, 1978; *Williams v. Artic*, 1982).

Among the 6 infringement cases that used public policy arguments, 2 of them, which were the same case that was held in the district court and in the court of appeals, used policy arguments regarding the public access and public benefit. In *Sega v. Accolade* (1992; 1993), Accolade developed game cartridges compatible with the 'Genesis' console developed by Sega, and argued that to gain the "public's need for access" to programs, fair use should be allowed. The district court judge commented that the public's need for access is fully satisfied by the copyright owner's marketing of the original. However, the judges in the court of appeals accepted Accolade's argument and argued that allowing a particular use of the original program results in the public benefit, and when humans cannot gain access to the unprotected ideas and functional concepts without making copies, it is against the public policy underlying the Copyright Act not to allow the use. Consequently, it was held that Accolade's game cartridges did not infringe Sega's copyright. In this case, the public policy argument was made in the context of other legal rules such as fair use and the functionality theory.

In the remaining 4 infringement cases, the policy arguments centered around possible consequences of allowing the use of the original programs such as innovation and competition, and the judges were split on that matter. When the policy considerations were argued in the context of the utilitarian aspect or functional use of the plaintiff's program, the judges decided that allowing the use of the program will preserve the market for innovation or otherwise it will result in too little competition. In *Foresight v. Larry Pfortmiller* (1989), Pfortmiller developed a digitizer based on the plaintiff's 'Drafix' program and used this enhanced program only in its business. The court held that this enhancement of the program falls within the adaptation for the exception of infringement, and argued that allowing this kind of utilization of the program would "preserve the market for improvements." In *Apple v. Microsoft* (1991), the judge argued that to accept Apple's desktop metaphor and look and feel arguments would result in "too much protection" and yield "too little competition" because the element of Apple's user interface is a purely functional purpose as much as the automobile. Therefore, considering the consequences for innovation or competition in terms of the utilitarian aspect of the programs led into arguing for a narrow scope for copyright protection.

In the other 2 cases the judges focused on the literary aspect of the program from the beginning of their arguments, or shifted the focus from policy considerations to the nature of the program itself. In *Pearl Systems v. Competition Electronics, Inc.* (1988), the defendant argued that ruling the use of a computer program as infringement would discourage innovation. But the judge shifted the focus of the issue from public policy to the idea versus expression dichotomy, by saying that granting a copyright does not give him or her the right to monopolize the idea. In *Lotus v. Paperback* (1990), Paperback argued that the judges should not find an infringement because the policy favors extremely narrow copyright protection in computer programs that are useful articles. The judge disagreed with the defendant's notion of the useful article, and argued that through copyright law Congress intends to explicitly give substantial protection to innovative expression in intellectual works, including computer programs.

In all of the cases in which the public policy arguments were used, the parties of the cases were both developers of different programs (in 7 cases) or both non-developers (in 1 case). Thus it remains unknown whether the nature of the parties would make any difference in the judges' use of policy considerations. However, it seems that the ways in which policy considerations are considered have a clear relationship to the context of the frame in which the arguments are placed. When the policy consideration on the intention of the Congress was combined with the frame of the nature of the program (work), the arguments were made in favor of the broad scope of copyright protection. The consideration regarding the public use and benefit consideration that was combined with the frame of use led the judge to argue against broadening the scope of copyright protection. When the policy consideration on innovation and competition was placed in the context of the nature of the program such as the idea versus expression dichotomy and in the context of the computer program as a literary work, the judges favored a broader scope of copyright protection. But when the policy considerations on innovation were placed in the context of a utilitarian element or functional use of the program, the judges argued against broadening the scope of copyright protection. Therefore, it is suggested that the policy considerations tended to be influenced by the use of other frames or legal rules rather than to operate as a decisive factor themselves.

Other than the policy considerations that were used in the above 8 cases, there are some cases that used legal theories relating to the issue of the public interest — publication/public domain doctrine and first sale doctrine — in infringement cases. In theory, these theories were designed to ensure the adequate access of the public to the computer programs and to encourage innovation by allowing the use of available codes. The first sale doctrine provides that the owner of a copy of the program can sell her copy without permission of the copyright holder (17 U.S.C. §109).

Among the 11 cases that used these theories, 6 cases used the publication/public domain doctrine and 5 used the first sale doctrine. Usually defendants made arguments based on these theories and judges responded to the arguments, more often unfavorably than favorably. It seems that the nature of the parties, whether the party was a developer of computer programs or not, was an important factor that related to how credible and convincing their arguments appeared to the judges.

When the plaintiff was a developer and the defendant was a non-developer (4 cases), judges never accepted the defendant's argument that used the doctrines of limited publication or first sale. In *GCA v. Chance* (1982), the plaintiffs manufactured and sold the computer machines and the defendants were in the business of repairing the machines. While the defendants argued that the plaintiff's program was already published when they used the program, the judge argued that the plaintiff's distribution of the program was a "limited" publication since the plaintiff had no intention of distributing its source code and object code to the general public. Similarly, in *Allen-Myland, Inc. (AMI) v. IBM* (1990), AMI was in the business of providing engineering services to owners of IBM large scale mainframe computers and argued that it did not infringe IBM's copyright in its 3090 microcode because the microcode was in the public domain. But the judge simply held that there was no evidence of supporting AMI's argument, thus the microcode was not in the public domain. In *ISC v. Altech* (1990),

Altech who serviced computer equipment and purchased and sold used computer equipment, argued that ISC is not entitled to the protection of its operating and applications programs under the first sale doctrine. But the judge decided that the doctrine of the first sale was not applicable because ISC did not sell the program to Altech but licensed it. In *Data Products v. William Reppart* (1990), the defendants for whom Data Products supplied their application program packages also argued that their use of the plaintiff's computer programs was legitimate and non-infringing due to the first sale doctrine. But the judge held that the doctrine was not applicable in the case since the defendant did not only use the software but made unauthorized "copies" of the material while the doctrine only extends to the original copy itself. The judges seem to have perceived that the theory of publication and the theory of first sale do not have applicability when the defendants were not developers themselves. The defendants failed to have appropriate resources to use certain legal theories, i.e., being engaged in software developing activities in these cases.

When both parties were not involved in any activities related to software development, such as in *Red Baron v. Taito* (1989) where Taito imported a game program called 'Double Dragon' and Red Baron owned copyright of the program, the appellate court judges also rejected the first sale doctrine argued by the defendant. The judges argued that the exhibition of the images in "sequence" of the game constitutes a "performance," and the first sale doctrine is limited to the "distribution" right, and does not apply to the "performance" right. There is only one case *Midway v. Strohon* (1983), where the plaintiff was a non-developer and the defendant was a developer. But in this case, the defendant's argument using the first sale doctrine was rejected on the basis that the judge considered the doctrine applicable only in patent cases.

Finally, when both parties of the case were developers of any kind of computer programs, the decisions were split. There are 4 cases in which the plaintiff was a developer of the original program and the defendant was a developer of another program, which the plaintiff allegedly infringed. In 3 of the cases the judges rejected the arguments of the defendants using the theories of first sale or public domain, while in 1 case the judge accepted the defendant's argument based on the theory of public domain. For example, in *Hubco v. Management Assistance, Inc.* (MAI) (1983), Hubco who developed an upgrading program for MAI's operating system software argued that because MAI publicly distributed its operating systems, Hubco's software did not infringe MAI's copyright. But the judge disagreed by saying that the important distinction is between "general publication" and "limited publication," and that MAI made a limited publication so it was not publicly available. Also, in *PRC v. National Association of Realtors (NAR)* (1991), the judge decided that NAR's modified program of PRC's software infringed the copyright of PRC because the original program was not made available to the public without restriction, so it was not publication as NAR insisted. In *Gates Rubber v. Bando*, the defendants who were former employees of the plaintiff's company argued that the plaintiff's copyright was not enforceable because the program was unprotected due to prior publication. The court held, however, that if any publication had occurred, it was a limited publication.

On the contrary, the judges of the court of appeals in *Data Cash v. JS&A* (1980) interpreted the concept of "limited publication" differently. They argued that a limited publication was really in the eyes of the law no publication at all, and thus JS&A's chess game program did not infringe upon the copyright of Data Cash's chess game program. The Data Cash case can be distinguished from the other 3 cases, in that the defendant's program in this case was a competing product which was similar in its function but was not found to have a clear relationship in terms of the developing process with the plaintiff's program. The defendants' programs in the other cases were an upgrading program for the plaintiff's program, a modified program of the plaintiff's program, or a similar program developed by the ones who had been involved with the development of the plaintiff's program. Therefore, when judges try to decide whether the use of the program is legitimate because the program is in the public domain or was already sold to the other party, they seem to consider the apparent connection between the two programs more importantly than the functional similarity of the programs.

In summary, there were only 11 cases that used the public access arguments using the publication or first sale doctrines, and these arguments were not usually accepted by the judges. Especially, when the parties involved non-developers of any computer programs, the argument using these doctrines were never accepted. Only when both parties were developers of different programs did the party that used the argument based on these theories have a chance to convince the judges, but they were not always successful. When the argument was accepted, it was when the defendant of the case could successfully use not only the legal theory but also the actor's resources of having developed another program that was not related to the plaintiff's program. Therefore, the most important concern in relation to the use of these legal theories seems to be the ways in which the defendant's program was developed (independently versus somehow using the underlying program of the plaintiff).

Preliminary Injunction Cases

Most of the arguments explicitly considering the public interest issue were made in preliminary injunction cases, since one of the four requirements of deciding for preliminary injunction is a factor of the public interest. Therefore, arguments in the cases deciding on a preliminary injunction are separately considered here. In an infringement action, preliminary injunction cases arguably have a stronger relationship with the issues of balancing equities than other final judgment or summary judgment cases. Because alleged infringers are only "preliminarily" enjoined from copying, manufacturing, using, or distributing the original program in these cases, decisions are made on the basis of different considerations from cases deciding on their merits. In determining whether to issue a preliminary injunction, courts require the satisfaction of some various combination of the following four factors: (1) the plaintiff has a likelihood of success on the merits of his claim; (2) the plaintiff does not have an adequate remedy at law and he or she will suffer irreparable harm without the injunction; (3) this harm is greater than the injury the defendant will suffer if the injunction is granted; and (4) the injunction will not harm the public interest. Some courts require that the plaintiff show either irreparable harm and likelihood of success, and other courts require irreparable harm and the existence of a serious question going to the merits and balance of hardship.

There are 47 preliminary injunction cases including 8 cases at the level of the court of appeals. The decisions in the preliminary injunction cases are more likely to be made in favor of finding an infringement (70%) than in other cases. Although judges tend to claim that none of the four or two factors of preliminary injunction cases should be definitive, not every factor is always explicitly considered, nor are the factors that are considered given the same weight in the arguments. For example, the issues related to the likelihood of success on the merits were dealt with in every case, and in an extensive way except for only one case. Moreover, the ultimate decisions of the cases regarding granting or denying an injunction were always consistent with the direction of the arguments regarding the likelihood of success on the merits. In this way, the likelihood of success on the merits actually seems to be the predominant factor in many cases. The arguments discussed to determine the probability of the merits have similar characteristics and structure with the main arguments in all the other cases. Therefore, these arguments will be analyzed together with the other arguments in other cases, which will be presented in the next section.

The second most frequently considered factor was the irreparable harm, but still 22 out of 47 preliminary injunction cases did not mention this factor at all. In the 25 cases that did mention this factor, the judges in 19 cases argued that the irreparable harm can be "presumed" if the plaintiff established the likelihood of success on the merits. This tendency of eliminating this factor altogether or of deciding that this factor was presumed became even clearer in later cases. Among the 19 cases in which the irreparable harm was presumed, judges of 9 cases provided some reasons why they thought that there was a possibility of irreparable harm as well. The reasons include that the plaintiff's reputation, although not sales, can be harmed, that video games have short-lived popularity, that the plaintiff invested large sums of money and time in developing the program, that the defendant's sales constituted only small percentage of total sales, and that the plaintiff was on the verge of bankruptcy.

In 2 cases no basis was provided, but the judges simply assumed and stated that there would be irreparable harm if an injunction was not granted. In 4 cases in which the judges did not presume the possibility of irreparable harm but argued that there was the possibility, the rationale given was that the plaintiff made a big investment in terms of time, money, and effort, or that the defendant's sales of the particular program were not significant in the defendant's business. In every case where the possibility of irreparable harm was considered, the judges decided that there was a possibility. And in every case in which it was decided that there was a possibility of irreparable harm, injunction was granted. It is interesting to find that while the "defendant's" "labor, time, and effort" (as opposed to the "creativity" and "independent production") are never acknowledged in the arguments that rule on the merits, the "plaintiff's" investment in terms of "time, money, and effort" is often considered a factor that makes a decision in favor of the plaintiff.

The factor of balance of harm was considered in 19 (40%) out of 47 cases. In 15 cases it was decided that the factor favored the plaintiff, and in 4 cases the factor favored the defendant. In some cases, judges explicitly stated that the balance of harm was a less important factor than the likelihood of success on the merits, and thus would not consider this factor (*Data General v. Grumman,* 1988).

In 4 of the 19 cases no reason or basis was provided upon why the judges thought the plaintiff's harm exceeds the defendant's harm. The reasons and rationales provided in the remaining 15 cases were related to the different positions and situations of the actors. In 9 cases the judges employed actual comparisons between the harms, or employed the situation in the industry as a rationale, i.e., that the defendant would experience the elimination of sales altogether while the plaintiff would experience only a decrease in sales, that the defendant was still marketing the product while the plaintiff is not, and that the plaintiff was better suited to withstand injury than the defendant. In these cases 4 cases were decided in favor of the defendant and 5 cases in favor of the plaintiff. In 6 cases judges employed the position of the actors in the case as a rationale, i.e., that the plaintiff's investment was large, that the program in issue was not a substantial part of the defendant's business, that the plaintiff's investment was much larger than the defendant's, that the defendant's loss of profit did not deserve equitable consideration due to its position as an infringer, and that the defendant's harm was its own fault. In all these cases the decision was made in favor of the plaintiff.

Therefore, when the actors' situation in the industry and the actual comparison of the harm were considered, the decisions were split and defendants sometimes were granted a favorable decision.

However, when the judges considered the position of the actors as an investor versus an alleged infringer in the case, the plaintiff always won the case.

The factor of the public interest was not mentioned or considered at all in 31 (70%) out of 47 preliminary injunction cases. Among the 14 cases in which the public interest was considered, 13 cases decided that the injunction should be granted. The basis of these arguments was that the public interest would be served by free trade and competition.

In 3 out of 14 cases the judges did not provide any rationale or explanation but simply argued that the public interest would be served by granting the injunction. This clearly contrasts with arguments relating to the likelihood of success on the merits, consider the rules and issues in a very detailed and extensive way. Among the remaining 11 cases in which the judges did provide rationales regarding the factor of the public interest, a judge in 1 case claimed that the public interest would be served by prohibiting unfair competition. In the other 9 (64%) cases the judges argued that the public interest would be served by rewarding the plaintiff's development, rewarding the author, encouraging individual effort and creativity, rewarding creative expression, encouraging innovation, and protecting the right of the copyright holder. The value of the public interest and access was strikingly equated with the value of authorship that was characterized by individual effort and creativity.

The analysis of the arguments and decisions in regards to preliminary injunction factors show considerations of the public interest, users, or equity were usually neglected. The three factors analyzed here are considered less frequently than the likelihood of success on the merits. Irreparable harm could be easily presumed by the establishment of success on the merits, and usually the basis to determine the possibility of irreparable harm was only that the plaintiff invested a large amount of money and effort. This is usually inevitable in many of the copyright cases. Consequently, the judges tend to make tautological restatements of the nature of the case.

The factors of the balance of harm and the public interest are even less seriously considered compared with the other two factors, and also do not benefit from any of the specific guidelines. Judges do not show consistency in dealing with the following conflicting bases to consider the balance of harm: the actual comparison of the dollar amount of harm, the actors' situation in the industry, or the actors' position in the case — as a plaintiff versus a defendant, and as a developer versus an alleged infringer. When the actors' position in the case is used as a sole consideration, this is again nothing more than a tautological restatement of the nature of the case, and as a result, the decisions were made always in favor of the plaintiffs.

The public interest factor was the least seriously considered factor. In addition, not only did the arguments centering around the public interest issue never deal with concerns of the users or the "public" as the users, but also was the most frequently used rationale for this factor rewarding the author's creativity and effort. The judges merely restated the assumption that the public interest will be automatically served by rewarding individual (authors') effort and creativity. In other words, it was assumed that by broadening copyright protection to authors (and probably copyright holders), the public interest will be enhanced. Therefore, the value of the public interest was trivialized into providing a monetary reward to the developers, and in the process, the value of "individual creativity" and "authorship" was created and reproduced as an important structural rule for later cases in the copyright cases regarding computer programs.

AUTHORSHIP , WORK, AND USE

I will now present detailed analyses of the legal arguments according to each issue of the cases, employing the frames of authorship, work, and use. As identified earlier, the issues include copyrightability in copyrightability cases, the ownership/authorship dispute, the validity of ownership, substantial similarity, copyrightable expression, and copying that constitutes infringement. The analysis focuses on the ways in which the plaintiffs, defendants and judges use frames, legal theories, and interpretations in their arguments. In order to identify the establishment of structural rules in copyright cases, and to define the conditions under which the structural rules are reproduced and transformed, I examine the ways in which the plaintiffs and defendants employ their resources and structural rules in their arguments, and the ways in which the judges respond to their arguments.

Copyrightability Cases

As expected by a large number of copyrightability cases in earlier time periods, arguments pertaining to the issue of copyrightability mainly occurred in the first time period, and the number of the arguments on that issue decreased over time. Among the 58 arguments that dealt with the issue of copyrightability, 25 were made in the first time period, 18 in the second period, 14 in the third period, and only 1 in the fourth period.

Unlike the infringement cases, copyrightability cases do not consider a question regarding the use of the plaintiff's program by the defendant. Thus the frames used in these cases consist only of the plaintiff's authorship (7 arguments) versus the plaintiff's work (50 arguments), except for one policy argument that was about the intent of Congress. The other frames such as the defendant's work, the defendant's authorship, the defendant's use, the public interest, or market consequences did not appear in the arguments pertaining to this issue.

All of the 7 arguments that used the frame of authorship involved the theory of originality. In only 1 argument the judge was responding to the plaintiff's argument while in 6 arguments judges were responding to the defendants' challenge of the originality of the plaintiffs' programs. Through these arguments, the judges clearly defined the concept of originality as a minimalistic requirement.

The first question regarding the originality of the plaintiff's computer program was raised in 1982 in *Apple v. Franklin*. Even though the preliminary injunction that Apple sought was denied in the district case (later preliminary injunction was granted in the appellate court), pertaining to Apple's operating system programs, the judge stated that an "original work" need not be a work of genius. This minimalistic view on the originality requirement was stated again later in 1986 in *M. Kramer v. Andrews*. When the defendants challenged the validity of the plaintiff's audiovisual work on the basis of the lack of originality, the judges argued that the standard for originality is minimal, which is enough if it is something "his own." Where the work is an audiovisual work, not a work of art, the judges argued, "true artistic skill" is not required.

In *Atari v. Oman* (1988), the district court agreed with the copyright register who was the defendant of the case and held that Atari's videogame lacked "minimal artistic expression," and admittedly independent efforts are too trivial or insignificant to support copyright. The district court's holding, however, was rejected by the appellate court, which argued that the usual standard of creativity for copyright is "minimal, modest, and very slight." In the 3 cases that followed, the judges consistently adopted this minimalistic view of the originality requirement by arguing: that originality means only that the work "owes its origin to the author," i.e., "independently created" (*NEC v. Intel*, 1989); that the defendant's files were substantially "re-worked" (*Service & Training v. Data General, 1990*); and that the standard of originality is minimal that it only requires "independent creation" (*Apple v. Microsoft*, 1991).

The analysis of the arguments in relation to the plaintiff's authorship suggests that the scope of copyright protection broadened by the minimalistic view of the originality requirement. This result is consistent with Jaszi (1991)'s argument that the concept of "authorship" continued to be strategically used to extend copyright protection to new kinds of subject matter, by making it dissociated from "genius" and then reassociated with the meanest levels of creative activity, as something more than a "merely trivial" variation. Moreover, not only was the requirement minimal, but the judges also considered "independent creation" the most important standard that determines the originality of a program, without building any objective standard for defining the characteristics that make a work "original." Therefore, the minimal standard for originality and the importance given to the "independent development" of the program is established as an important structural rule in copyright cases regarding computer programs. As will be discussed later, the judges' view of originality explains why they make infringement decisions based on the degree of the defendant's developing activity "on his own," rather than on the functional similarity or possible market effect of the defendant's program.

The arguments that used the frame of work were made more frequently in earlier cases. Twenty-four (48%) of the 50 arguments were made in the first time period, 17 (34) in the second period, and 9 (18%) in the third period. There were no arguments that used the frame of work in the fourth period. This seems to be because the copyrightability of computer programs as a subject matter was a critical question when the initial cases regarding software copyright began to be decided. After many cases, it had become established as a structural rule that the computer software is copyrightable as a subject matter, thus this issue ceased to be considered in later cases.

Among the arguments that used a frame of work, most of them (44 out of 50) were responding to the defendant's challenge against the copyrightability of the plaintiff's program. Forty-one of them rejected the defendant's arguments and only 3 of them accepted the defendant's arguments. There was only one argument that rejected the plaintiff's argument that the program is copyrightable.

Most of the arguments that used a frame of work were about whether the computer program is copyrightable. In most of the arguments (45 arguments, 90%), it was established that it is a copyrightable subject matter. The first case *Synercom v. University Computing Company* (1978) employed the theory of communication and expression to determine the copyrightability of the input formats of the Synercom's statistical analysis program. The defendants argued that the input formats are not subject to copyright because they are not intended to convey information. The judge rejected this argument saying that forms which communicate information can be the subject of copyright, and the critical question is whether the material undertakes to "express." The computer program's input formats, therefore, were decided to be copyrightable as it communicates the selection arrangements and the sequences, which is expression. Citing this argument in Synercom, the judge in *Digital v. Softklone* (1987) argued that screen is a form that clearly expresses and conveys information and therefore, is copyrightable.

The theory of communication was used in the other 4 arguments. In *Apple v. Franklin* (1982), the judge argued that the scope of copyright is limited to the material with a communicative purpose, so that it can create human interaction. This argument that tried to limit the scope of copyright helped Franklin in the district court, but it was explicitly rejected in the court of appeals (1983), which argued that the 1976 Copyright Act suggested that programs are considered copyrightable as literary works whether or not it is a medium of communication to human being. The question of communication in the issue of copyrightability was considered once again in *Williams v. Artic* in 1982, where the defendant argued that a "copy" must be intelligible to a human being. The judge, however, held that the program can be fixed by any method, including with the aid of a machine. In this way, a strict communication requirement was generally rejected by the courts and the courts began to rely more on the fixation requirement.

The 1976 Copyright Act states that "copyright protection subsists . . . in original work of authorship "fixed in a tangible medium of expression" . . . from which they can be perceived, reproduced, or otherwise communicated, either directly or with the aid of a machine or device." Two arguments that focused on the fixation requirement were also made in response to the defendants' challenge against the copyrightability of computer programs. The defendants in both *Midway v. Artic* (1982) and *M. Kramer v. Andrews* (1985) questioned whether the changing images of the audiovisual screen of videogames can be copyrightable because they are not "fixed" in a tangible medium of expression. Judges held that audiovisual are fixed in the computer program, thus both the images (Midway) and the underlying computer programs (M. Kramer) may be copyrighted. Consequently, arguments regarding the communication and fixation requirement have undoubtedly established that both literal and non-literal elements of the computer program, including the status screen and audiovisual display, are a copyrightable subject matter.

A related legal theory is that of idea versus expression, which states that expression, but not ideas, are protected by copyright in order to prohibit the monopolization of an idea. Twenty-five of the 28 arguments that used this theory were made in response to the defendants' arguments against the copyrightability of computer programs, and 3 of them did not explicitly mention who initiated the arguments. Judges tended to disagree with the defendants' arguments using this theory (22 out of 25) and held that the program is copyrightable expression rather than ideas. For example, in *Whelan v. Jaslaw* (1986), which was later extensively cited although often criticized, the court of appeals held that copyright protects "non-literal" aspects of the program, i.e., structure, sequence, and organization because the "purpose or function of a utilitarian work would be the work's idea and everything that is not a purpose or function is expression." In *Broderbund v. Unison* (1986), Unison argued that the idea underlying the menu screens, input formats, and sequencing of screens in the plaintiff's program is indistinguishable from its expression (merger doctrine), and thus are not copyrightable. But the judge, following *Whelan v. Jaslaw*, rejected this argument saying that there are many ways of expression in the case of the plaintiff's program, thus rules and instructions can be protected by copyright.

In order to determine whether computer programs or any elements of the programs are ideas or expression, courts usually examined the characteristics of the computer program (functional or artistic). Some of these arguments explicitly used the metaphor of utilitarian work, artistic work or literary work in relation to the idea versus expression doctrine. Due to the significant influence of the use of metaphor on the ways in which the decisions are made, the arguments and decisions explicitly using metaphor will be separately discussed later in this section.

The judges who made arguments using this theory of idea versus expression usually held that the work is copyrightable. When they decided that it is not copyrightable in 2 out of 20 cases (even though both of the cases were reversed in the appeals courts), it was always related to the fact that they considered the program a functional work, or focused on the functional aspect of the program. For example, in *Atari v. Oman* (1988), when Atari tried to register its videogame for copyright, the copyright register argued that copyright protection does not extend to games because the game and the expression is merged, and its arrangement of images are dictated by functional requirements. The district court agreed with the defendant, but the court of appeals (1992) reversed the holding because the judges considered the plaintiff's arrangement of images not dictated by functional requirements or merged with ideas. Another case is *Apple v. Franklin* (1982), in which the judge accepted the defendant's argument that ROM is an object that merges its utilitarian function and expressive purpose so that they are inseparable. But the judges in the court of appeals (1983), reversing the district court's ruling, rejected the view that the ROMs are utilitarian objects or machine parts, but regarded computer programs as literary works, which are protected by copyright law.

There are other arguments in relation to the copyrightability of the plaintiff's work focusing on the nature of the work, but without using any identifiable theories. All of these arguments were made in favor of granting copyrightability. In regards to whether ROM chips are a "copy," or regarding the distinction between the game and the program, many of these arguments used metaphor as a rationale for their arguments. The use of metaphors is analyzed in the next section.

The arguments in the copyrightability cases were always made in a way to grant copyright protection to the plaintiff (excluding the arguments and decisions that were later rejected and reversed). The questions such as which party initiated the arguments, which particular frame or theory was used, or what are the characteristics of the parties (developers, copyright holders, neither) did not matter. In conclusion, the copyrightability cases and arguments, which centered around originality as the plaintiff's authorship and the plaintiff's work as a copyrightable subject matter, have clearly established structural rules that: 1) computer software is copyrightable as a subject matter and the protection extends to videogames and operating programs as well as application programs, to literal and non-literal elements and to programs embodied in ROMs and diskettes; and 2) only a minimal amount of the originality shown by the evidence of the plaintiff's independent development (on his own) is required to grant copyright.

Metaphor

In earlier cases, the focus of the arguments was often about which law should be applied, between the Copyright Act of 1909 and the Copyright Act of 1976. Almost all the cases held that the parties should comply with the 1976 Act. After this issue was settled, the use of metaphor in cases regarding software copyright became frequent. As the new technology of computer programs poses difficult problems to the copyright cases, many judges and legal actors tried to find an analogy between computer programs and other traditional works that had been protected by copyright law. Some of the arguments relied on the 1976 Copyright Act that states that "works of authorship include literary works, musical works, dramatic works, choreographic works, pictorial, graphic, and sculptural works, audiovisual works, and sound recordings."

Although the arguments using a metaphor were made in the copyrightability cases most frequently (15 out of 33 arguments), they are also found in the ownership dispute cases and the infringement cases. But the arguments that used metaphor in the other cases also were placed in the context of determining the copyrightability of certain elements of programs. Therefore, the analysis of the metaphor arguments will include all the arguments, regardless of the issue of the cases.

Among the 115 cases judges in 27 cases mentioned some kind of metaphor in making decisions. In some cases the judges were responding to the plaintiffs or defendants who used metaphor in their arguments. In other cases the judges used metaphor of their own. The metaphor most frequently used by the judges was the literary work (9) and the audiovisual work (9), followed by the utilitarian work (6) and the artistic or pictorial, graphic, sculptural work (2).

The issue of whether software program is characterized as a utilitarian work, a literary work, an audiovisual work or an artistic work has beneath it important implications about the scope of protection. The most critical distinction is whether computer programs were considered a utilitarian work or a literary and artistic work. For example, when Microsoft succeeded in persuading the judge to think of the Apple interface as a utilitarian work, it practically won the case on that issue (*Apple v. Microsoft*, 1991). Apple had argued that the interface was artistic and fanciful, and hence should enjoy a broad scope of protection. Apple analogized the interfaces to paintings and music, while Microsoft analogized them to automobiles.

The metaphor arguments turned out to be powerful and decisive, in that the use of different metaphors always resulted in different decisions in the copyrightability and the infringement cases. In 6 cases when judges considered the computer program as a utilitarian work, it was always held that the defendant did not infringe the copyright of the plaintiff's program because it was not a copyrightable work. For example, in *Synercom v. University Computing Company* (1978), the judge rejected Synercom's argument that the order and sequence of the data was the expression, not the idea. The judge's rejection was based on its famous analogy of the "figure-H" pattern of an automobile stick, which the court decided was not protected by copyright. Also, in *Sega v. Accolade* (1992), which involved the plaintiff's computer program for a video entertainment system, the court of appeals argued that copyright protection differs according to the nature of the work, and that functional and factual aspects receive less protection and computer programs are in essence utilitarian articles.

All the other arguments used a literary work, artistic work, and pictorial, graphic, and sculptural work as a metaphor for computer programs, and resulted in the decision that the work was copyrightable and/or the defendants did infringe on the plaintiffs' copyright. In *Midway v. Artic* (1982), Midway argued that its 'PacMan' games are copyrightable as an audiovisual work while Artic argued that the 'PacMan' on the ROM and the 'PacMan' games themselves are utilitarian objects. The judge rejected Artic's argument and decided that Artic infringed Midway's copyright. Also, in *Johnson v. Uniden* (1985), the defendant argued that the plaintiff's computer code is not copyrightable because a computer program is a "useful" as opposed to a literary work. But the judge held that a computer program is a "literary" work, thus the "useful work" doctrine is not applicable in such a case.

In addition, the cases that regarded videogames as an audiovisual work held that the displays of videogames are copyrightable as an audiovisual work, regardless of the requirement of the fixation, communication, or originality (*Atari v. Amusement*, 1981; *Midway v. Dirkschneider*, 1981; *Stern v. Kaufman*, 1981; *Midway v. Artic*, 1982; *M. Kramer v. Andrews*, 1985; *Red-Baron v. Taito*, 1989). Regarding videogame programs and their audiovisual displays that were a new subject for copyright, the arguments and decisions that employed the notion of an audiovisual work firmly established the structural rule that videogames are copyrightable as a subject matter and that the other requirements for copyright do not have to be strictly applied for videogames. Consequently, the scope of copyright protection for videogames became even broader than that for other computer programs.

It has been shown that the judges' use of metaphor is a decisive factor in decision making. However, it is not clear how the judges determine which metaphor to accept or reject when they face opposing metaphors argued by different parties. When the judges accept or reject the parties' arguments, they tended not to provide any basis or rationale for why they consider a program in a different way. Further, it was found that the nature of the plaintiffs or defendants (whether they were developers or non-developers) or the topic of the case (copyrightability or infringement) does not have any significant relationship to the metaphor used by the judges or to whether the judge accepted or rejected the parties' arguments. In order to identify how the metaphor arguments may operate, I examined the frames regarding the authorship, the work and the use that are implied in some cases.

Although the metaphor arguments were made in 9 copyrightability cases and 17 infringement cases, the basis for the decisions was whether the plaintiffs' computer programs were copyrightable or whether their elements were a copyrightable expression in the first place, even in the infringement cases. Thus the metaphor arguments basically focused on the nature of the work, more likely on the plaintiff's work. But in some cases there was a difference in the implicit notions of authorship, work, and use. I examined the interaction between the concepts of authorship, work, and use implied in the metaphor arguments that was apparent in some cases.

When the judges considered the computer program to be a literary work or artistic work, the metaphor arguments tended to imply a process of creation. For example, in *Broderbund v. Unison* (1986), Unison argued that the plaintiff's program 'The Print Shop' does not fall within the definition of "pictorial" or "graphic" works, since the program has mechanical or utilitarian features rather than the artistic aspects which are protected. The judge argued that the structure, sequence, and layout of the audiovisual displays of the plaintiff's work are dictated primarily by "artistic considerations" of the creators and not by utilitarian ones, so it is protected by copyright. Also in *Digital v. Softklon* (1987), the judge argued that the status screen, as a literary work, meets the requirement of an original work. The defendant in *M. Kramer v. Andrews* (1985) argued that the plaintiff's work is invalid because the work lacks originality, but the judges argued that the standard for originality is minimal, and artistic skill is not required where the work is audiovisual work. The judge followed the structural rule in copyright law that the originality standard is minimal. Consequently, his arguments expanded the scope of copyright.

Therefore, when the computer program was considered a utilitarian work, the argument focused on the nature of the work itself, isolated from the process of development or creation. However, when the program was viewed as a literary work, the arguments usually mentioned authorship, originality, or the process of software creation. It seems that when the work is considered an artistic or literary work, it becomes more persuasive and convincing that the author of the work should be compensated. But when the work is considered useful and mechanical, the focus of the argument becomes detached from the consideration of authorship. Thus it becomes easier to argue against providing copyright protection, of which the main concern in the courts seems to be rewarding the authors.

On the other hand, in some cases that involve an alleged infringement of a videogame copyright, arguments that used the metaphor of an audiovisual work included the ones that responded to the defendant's arguments regarding the use of the program. In *Atari v. North American* (1981) the defendant and the district court judge mentioned extensively the defendant's "effort to avoid infringement" in the use of the plaintiff's program and decided that North American did not infringe on the copyright of Atari's 'PacMan' video game programs. The judge in the court of appeals (1982), however, viewed North American's effort to avoid copying as an attempt to disguise an intentional appropriation of Atari's game, and instead argued that games can be copyrighted as pictorial or graphic works and the repetitive sequence of a game is considered copyrightable as an audiovisual work. The case was reversed and decided that North American infringed on Atari's copyright. The shift of the focus from the defendant's use to the nature of the plaintiff's work resulted in a decision that found an infringement.

In conclusion, in many of the arguments that used metaphor, the critical distinction lies in the difference between work and authorship. The arguments and decisions regarding the metaphor have firmly established the copyrightability of computer programs and audiovisual displays of videogames, by focusing on the frame of the plaintiff's work. The only cases in which the copyrightability was denied, were when the judges viewed the computer program as a utilitarian work. The metaphor of a utilitarian work was presented as an alternative to considering the computer program as a literary work or artistic work, which inevitably relates to the notion of authorship and creativity. Metaphors in copyrightability arguments tend to reflect the tension between the plaintiffs who developed the original program and the defendants who may benefit by isolating the author from the work. In the case of the audiovisual work, it is presented as a work of authorship that is protected by copyright regardless of the degree of originality or fixation. Also the minimal requirement of the originality test was applied and reinforced here. Therefore, metaphors in some of the infringement arguments reflect the tension between the defendants who try to use the plaintiffs' programs and the plaintiffs who are often not developers themselves and try to focus the argument on the notion of work that is isolated from the notion of use.

Ownership/Authorship Dispute Cases

17 of the judges' arguments in 13 cases were made in the context of deciding the rightful author of the computer program when it was not clear who developed (or co-developed) the program, or in the context of deciding who owns the copyright of the program. Naturally, all the arguments in the authorship/ownership cases used the frame of authorship. None of the arguments used the frame of work or use. The analysis of the frame of authorship in copyrightability cases demonstrates that the individual creation is emphasized while the originality requirement in general is minimized. The arguments in the authorship/ownership dispute, which consist of the work-for-hire doctrine and the joint authorship issue, reflect another dimension regarding how the concept of authorship transforms itself in copyright law.

In most of the cases (10) both the plaintiffs and the defendants were somehow engaged in the development of a computer program, and the judges used the work-for-hire doctrine in deciding who was the rightful author. In one case the defendant was not engaged in any kind of developing activity but questioned the plaintiff's authorship of the program. Two cases decided whether the plaintiff and the defendant were joint authors of the program. These authorship/ownership dispute cases began to appear relatively recently. Nine of the 13 cases were held in the 1990's.

The 2 cases regarding joint authorship are actually the same case *Ashton-Tate v. Ross* (1989; 1990) that were held in the district court and the court of appeals. Although the original frame in the arguments was that of authorship, the frame of work was combined as the theory of idea versus expression was used. Ashton-Tate received a list of user commands for the program 'MacCalc' that Ross was developing, and created a similar program 'Full Impact.' Ross claimed a joint authorship in 'Full Impact' but the judges shifted the focus of the arguments to the nature of the work by asking whether Ross' contribution in terms of the list of commands was an idea or an expression. The judges argued that the defendant's contribution is considered only ideas because it's nothing "innovative" or "novel," and held that Ross does not have joint-authorship. Consequently, the judges applied a different level of the authorship requirement to the defendants, as compared to the very minimal requirement for the plaintiff's authorship, by shifting the focus of arguments from the defendant's authorship to the nature of the plaintiff's work.

In *Nintendo v. Elcon* (1982), the defendant who did not participate in the development of the plaintiff's video game questioned the validity of the plaintiff's authorship, arguing that the plaintiff itself did not develop the program but hired someone else. The judge responded that according to the work-for-hire doctrine, the plaintiff's copyright is valid because Nintendo was an employer of the person who developed this program while the person who developed the program was merely a "technical assistant." In all the other work-for-hire cases, both parties were involved with the developing process of the program in some way. A critical question posed in all of the work-for-hire cases is whether one party was an employee of the other party or not, because most judges follow the rule in 17 U.S.C. §101(1), which was again established in *Community v. Reid* (1989). *Reid* discussed the presumption that the one who creates the work is the owner for copyright purposes, and stated that this presumption may be overcome if the work is made for hire. In order to decide if the work is made for hire, *Reid* applied a 2 step analysis to determine: 1) if the creator is a true employee of the employer or merely an independent contractor; and 2) if the product was prepared within the scope of the employment. And the product is within the scope of the employment if: 1) it is of the kind he is employed to perform; 2) it occurs substantially within the authorized time and space limits; and 3) it is actuated by a purpose to serve the master.

Therefore, on the one hand, the work-for-hire doctrine alienates the work from the author by taking rights from the author and granting them to the employer, and it can be considered an indication that the authors' rights began to be deprived of as some scholars argued. On the other hand, the concept of authorship, which was developed in the earlier copyrightability cases, seems to remain in the work-for-hire doctrine. The importance given to the "independent creation" in the concept of authorship in copyrightability arguments is also found in this work-for-hire doctrine, in that the important premise to be an author of the work one creates is to be an "independent contractor" rather than an employee. Among the multi-dimensional factors to take into account, judges weigh different factors and questions in a different way in the work-for-hire cases. The analysis of these arguments reveals how the individual Romantic vision of authorship still remains central, but in a somewhat distorted way, in work-for-hire cases.

The question regarding whether the developer was an employee appeared in every case. In some cases, especially in earlier cases, the only question was whether the developer was an employee. Once the judge decided on that matter the question of who the author is was automatically decided accordingly. In *BPI v. Leith* (1981), judgment was made for the developer of the program when the judge held that he was not an employee of BPI. *Graham v. James* (1992) held against the developer of the program when the judge held that James was an employee of Graham. Also, *Aymes v. Bonelli* (1991) held for the developer of the program in the district court and then held against the developer of the program in the court of appeals (1992), purely on the basis of the judges' different interpretation and application of the *Reid's* test of the "hire" and "employment" concept.

Later cases tend to introduce other factors in connection with the discussion of the matter of employment. There are some cases where, despite a finding that the developer was an employee, the other factors played a larger role and the decision was made differently. For example, in *Avtec v. Peiffer* (1992), the court admitted that Peiffer was an employee, but it still decided that he was the rightful owner of the program because he did not prepare the product within the authorized time and space limits but developed the program during his non-working hours and did not create it for Avtec. In addition, in *Kelstall-Whitney v. Mahar* (1990), the court found that Mahar was an employee. But when Mahar argued that he developed the program on his own time "independently," the court accepted the argument and held that it was Mahar who had the "initial idea," wrote the source code, after working hours, and with no wage compensation.

In other cases, other factors work complementary to the notion of employment. For example, in *Mercer v. MacLean* (1991), the court of appeals considered the factors in *Reid* and decided that Mercer-MacLean was not in a master-servant relationship to constitute employment because he wrote the program after he left Mercer. Thus, the district court's holding was reversed and it was held that MacLean may be the author of the program. At the same time, the court of appeals also pointed out that MacLean had the required "skill and creativity" to develop the program. Another clear example suggesting that "independent creativity" was considered important is *Whelan v. Jaslaw* (1985). When Jaslaw sought co-authorship with Whelan who developed a dental lab program for Jaslaw, the court held that the work-for-hire doctrine was not applicable because Whelan was an "independent contractor." At the same time, the judge noted that Whelan alone was the author because her "expertise" and "creativeness" designed the methods, while Jaslaw explained to Whelan only the "functions" to be performed by computer.

The analysis of the arguments in authorship/ownership dispute cases keenly reveals how the notion of authorship interacts with the notion of the work in copyright arguments. The work-for-hire doctrine provides a place in which the alienation of the author from the work occurs, and the ownership rights are transferred from developers to employers, in that the "author" of the "work" is the person on whose behalf the "work" was made, not the individual who created it. The work-for-hire doctrine thus provides a rare opportunity for the parties who are not developers to possibly prevail in authorship cases. At the same time, the notion of "employment" which is critical in deciding the applicability of the "work-for-hire" doctrine is contrasted with the notion of "independent contractorship," suggesting that the activity of "independent" creation is considered important. In addition, the values that are constantly emphasized in conjunction with the employment arguments are "skill and creativity," "expertise," "creativeness," and even "ideas," all of which are rooted in the Romantic vision of the author-genius. Therefore, while the author is being alienated from the work when a work is deemed to have been made "for-hire," the individualistic Romantic notion of the authorship seems to be still central to the conceptualization of the authorship-ownership disputes.

Moreover, even when the "employer" was considered the author of the program, the values of creative "ideas" or "inspirations" as opposed to "labor" were emphasized. For example, in *Aymes v. Bonneli* (1991), the judge argued that because Aymes performed work under "supervision and direction" of Bonneli, the work belonged to Bonneli even if Aymes had not been an employee. In this way, the employers' claims are ironically rationalized in terms of the Romantic conception of "authorship" with its concomitant values of "creativity" and "inspiration," as Jaszi (1991) pointed out.

Infringement Cases

As the structural rules regarding copyrightability of comptuter programs are established, most later cases involved the issue of infringement. 186 arguments were made in infringement cases, which comprise the arguments made most frequently in the data, and these arguments tended to increase over time. In the first time period the infringement arguments were 61% (42 arguments) of the total arguments, 72% (49 arguments) in the third period and 89% (70 arguments) in the fourth period. In the second period, however, the infringement arguments slightly decreased to 56% (25 arguments) while the copyrightability arguments slightly increased from the first period. This is because the second period was when the copyrightability of new subject matters such as videogame programs and their audiovisual displays were being decided. The arguments in the infringement cases were more likely to be made in favor of broadening the scope of copyright rather than limiting (69% versus 31%), but the discrepancy was smaller than in the copyrightability cases (90% versus 10%).

Some interesting changes appear in infringement cases. While the concept of work and the concept of author were separated in ownership/authorship dispute cases, in infringement cases the concept of work did not replace the concept of authorship but worked in conjunction with the authorship construct. In addition, many of the arguments in infringement cases began to deal with the defendant's work, the defendant's authorship, while none of the copyrightability arguments focused on the defendants. Also, the frame of use is introduced and interacts with the frame of authorship and that of work. Except for one argument, all the arguments that used the frame of use were made in infringement cases, including the nature of the defendant's use of the plaintiff's program, public use/benefit, and market consequences. The most frequently used frame in infringement arguments was the frame of work that was used 60% of the time, followed by the frame of use (30%) and the frame of authorship (10%). In copyrightability cases, the frame of work was used 86% of the time, and the frame of authorship was used for 12% of the time. Also, many of the arguments in infringement cases began to focus on the defendant's work, the defendant's authorship, and the defendant's use (44% of the arguments) in infringement cases, while none of the copyrightability arguments focused on the defendants.

To determine whether the defendant infringed the plaintiff's copyright, the courts employ different steps of analysis. First the court confirms if the plaintiff owns a valid copyright for the program in dispute. Because the copyrightability of computer programs as a subject matter and the minimal standard of originality required for the plaintiff had been solidly established as important structural rules of copyright cases, the courts tend not to refute the plaintiff's ownership as invalid. Next the court investigates whether the defendant copied the plaintiff's program. Acknowledging the difficulty of showing direct copying, the courts note that copying can be inferred from access and substantial similarity: that the defendant had access to the plaintiff's program, and the two programs are substantially similar. The access is rarely in dispute in copyright cases regarding computer programs probably because the programs in dispute are usually commercial products that are easily available. Thus the arguments in infringement cases often center around identifying substantial similarity. Once it is decided that copying had occurred, it is presumed that the defendant had infringed the plaintiff's copyright. But the defendant can raise a defense that the copying was legally allowed, and courts usually consider the question if raised. Thus the arguments in infringement cases can be categorized into 4 major issues upon which infringement decisions are based: 1) ownership of a valid copyright, 2) copying — substantial similarity), 3) copying — copyrightable expression as a scope of copying, and 4) copying that constitutes infringement.

Among the 186 arguments in infringement cases, the most arguments were made in the context of infringing use (72), followed by substantial similarity (54), copyrightable expression (39), and ownership of a valid copyright (21). The arguments regarding the copying as infringement were a steady majority of the arguments most of the time (36%, 32%, 47%, and 43% of the arguments in each time period), although arguments regarding the substantial similarity were the majority in the second time period (52%). The arguments regarding copyrightable expression also greatly increased in the fourth period (6% to 33%), while the arguments in substantial similarity decreased over time (33% and 19% in the third and fourth periods).

The judges were most likely to argue in favor of broadening the scope of copyright (95% of the time) when the arguments were made in the context of the validity of a copyright ownership, followed by the context of copying as infringement (72%), copyrightable expression (67%), and substantial similarity (54%). All the arguments that were made regarding the validity of copyright ownership, except for one, were in favor of deciding that the copyright is valid.

Also, some differences are found in the use of frames according to these issues. The arguments regarding the copying of the substantial similarity, copyrightable expression, and valid ownership of copyright used the frame of work most frequently (91%, 87%, and 62% of the arguments respectively), whereas the arguments regarding the copying as infringement used the frame of use most frequently (75%). Except for 2 arguments, all the 57 arguments that used the frame of use were made in the context of copying as infringement. The detailed analysis of the use of frames, legal theories, and interpretations in legal arguments according to each issue is presented as follows.

Valid Ownership

Twenty-one arguments were made in relation to whether the plaintiff has a valid ownership of the program. Basically, these arguments have similar characteristics with the arguments in copyrightability cases, but they do not lead to a separate decision on copyrightability; rather they are placed in the context of defining the validity of a copyright as a pre-requisite to find an infringement. As in the copyrightability cases, the arguments on the validity of ownership tend to use the frame of work most often (13 out of 21 arguments), and most of them (12 out of 13 arguments) were about the plaintiff's work rather than the defendant's work. Except for one case the judges' arguments did not refute the validity of the plaintiff's copyright, even in the 3 cases where the defendants were not found to have infringed on the copyright.

Only 2 arguments used the frame of use. The defendants of the two cases in the fourth period challenged the validity of the plaintiffs' ownership using the frame of public interest/benefit (*Gates Rubber v. Bando*, 1992; *PRC v. National Association of Realtors*, 1991). Both of these arguments relied on the doctrine of publication arguing that the plaintiff's published programs do not have valid ownership, and were rejected by the judges.

The frame of authorship was used in 6 arguments, 4 of which were on the plaintiff's authorship and 2 on the defendant's joint-authorship claim. As demonstrated in the analysis of the arguments in authorship/ownership dispute cases, the notion of authorship was constructed differently when it was applied to the defendants than to the plaintiffs. In all of the 4 arguments that used the frame of the plaintiff's authorship, the defendants challenged the validity of the plaintiffs' copyright based on the lack of originality. The judges rejected all of them by shifting the focus of arguments from the authorship to the nature of work, or applying the minimal requirement of authorship that had been established. For example, the defendants in *Stern v. Kaufman* (1981) made an argument in relation to the issue of the distinction between the program and the audiovisual display, arguing that Stern's videogame display is not an original work because Stern registered the audiovisual material, but not the underlying computer program. The judge, shifting the focus of the argument from the issue of originality to the nature of the work, held that copyright protection extends to an audiovisual work and the plaintiff's game is a copyrightable subject matter as an audiovisual work. The judge in *Johnson Controls v. Phoenix* (1989) explicitly stated that the standard of originality required for a copyright is minimal, rejecting the defendant's challenge against the validity of copyright in the plaintiff's program. *Dynamic Solutions v. Planning & Control* (1986) also held that the plaintiff's program is original, because the plaintiff's "contribution" is substantial. The judge in *Allen-Myland v. IBM* (1990) claimed that the plaintiff's work can be considered original if the work is viewed as a whole.

In rejecting 2 joint authorship arguments made by the defendants, the judges in *Softel v. Dragon* (1992) and *S.O.S. v. Payday* (1986) relied on *Whelan v. Jaslaw*, in arguing that the defendant's "contribution" was not sufficient and that the defendant was only a supplier of "ideas" who did not translate the work in a tangible medium of expression. As in the authorship/ownership dispute cases, the defendant's joint authorship arguments never received the benefit of the "minimal" requirement of originality that was usually applied to the plaintiffs. In addition, in *S.O.S. v. Payday*, the judge again shifted the focus of argument from the authorship to the work itself by introducing the idea versus expression theory to determine the authorship. Contrary to the work-for-hire cases in which an employer as a supplier of ideas and supervision was deemed an author, this case alienated the defendant's authorship from the defendant's work by using the idea versus expression theory.

Similar to the copyrightability arguments, most of the arguments (12 out of 13) regarding the frame of work were made by the defendants who tried to challenge the validity of the plaintiffs' copyright, usually using the idea versus expression dichotomy (7 arguments) or the fixation/communication requirement (3 arguments). The judges rejected all but one of the defendants' arguments.

Therefore, the analysis of the arguments regarding the validity of the ownership of copyright in infringement cases reveals that, no matter what kind of frame or theory was used in the defendants' arguments judges tended not to refute the plaintiff's copyright ownership as invalid. When the frame of authorship was used, the requirement of the authorship changed depending on whether the prospective author was the defendant or the plaintiff. And when the frame of work was used, the computer software was simply considered a copyrightable subject matter. Even when the case did not find an infringement eventually, it was on the ground of other issues such as substantial similarity or copyrightable expression. It seems that through the arguments and decisions of the copyrightability cases, the minimal standard of originality required for the plaintiff and the copyrightability of computer software as a subject matter had been solidly established as important structural rules of copyright cases regarding computer programs. Furthermore, these established structural rules seem to have constrained future arguments as the copyrightability arguments in copyrightability cases and in the issue of the validity of ownership have decreased.

Substantial Similarity

As discussed above, copying can be inferred by showing access and substantial similarity in the infringement cases. Since the access was rarely in dispute, the substantial similarity becomes a critical question to be answered in finding an infringement.

The cases regarding substantial similarity usually involve two different programs that are created by different developers. For the first time the defendants were also developers themselves. While the plaintiffs were more likely to win in infringement cases in general, when the focus of the cases was substantial similarity the defendants had almost the same chance to win the case. Analyzing the legal arguments in these cases help us understand why this was the case.

The arguments regarding substantial similarity naturally shift the focus of the arguments from authorship to work. Thus the frame of work was constantly used in similarity arguments to compare the characteristics of the two programs. Forty-nine (91%) out of 54 arguments used the frame of work and 5 arguments used the frame of authorship. The arguments using the frame of work focused on the nature of the defendant's work rather than the plaintiff's work except for one argument. All of the arguments that used the frame of authorship were about the defendant's authorship rather than the plaintiff's authorship. None of the arguments used the frame of use.

While most of the arguments using the frame of the defendant's authorship (4 out of 5) were in favor of deciding that copying did not occur, arguments using the frame of the work were evenly distributed. Twenty (41%) arguments found that there was copying, and 23 (57%) arguments did not find that there was copying.

When the defendants were not developers of any of the programs, they never used the frame of authorship. But when the defendants were developers they were able to use the frame of authorship as well as that of work. Interestingly, when the party who was making any kind of argument was a non-developer whether the party was the plaintiff or the defendant, judges never explicitly accepted her arguments. It seems that being a developer of any computer programs rather than being only copyright holders or retailers becomes an important resource in making copyright arguments. To reiterate, in order to have this advantage in making arguments, the party did not have to develop the original program or any programs in issue in the case, but any kind of computer programs.

In 4 of the 5 arguments that used the frame of authorship, judges rejected the plaintiff's argument that the defendant's work is substantially similar to their program by shifting the focus from the work to the skills and expertise of the defendants. Whenever the judge focused on the defendant's developing activities, the judge decided that the defendant did not copy the program. For example, in *Plains Cotton v. Goodpasture* (1987) where Plains Cotton argued that they had an evidence of similarity between the two programs, the judge changed the focus of argument toward the fact that the defendant had "experience and knowledge" and held that the defendant did not copy. Therefore, when the judges decided to use the frame of authorship instead of the frame of work in order to find substantial similarity, it usually worked in favor of the defendant whose creativeness was considered in the arguments. The judge's arguments in *NEC v. Intel* (1989) also clearly illustrates how the defendant's knowledge and skill was emphasized. When Intel argued that there was copying, the judge stated that the developer of the NEC's program does have the "expertise and talent," as opposed to Intel's argument that he was inexperienced. The judge also mentioned that the program had been "independently created," and thus it was not copying. Responding to the similarity argument of the plaintiff, the judge in *Micro Consulting v. Zubeldia* (1990) also emphasized that just being "created independently" by the author-defendant meets the originality requirement. The judge in *Integral v. Peoplesoft* (1991) also decided in favor of the defendant when the defendant argued that its employees had the necessary "skills, knowledge, and experience" to develop the program "independently."

In the remaining one argument in *Lasercomb v. Holiday* (1989) that used the frame of authorship, while the defendant used the concept of the "laborious and expensive process," the plaintiff used the concept of "independent creation," arguing that the defendant could not have independently created its program without consulting the plaintiff's program, which the plaintiff admitted was true. As expected, the court chose the plaintiff's view, which had already been accepted by other courts.

Therefore, when the focus of argument in similarity cases shifted from work to authorship, and the frame of authorship involved the defendant's "expertise and knowledge" and "independent creation," the arguments were made in favor of the defendants. But earlier it was demonstrated that, in the case of other issues, the frame of authorship was applied differently to the plaintiffs and to the defendants: the minimalistic view of originality was not applied to the defendants, but instead a higher standard was considered. The critical difference between the authorship arguments in the similarity issue and those in the other issues was that all of the defendants in substantial similarity cases were developers themselves. It is suggested that the concept of "independent creation" and "expertise" have become important structural rules in the copyright cases that constrain the legal actors' arguments but also enable some parties who have traditionally been in a disadvantaged position, when they have and employ their resources effectively in making arguments, i.e., by being developers themselves and presenting themselves as independent creators to the judges. In the process of these actors' interactions through the use of the structural rules and resources, the possibility of a structural change was found.

The majority of the arguments in similarity cases used the frame of work. Various tests were conducted to determine similarities and differences between the characteristics of the two programs. Traditionally copyright cases have used a two-prong test that consists of both lay observer test and expert testimony. Other tests have been also used and applied including intrinsic versus extrinsic tests, but a basic form of the tests is similar to this two-prong test. First the courts ask a lay observer if the similarity in the specific and overall appearances can be determined, and then introduces expert testimony that usually consists of an analytic dissection or laundry list of specific differences. In the case of computer programs, in earlier cases, courts tended to employ this two-prong test and ask if the similarity in the specific and overall appearances can be determined by a "reasonable lay observer" and considered expert testimony (*Midway v. Dirkschineider*, 1981; *Atari v. North American*, 1981; *Nintendo v. Bay Coin*, 1982; and later *Soft Computer v. Lalehzarzadeh*, 1988; *NEC v. Intel*, 1989; *Accolade v. Distinctive*, 1990). In the first 4 cases employing this "reasonable observer test" or "intrinsic test," the courts found that there were substantial similarities.

However, this lay observer test began to be criticized by other courts in that it captures the "total concept and feel" that was not supposed to be protected in copyright law. In *Micro Consulting v. Zubeldia* (1990) as well as in *Autoskill v. National Education* (1992), the plaintiff claimed that "total concept and feel" is similar between the programs, so an intrinsic test should be applied. But the judge argued that the test of total concept and feel had been widely criticized as it was geared toward simplistic works, thus served no purpose in the realm of computers, where expert testimony was needed. The judge used instead a "laundry list" of specific differences suggested by the defendants as an extrinsic test. Also, the judges in the court of appeals in *Computer Associates v. Altai* (1992) argued that due to the nature of computer programs that are impenetrable by lay observers, the "reasonable person" doctrine employed in other areas of copyright law should not be so much observed in software copyright cases, and that the use of expert evidence was warranted. There were some courts that still used the lay observer test, but the last 3 cases that used this test found that the two programs were not substantially similar. Therefore, the courts constantly emphasized the importance of the expert testimony over the lay observer test in software copyright cases (*Midway v. Bandai*, 1982; *Computer Associates v. Altai*, 1992). More courts began to use the extrinsic test, that involves expert testimony, analytic dissection and detailed analysis of the two programs (*Pearl v. Competition*, 1988; *Midway v. Strohon*, 1983; *Telemarketing v. Symantec*, 1989; *Micro v. Zubeldia*, 1990). Surprisingly, not only in the cases in which literal elements were the issue, but also in the cases where non-literal elements such as screen display or user interfaces were the issue, a lay person's opinion was not considered. This is a big departure from the cases regarding traditional literary work and artistic work, where both lay person's and expert opinions are introduced irrespective of the lay person's ability to observe similarities.

Although some courts used both extrinsic and intrinsic tests as a 2-step test (*Brodurbund v. Pixelliite*, 1986; *Digital v. Softklone*, 1987; *Manufacturers v. CAMS*, 1989; *Integral v. Peoplesoft*, 1991), even the courts that considered both tests tended to rely on the expert testimony in deciding the issue, explicitly giving a greater weight to the extrinsic prong of the 2-step test (*Gates Rubber v. Bando*, 1992). Moreover, some judges transformed the concept of a reasonable person into someone who has expertise in computer programs. In *Integral v. Peoplesoft* (1991), the judge stated that a "reasonable person" is defined as a reasonable person in the intended audience, and in this case the person would be with some knowledge of human resource management systems, which was the software system of dispute in the case. The judges in *Atari v. Nintendo* (1992) also stated that in the context of computer software, the "ordinary reasonable person" is a computer programmer. Consequently, more and more of the plaintiffs and defendants tried to use expert testimony. Moreover, when the experts of the two parties presented different views, the judges often decided whose testimony was more credible on the basis of the background and expertise of each expert, rather than creating an objective way to evaluate the testimony (*NEC v. Intel*, 1989; *Plains Cotton v. Goodpasture*, 1987; *Integral v. Peoplesoft*, 1991; *Autoskill v. National Education*, 1992; *Yamate v. Sugerman*, 1991).

In this process, the importance given to the expertise and skills in the authorship arguments was found even in the arguments that used the frame of work in the area of similarity tests. The analysis of the similarity tests shows that computer programs were differentiated from other works of authorship, unlike in copyrightability arguments where computer programs were constantly analogized to other works of authorship such as literary work, artistic work, or audiovisual work. By pointing out that these are cases pertaining to the realm of computer programs, not to other traditional works of authorship, courts tried to use a different test (expert testimony rather than lay observer test, and extrinsic test rather than intrinsic test) and/or to use the same test but placed a totally different meaning on it (computer expert as an ordinary lay observer).

The values of scientific expertise and skills were constantly emphasized and reinforced by the copyright cases regarding the protection of computer programs, which at first rejected the relevance of a lay observer test but adopted analytic dissection and expert testimony, and then decided the credibility of the testimonies based on the scientific background of the testifier rather than the testimony itself. The use of expert testimony and analytic analysis became an important structural rule in the copyright arguments and decisions regarding computer programs. The value of artistic creativity that has been emphasized and reinforced in other areas of copyright law was transformed into that of "scientific expertise and knowledge" in software copyright cases. In addition, the concept of scientific skills and expertise itself has been limited to those related to developing programs rather than understanding programs.

In addition, the courts used the idea versus expression dichotomy as another rationale in finding the expert's opinion important in copyright law. That is, copyright is infringed only when the similarities between the two programs relate to the "expression" or the programs, because similarities in ideas that are not protected by copyright law do not constitute infringement. Consequently, the courts' position is that identifying similarities in "expression" requires detailed analytic skills. Also notable is the fact that the expression in this case focused on the expression in terms of literal elements rather than that in terms of display or interfaces. Therefore, despite the fact that more and more cases deal with non-literal elements of computer programs rather than literal elements, courts tended to view skills related to literal elements such as computer language and codes to be more relevant. The analysis of the ways in which substantial similarity tests are employed shows that the values of scientific expertise and skills were constantly emphasized and reinforced by these cases.

But the similarity tests themselves did not determine whether the judges would find similarity when the tests were applied without having any relation to other legal theories, even though the judges were slightly more likely to find similarity than not (found similarity in 13 out of 19 arguments). In general, the chances of finding similarity were quite evenly distributed: 54% of the arguments found similarity and 46 % did not. However, when the theory of idea versus expression was introduced in analytic dissection to determine similarities, the arguments tended to limit the scope of copyright. More often than not (13 out of 19 arguments) arguments that used the theory of idea versus expression did not find that the two programs were similar.

One of the most important rules in copyright law is that only the expression, but not ideas, is protected against copying. The idea versus expression doctrine has some corollaries such as merger doctrine, limited ways, *scenes a faire*. Merger means that there is practically only one way to express an idea, thus if the idea is indistinguishable or inseparable from, or limited by its expression, copying the expression will not be barred. *Scenes a faire* is a doctrine that allows the use of the expression when using that expression is inevitable as an ordinary, stereotyped, industrial standard.

It was found that if the relevance of this doctrine was admitted it became one of the most important exceptions of deciding that there was copying. Except for the 3 arguments in which the relevance of the idea versus expression theory was rejected, all of the remaining 16 arguments that used the idea versus expression doctrine in the context of the similarity issue were made against deciding that the defendant copied the plaintiff's work. For example, in *Frybarger v. IBM* (1987), the court decided that similarities between the two programs were confined to ideas and concepts, so they are non-infringing. Also in *Micro v. Zubelda* (1990), no substantial similarity was found between the programs at the level of protected expression. A few examples of arguments using the merger doctrine or *scenes a faire* are as follows. *Atari v. Amusement* (1981) decided that Amusement did not infringe on Atari's copyright because, given the requirements of the idea of a game, most of the similarities between Atari's videogame 'Asteroids' and Amusement's videogame 'Meteors' are inevitable. This case influenced *Frybarger v. IBM* (1987), where the judge held that IBM did not infringe on Frybarger because when idea and expression are inseparable, only virtually identical copying is barred. *Data East v. Epyx* (1988) also held that the elements of similarities between the two videogames necessarily follow from the idea of a karate game, or inseparable from, indispensable to, or standard treatment of, the idea of the karate, so they are not protectable. *NEC v. Intel* (1989) held that if the underlying ideas of the similar routines found are capable of only a limited range of expression, they may be protected only against virtually identical copying, which the defendant's program does not have. Finally, *Integral v. Peoplesoft* (1991) found that the similarity of system modules compares functions, not expressions, thus cannot be the evidence of copying.

The analysis of the arguments that used the frame of work shows that when the arguments centered around the comparison between a work and a work, when the Romantic notion of authorship was severed from the notion of work, the defendants were able to use the structural rule on a more equal footing. Using the idea versus expression theory in the context of comparing the similarities of the two works, as opposed to in the context of determining the copyrightability of the plaintiff's work, the defendants gained a more solid ground to compete with the plaintiffs.

This result suggests that the same frame of work that invariably favored the plaintiffs in copyrightability or valid ownership arguments was somehow used in a different way in similarity arguments. That is, the frame of work in similarity arguments encompassed both the defendant's work and the plaintiff's work, thus often changed the focus of the argument from the plaintiff to the defendant. As a result, when the defendants who are themselves developers of programs and videogames could effectively use the frame of work on their behalf, they have transformed the meaning of the "work of authorship" protected in copyright law to the one that includes the work created by the defendants.

In conclusion, differing from the arguments regarding copyrightability or the validity of the ownership of copyright, which invariably favored the plaintiffs, arguments regarding the similarity issue gave the plaintiffs merely a slightly greater chance to prevail on the merits. Many of the defendants could employ their resources of being developers in their use of frames (of authorship and of work), and transformed the frame of authorship to emphasize scientific expertise and knowledge and the frame of work as encompassing the work created by defendants as well. This is a process by which structural rules were transformed by the legal actors' use of rules and resources.

Copyrightable Expression

When arguments using the idea versus expression dichotomy were placed in the context of similarity arguments, the question was whether the "similarities" were the expression or the idea. The idea versus expression theory can also be applied to arguments in the context of copyrightable expression in infringement cases. In that case, the question becomes whether the "plaintiff's work" was copyrightable expression. Thus, the issue of copyrightability of the plaintiff's computer program was considered in conjunction with the similarity test in many courts, especially in later cases. Among the 39 arguments that dealt with the issue of copyrightability of the plaintiff's programs in relation to similarity arguments in infringement cases, 26 (67%) arguments were made in the fourth time period.

Various tests were used to determine the copyrightable expression in infringement cases. The most frequently used tests were the "Whelan test" and the "abstraction-filtration-comparison" test used by Judge Learned Hand in *Nichols v. Universal.* The Whelan test comes from a holding of *Whelan v. Jaslaw* (1985) that the purpose and function of the utilitarian work is a part of ideas and everything else is the expression. Judge Hand's 3-step test involves conducting an analytic dissection (as in the extrinsic test), removing elements of ideas from those of expression, and then comparing the plaintiff's expression and the defendant's expression. The first 2 steps involve the nature of the plaintiff's work while the last step involves the similarity between the two works. Some courts used only a portion of the test. Courts have used different combinations of different tests, but they can be divided into the test of the similarity that involves the nature of the two works and the test of the copyrightable expression that involves the nature of the plaintiff's work. It depends on the court whether it will consider the copyrightable expression requirement, and if it does, whether the copyrightability test is conducted before or after the similarity test.

Thirty-four (87%) of the 39 arguments used the frame of work and 5 used the frame of authorship. Most (32 out of 34) of the arguments that used the frame of work focused on the plaintiff's work. Arguments that used the frame of work in the copyrightable expression issue were more likely to decide that the plaintiff's program was copyrightable expression than it was not copyrightable expression (13 cases versus 6 cases).

By considering the issue of copyrightable expression in infringement cases, the arguments regarding the issue of copying were turned into the arguments regarding copyrightablility. Consequently, the arguments related to the issue of copyrightable expression in the infringement cases show a striking similarity with the arguments made in the copyrightability cases in terms of the use of the frame, theories, and structural rules derived from the arguments and decisions. For example, in *Atari v. North American* (1982), the judges in the court of appeals argued that the repetitive sequence of a game is considered copyrightable as an audiovisual work and held that the plaintiff's work was copyrightable expression by applying the abstraction test. Other cases also employed the traditional copyrightability arguments such as that ROMs are copyrightable (*Midway v. Strohon*, 1985), that the program is a "literary" work that is copyrightable (*Johnson v. Uniden*, 1985), that the program can be copyrighted as an audiovisual work or a literary work (*Whelan v. Jaslaw*, 1985), etc.

In the cases where the courts decide that the plaintiff's work is not copyrightable expression, it was usually when the defendants used the merger doctrine or functionality theory that is related to the idea versus expression dichotomy (*Computer Associates v. Altai*, 1991). For example, the judge in *Williams v. Bally* (1983) held that many elements of the plaintiff's game are not protected because they are utilitarian, and once these elements are put to aside, relatively little remains to be determined for substantial similarity.

Another similarity between the copyrightable expression arguments and the copyrightability arguments lies in that the nature of the actors does not seem to make any difference to whether the judge will decide that the work is copyrightable or not. Regardless of whether the plaintiffs were developers or not, the judges were more likely to decide that the work was copyrightable. The nature of the defendants did not make a difference, either. Whether the defendants were developers or non-developers, the judges were always more likely to decide that the plaintiff's work was copyrightable expression.

The ways in which the frame of work was used in the arguments regarding the copyrightable expression were considerably different from the ways in which that was used in the arguments regarding substantial similarity. In similarity arguments, the focus of the arguments was on the defendant's work and on how similar or different the defendant's work is from the plaintiff's work. On the contrary, in copyrightable expression arguments, the arguments centered around the copyrightability of the plaintiff's work or even the copyrightability of computer programs in general as a subject matter, which had already been decided in copyrightability cases. In this way, the infringement arguments were transformed into the traditional copyrightability arguments and decisions, and copyrightability arguments which generally favored the plaintiffs are being repeated in infringement cases. As a result, the arguments that used the frame of work in copyrightable expression issue were twice more likely to be made in favor of the plaintiffs than of the defendants. In this process, the structural changes that occurred in similarity arguments were diminished, and the structural rules regarding the computer software as a subject matter were reinforced.

Four of the 5 arguments that used the frame of authorship found that the plaintiff's work was copyrightable and 1 argument found it was not copyrightable. These arguments were often complementary to arguments using the frame of work by being made in conjunction with them without any further discussion (*Stern v. Kaufman*, 1981; *Apple v. Microsoft*, 1991). Two of the arguments were about originality of the plaintiff's work. For example, the defendant in *Johnson v. Uniden* (1985) argued that the plaintiff's program is not copyrightable because it was derived in large part from a preexisting material in the public domain, thus he cannot have infringed Johnson's copyright. But the judge responded that as long as the work contains originality, the mere fact that it is a derivative work does not bar copyrightability, and stated that the originality test is a modest one, requiring only a "faint trace" of originality. The judge in *Lotus v. Borland* (1993) also stated that the originality requirement is minimal. Even when the focus of the argument shifted from work to authorship, the focus remained as the "plaintiff's" authorship rather than the defendant's, and the arguments still relied on the established rule that the originality requirement for the developer of the underlying program is minimal.

The analysis of the arguments in the copyrightable expression issue reveals that many of the later infringement arguments were turned into the traditional copyrightability arguments, which benefited the plaintiffs even when the plaintiff was not a developer of computer programs, by introducing the requirement of showing copyrightable expression of the plaintiff's work. This result is ironical given that the requirement of the copyrightable expression was at first introduced as a means to prohibit the monopoly of ideas by the plaintiffs. Even though most (87%) of the defendants in these cases were developers, due to the nature of the issue that focused on the copyrightability of the plaintiff's program, their use of the frame was limited. This is an example of when the structural environment constrains the actors from fully employing their resources, the actors fail to have the opportunity to make an effective argument and probably change the structural rule in their favor. In this process in which the frame of work and the frame of authorship operated in the same way as they did in copyrightability cases, the structural rules related to the concept of the minimal requirement of originality and to computer software as copyrightable subject matter, were reproduced and reinforced.

Infringing Use

When direct or indirect evidence shows that copying had occurred, in most cases courts hold that the defendant had infringed the plaintiff's copyright. But the defendant may still argue that their use of the plaintiff's program was not illegal but legitimate. There are 72 arguments regarding the question of whether the plaintiff's copying is legitimate or infringing. As in the copyrightable expression arguments, these arguments imply that the copying did occur or that the question of copying does not matter if it is decided that copying is legitimate. The arguments regarding the infringing copying of the plaintiff's program constitute the majority (72 arguments, 39%) of the infringement arguments, and tended to increase proportionately over time.

The arguments regarding the issue of copying as infringement are the only arguments that employ a variety of frames related to the "use" of the plaintiff's work, including the use by the defendants and by any potential users. The judges used the frame of use most frequently (54 arguments, 75% of the time), followed by the frame of work (16 arguments, 22%) and the frame of authorship (2 arguments, 3%). Among the arguments that used the frame of use, most arguments (36) focused on the defendant's use, followed by the public use and benefit (12). The arguments focused on the consequence on the market or innovation least frequently (6).

When the frame of work was used, judges tended to argue that the copying constitutes infringement (10 of 16 arguments). Among the 16 arguments, 11 focused on the defendant's work and 5 focused on the plaintiff's work. When the focus was on the plaintiff's work, arguments were made in favor of the plaintiffs, but when the focus was on the defendant's work, the arguments were split. Among the 5 arguments that focused on the plaintiff's work, one case was reversed in the court of appeals, one argument was rejected because the defendant simply misunderstood the law, and one case was placed in the context of the fair use, which will be analyzed later. In the remaining 2 cases that are actually the same case in different levels of courts, the judges held that the copying constitutes infringement. In *Data Cash v. JS&A* (1979), the plaintiff argued that ROM is a copy, but the judge used the analogy of a piano and argued that ROM is not a copy so there is no infringement. The court of appeals (1980) reversed the case and held that there is infringement because ROM is a copy. Since the district case was decided before the rule regarding the copyrightability of ROM was clearly established, the plaintiff in *Data Case v. JS&A* could not employ the rule on their benefit. But in the court of appeals of *Data Case v. JS&A* and also in a later case *Midway v. Artic* (1982), the plaintiffs and the judges were able to use this rule that ROM is a copy. Also when the defendants in *Sega v. Accolade* (1992) argued that the disassembly of the object code does not constitute infringement because it is necessary in order to gain an understanding of the code, the judges changed the focus of argument and asked instead whether the object code is eligible for the full range of copyright protection. As in most of the copyrightability arguments, the judges held that the object code is copyrightable, thus the defendant infringed the plaintiff's copyright.

When the arguments focused on the defendant's work, the judges were split but they were still more likely to decide in favor of the plaintiffs: in 7 out of 11 arguments the judges held that the copying was an infringement and in 4 arguments they decided that the copying was not an infringement. Some of the defendants used theories used in the copyrightability arguments such as the idea versus expression, and the judges rejected the arguments (*Johnson v. Uniden*, 1985; *Johnson Controls v. Phoenix*, 1989). In some of the earlier cases judges held that the defendant's work is a derivative work, thus constituting an infringement of the copyright (*Midway v. Artic*, 1982; *SAS v. S&H*, 1985; *Forry v. Neundorfer*, 1987). But in other cases the judges decided that the defendant's work is not a derivative work because they are not substantially similar (appeals in *Vault v. Quaid*, 1988) or because they are not fixed in a separate form (*Lewis Galoob v. Nintendo*, 1991).

It was found that the nature of the parties did not make a significant difference to the ways in which the arguments that focused on the defendant's work were made. The arguments that used the frame of work were usually made in favor of the plaintiffs. But when the focus was on the defendant's work instead of the plaintiff's work, the defendants were sometimes able to prevail. All the cases that were decided in favor of the defendants involved the issue of derivative works, in which the separation of the notion of work from the notion of the plaintiff's authorship provided room for the defendants to shift the concern toward their own authorship and their work as a product of independent developing activity.

The frame of the use was employed in 55 arguments in the issue of copying as infringement. Usually the defendant's argument was that their copying of the plaintiff's program was not infringement because the program was used for legitimate reasons. The basis of most of their arguments relates to the theories of fair use and adaptation, which are a product of the recent amendment to the copyright law.

Before the theories of fair use and adaptation became prevalent in software copyright arguments, some parties and judges made arguments in terms of "legal use" or "legitimate purposes," without specific supporting doctrines. All of these arguments were made in favor of the plaintiffs. The first argument regarding the defendant's use was introduced by the judge in *Midway v. Artic* (1982), when the defendant argued that copies of the plaintiff's circuit boards are not infringement because they are useful devices. The judge pointed out that because the printed circuit boards were not used for "innocent purposes," they constitute infringement. Some of the defendants in other later cases argued that their use was legitimate because its purpose was to achieve compatibility or standardization (*Lotus v. Paperback*, 1990), that their copying should be permissible as "repair" of the patented machines (*Allen-Myland v. IBM*, 1990), and that the reverse engineering and disassembly of the object code is intermediate copying, which is not infringement (*Sega v. Accolade*, 1992). All of these arguments were rejected. Even though *Sega v. Accolade* was reversed in the court of appeals (1993), the reversal was on the ground of fair use.

The defendant in *Atari v. JS&A* (1983) first made an argument based on the issue of "adaptation" as an exception of infringing use, pursuant to 17 U.S.C. §117, which stated that copying is not an infringement when a new copy is an essential step in the utilization of the computer program and when such a copy is for archival purpose only. The judge was reluctant to accept this argument saying that no other court had interpreted §117, and the legislative history was scant. Interpreting §117 according to a report made by a National Commission on New Technological Uses of Copyrighted Works (CONTU Reports), the judge held that the archival exception is not applicable because it is to protect the use of a copy specifically against the risk of being destroyed by mechanical or electrical failure. The judge in *Micro-Sparc v. Amtype* (1984) followed this interpretation when the defendant relied on the adaptation doctrine to argue that their service to type the published written programs in magazines and to sell the disks was legal. The defendant used the theory of utilization of the program as well as that of archival copying. The judge responded that Nimmer on Copyright and the CONTU Reports strictly limit the exception to "inputting" of the program and its use by the purchase of the program, thus creating and selling disks does not fall into the concept of "utilization." The interpretations of §117 which resulted in the narrow scope of possible exceptions in these two cases became an established rule in copyright law regarding computer programs, which influenced almost all the cases that later relied on this theory (*Allen-Myland v. IBM*, 1990; *ISC v. Altech*, 1990; *Cmax v. UCR*, 1992).

Although the doctrine of adaptation may have been designed to provide exceptions in infringement decisions defending the defendant's use of the program, the relative focus of the above arguments regarding the adaptation was on the nature of the program that need to be loaded into a diskette and are subject to the risk of being destroyed, rather than on the nature of the defendant's use. This may have had a significant influence on the ways in which the arguments were made, because a particular nature of the defendant's use of the program can be argued to have a relationship with the defendant's independent production. In other words, the defendants could have argued that their use of the plaintiff's program did not influence the process of "independent" creation of their own programs. But when the focus of the arguments that used the adaptation theory was placed more in the frame of work than in the frame of the defendant's authorship, the arguments almost always led to finding an infringement, even when the defendant was a developer. In this situation, even the defendants who had the resource of having developed their own programs could not benefit from this doctrine.

On the other hand, there were 2 cases that used the doctrine of adaptation and were made in favor of the defendants. One of such cases is surprisingly *Vault v. Quaid* (1988) in which the defendant's program allowed a user to make copies of programs contained in floppy diskettes which had a serious potential of creating a large number of infringing copies. The judges in Vault simply refused to follow the interpretation of the previous cases that adopted the view of the CONTU Report and Nimmer. They argued that the statutory reading itself does not suggest the narrow conception of the exception, and focused on the fact that the defendant's use of the plaintiff's program did include "non-infringing" use. Thus the judges focused their arguments on the nature of use rather than on the nature of work. The judge in *Foresight v. Pfortmiller* (1989) also refused to follow the narrow interpretation of the previous cases, by arguing that Pfortmiller enhanced the plaintiff's program and used it only in its business and did not sell. Therefore, distinguishing the use of Pfortmiller from the nature of the defendant's use in other court cases, the argument in this case remained focused on the frame of use.

It was found that most of the arguments that used the doctrine of adaptation focused on the nature of the work in the process of interpreting the statute, thus the judges decided that the defendant's copying of the plaintiff's work could not be an exception to finding an infringement. However, when the arguments remained focused on the nature of the use and the defendants were also developers themselves, the judges sometimes decided that the copying did not constitute infringement. It seems that the arguments can be made in favor of the defendants when the defendants effectively employ their resources (being a developer and being perceived as a developer) and the structural rules (valuing the independent creativity of developing computer software), i.e., when they employ the frame of use in relation to the fame of authorship by arguing how the defendants' program still involves a process of independent creation despite their use of the plaintiff's program.

Scholars have noted that in early cases regarding the adaptations of the works of authorship in other areas of law, the new creator of an unauthorized adaptation was not deemed to be an infringer but regarded as a new author. For example, Kaplan (1967) noted that the infringement problem was being answered by looking not so much at what the defendant had taken as to what he had added or contributed. But as in other contemporary cases, showing how much of his work he did not pirate does not seem to mean that he did not infringe the copyright in software copyright cases.

The defendants involved in the arguments regarding the issue of copying as infringement invariably focused on the frame of use, and when the frame of use was used, judges tended to argue and decide that the copying constituted infringement (41 of 54 arguments). This seems to be related to the fact that the defendants including those who were developers themselves were not able to shift the focus of the argument toward the nature of their developing activity. There were only 2 arguments that used the frame of authorship, and these arguments failed to employ the structural rules established in the authorship arguments in copyright law. The arguments using the frame of authorship were made by a plaintiff once and by a defendant once. Both of them were rejected because they used the "sweat of the brow" arguments that had been widely criticized in other areas of copyright law. Responding to their arguments that considerable "time, effort, and money" went into developing the program, judges stated that the "sweat of the brow" evidence is not to be considered in a copyright case (*Autoskill v. National Education*, 1992; appeals in *Sega v. Accolade*, 1993). Thus, the actors in these cases failed to use the structural rules on their behalf, even when one of them had the resource to effectively use the rule because the defendant was a firm that developed a program. By explicitly rejecting the value of "labor" and "effort," as opposed to "expertise" and "independent creation," the judges' arguments and decisions in these cases have refined and reinforced the existing structural rule regarding authorship.

Fair use is a doctrine that recently began to be used in copyright cases regarding computer software. The theory was first used in an argument of a defendant in a case decided in 1990, and the theory was frequently used each year from then on. Section 106 of the 1976 Copyright Act states that "the fair use of a copyrighted work, including such use by reproduction in copies or phonorecords of by any other means specified by that section, for purposes such as criticism, comment, news reporting, teaching (including multiple copies for classroom use), scholarship, or research, is not an infringement of copyright." Four factors are suggested to be considered to determine whether the use made of a work in any particular case is a fair use: the purpose and character of the use, the nature of the copyrighted work, the amount and substantiality of the portion used in relation to the copyright work as a whole, and the effect of the use upon the potential market for or value of the copyrighted work (§106, 1976 Copyright Act). Courts differ in terms of which factors they consider and which factors they weigh heavily. Since these 4 factors involve different frames, the ways in which the courts responded to the arguments that used this theory provide an understanding of the values created, maintained, and reinforced in the copyright arguments and decisions regarding computer programs.

There are 9 cases in which the theory of fair use was applied and discussed, one of which was reversed in the court of appeals. Among them, only 2 cases decided that the defendant's use of the plaintiff's program was a fair use. Most of the cases considered all the 4 factors and weighed each factor as the same. And in many cases considerations of each factor provided consistent results for the decision making. For example, in *Cable/Home v. Network* (1990), the judges held that the defendant's device to de-scramble the plaintiff's program was made for commercial use, that the plaintiff's program was copyrighted, that a qualitative evaluation indicated the two programs were substantially similar, and that the defendant's device had a negative effect on the plaintiff's market. The fair use arguments in *Allen-Myland v. IBM* (1990) and *Kepner-Tregoe v. Leadership* (1992) were also similar.

The court of appeals in *Atari v. Nintendo* (1991) was the only court that did not explicitly mention the 4 factors. But the court implicitly focused on the first factor by saying that the reverse engineering is not a fair use because its use was beyond understanding and distinguishing unprotected ideas but the use included commercially appropriating the program. In the cases that did not find a fair use, the issue of commercial use was present in every case, but the factor of the market effect was often considered the least important. For example, in *Lotus v. Borland* (1992), all the other 3 factors were explicitly considered and decided in favor of the plaintiff. But the judge argued that the effect on the market can be presumed by a commercial use, thus a likelihood of negative effect on the market is enough to decide that it was not a fair use. In *Softel v. Dragon* (1992), 2 factors were found to work in favor of the plaintiff and 2 factors were found to work in favor of the defendant. The judge argued that the purpose was solely for profit and the portion used by the defendant was qualitatively substantial, which worked against finding a fair use. But it was found that the work is a utilitarian, functional, and factual work and that there was no evidence that the defendant's use would affect the potential market, both of which worked in favor of finding a fair use. Then the judge decided against finding a fair use based on a "good faith" concern.

On the other hand, courts that found a fair use emphasized the importance of the effect on the market while considering the purpose of use and the amount of copying less importantly. For example, *Lewis Galoob v. Nintendo* (1991) held that the effect on the market is the single most important factor while it admitted that the defendant's videogame accessory was made for a family's noncommercial home use (focusing on the end user's use rather than the defendant's use of the program), that the plaintiff's games were published work which gains less protection, and that the portion copied is not an important factor. The judge provided a detailed analysis of market analysis in arguing that most of the defendant's works are no longer in the market, so the program cannot affect the sale of products and future harm is not likely to occur, and that the defendant's product would encourage rather than discourage enthusiasm over video games in general. The court of appeals in *Sega v. Accolade* (1993) also argued that the issue of commercial use is insignificant and can be rebutted by the fact that the defendant's work involved intermediate use only and that the public benefits from the compatibility gained in the defendant's work. The judges also argued that even a wholesale copying should be allowed if it increases the public use, and the minor economic loss of the plaintiff caused by the defendant as a legitimate competitor should not bar a finding of fair use.

The arguments that used the theory of fair use resemble various arguments that are considered in copyrightability and infringement cases. The judges who considered the theory of fair use were more likely to decide that the defendant's work infringed the plaintiff's program. When the arguments used the issues of the defendant's use, substantial similarity, or the nature of the plaintiff's work, the judges tended to decide against the defendants. However, when the market consequences were seriously considered and extensively discussed, the judge found in favor of the defendants. But the market consequences were rarely considered and usually speculated when considered, as similar to the finding in the preliminary injunction arguments. The same was true with the issue of public benefit and public use. When the judge acknowledged the issue raised by the defendants in *Sega v. Accolade* (1993), it worked in favor of the defendant. However, the public interest was the least frequently considered concept in the fair use arguments.

Beside the arguments regarding the theory of fair use, there were 6 arguments that used the frame of the consequence on the market and innovation, most of which were initiated by the defendants and the plaintiffs rather than the judges. The judges rejected all of them. In these cases the judges simply rejected the defendants' arguments that finding an infringement would discourage innovation (*Pearl v. Competition*, 1988), and would drive competitors out of the market (*Data General v. Grumman*, 1988; *Sega v. Accolade*, 1992). In one case the judge ignored the plaintiff's argument that used the theory of market consequence by shifting the focus to other issues. In *Vault v. Quaid* (1988), the plaintiff used the argument regarding the impact of the defendant's software that allows a user to make copies of programs. Responding to the plaintiff's argument that they lost customers, the judges argued that even if the plaintiff did lost customers, the purchasers of the program, not the defendant who made the program, were responsible. Thus the concern of market consequence that the plaintiff raised was ignored and the focus of argument was shifted to the issue of deciding the responsible party. On the contrary, in another case the judge responded to the defendant's argument that was not directly related to the market consequence by introducing a marketplace concern. The judge in *Midway v. Artic* (1982) responded to the defendant's analogy of a speeding-up kit used on the plaintiff's videogame to speeding-up of a phonograph record, by pointing out the difference between phonograph record and videogame in terms of the demand in the market. The judge argued that since there is enormous demand for speeded-up videogames but little if any demand for speeded-up records, the defendant's kit infringed the plaintiff's copyright.

Whenever the judges considered the market consequences in their arguments regardless of whether they were initiated by the defendants, the plaintiffs or the judges themselves, they decided that the copying does constitute infringement. Only when the argument regarding the market consequence was placed in the context of fair use, was it decided that the copying does not constitute an infringement. Otherwise, arguments that used the frame of market consequence were always rejected whether the argument was made by the plaintiff or the defendant.

The arguments that used the frame of the public interest were analyzed in the previous section on the framework of the public interest versus the private property right. It was found that the arguments regarding the public access and benefit were infrequently made and these arguments were usually rejected by the judges. Especially, when the parties involved non-developers of any computer programs, the argument using the frame of the public interest (especially the doctrines of publication and first sale) were never accepted. Only when the parties were developers of different programs the party that used the argument based on these theories had a chance to convince the judges, but they were not always successful. The most important consideration seemed to be whether the program had a direct linkage with the plaintiff's program or was independent created. Therefore, it is suggested that the value of the independent creation is still emphasized in the arguments using the frame of the public interest, thus the structural rule regarding the authorship that works in the copyrightability cases still prevails in the arguments regarding the public interest.

In conclusion, when the arguments used the frame of the defendant's use, judges generally decided against the defendants. At first the judges did not have clear structural rules to rely on when the arguments regarding the nature of the defendant's use of the program were introduced. Drawing on the available rules relating to the nature of work, judges began to focus the arguments on the issue of copying as infringement on the plaintiff's work rather than on the defendant's development activities. As the decisions were being made against the defendants as a result of these arguments, the defendants failed to establish a structural rule regarding their use of the program in their favor.

It was found that the nature of the actors influenced the ways in which they make arguments. For example, when the plaintiffs were non-developers, all of their arguments used the frame of use, while when they were developers their arguments included all the frames of work, authorship, and use. In the same vein, when the defendants were non-developers, they used the frame of use almost exclusively, while the defendants who developed their own programs used the frame of use more frequently, but also used the frame of work. Even though the nature of the actors constrained and enabled the plaintiffs and the defendants in a similar fashion, the result of this influence was different to the plaintiffs and to the defendants due to the mechanism by which the established structural rules operated. When the non-developing plaintiffs used the frame of the use, it did not work against them if the judges shifted the concern toward the nature of the plaintiff's work. This is because the structural rule regarding the nature of the plaintiff's work usually granted the copyright protection to computer programs. However, the use of the frame of use clearly worked against the defendants including the ones who developed their own programs, because the focus on the nature of work deprived them of the opportunities to shift the concern toward their independent developing activities.

The implication of these interactions between the structural rules and the actors' resources is clearly reflected in the ways in which the decisions were made according to the nature of the actors, in the arguments regarding the issue of copying as infringement. Differing from any other issues from the copyright cases, in the issue of copying as infringement, it was found that when the defendants were developers, it was more likely to be decided in favor of the plaintiffs if the plaintiffs were non-developers (100% in favor of the plaintiffs) than if the plaintiffs were developers (56%). In other words, the plaintiffs who are non-developers than the plaintiffs who are developers have a better chance to win the case against the defendants who are developers. The apparent paradox is solved by examining how the plaintiff's tendency to employ the frame of use when they were non-developers, which was a constraint of the structural rule and their resources, actually helped them to render the decisions in their favor. On the contrary, the tendency of the defendants to rely on the frame of use became a real constraint for them. This may be unintended but real consequences of the interaction between the structural rules and resources, where the apparent structural constraints turned out to be enablements for certain actors.

Finally, it is found that parties had been reluctant to use arguments related to the concept of the public interest or the concept of market consequences. Although those arguments began to appear recently, introducing the frame of the public interest or the market consequence generally did not help the parties who made the arguments. Whether the reluctance of making arguments using the frame of the public interest and market consequences comes from the judges' tendency to reject the arguments or their tendency to ignore them is not clear. But it is suggested that those concerns regarding the public interest and the marketplace have yet to be established as identifiable structural rules in the copyright cases of computer programs.

Part III

Process of Structuration in Copyright Cases

CHAPTER 8

Reassessing the Role of Communication

The findings of this book demonstrate the importance of communicative activities in the process of structuration. As will be discussed in more detail in this chapter, the actors' use of their resources of being a developer in making legal arguments was found to be the most influential on the judges' decision-making process than any other factors. The framework of authorship, work, and use helps us understand the legal actors' relationships and struggles that are manifested in their legal arguments, because the construct of authorship and its interaction with other concepts, which are transformed and reproduced through the decision-making process, reflect and generate the underlying values of the legal system and the society.

It was found that in copyright cases regarding computer programs, the plaintiffs were more likely to prevail than the defendants, and there was more consensus in granting copyright to the plaintiffs than in holding that the defendant infringed the plaintiff's copyright. Various factors were examined which may have influenced the ways in which the copyright decisions were made. Some of the factors that have traditionally been acknowledged as having an influence in other areas of law, such as the judges' political or educational characteristics and the human and financial resources of the parties, were not found to be related to the copyright decisions regarding computer programs. The most important variable that relates to decision making was the nature of the actors, i.e. if they were developers of computer programs or not. Although the judges tended to grant copyright to the plaintiff's program regardless of the nature of the plaintiffs and the defendants in copyrightability cases, infringement decisions were clearly related to the nature of the defendants, i.e., if the defendant developed his own program or not.

The importance of being a developer was manifested in another dimension in the decision making, regarding the nature of the computer program. Although the nature of the plaintiff's program did not relate to the ways in which copyrightability and infringement decisions were made, the nature of the defendant's program turned out to be related to decisions in an interesting way. Judges tended to grant copyright to the plaintiff's program regardless of whether it is an application program or a videogame, and whether the aspects in dispute are literal or nonliteral elements of the program. However, in making infringement decisions that usually involve two programs developed by the plaintiff and the defendant, the judges found an infringement even more likely when the defendants developed products that have characteristic that are not clearly harmful to the plaintiff or other users such as accessories to the plaintiff's program or a device to enhance the plaintiff's program, than when they developed competing products which are functionally so identical that the plaintiff is very likely to suffer from it. This finding clearly illustrates that the central question that the courts considered was the independent developing activity of the defendant rather than any other related concerns such as the function of programs or market consequence of the defendant's program.

This finding posed an interesting question when it is compared to some critics' argument that the authors' rights are taken to be given to the copyright holders in the U.S. copyright law, which has been shaped through the struggle between authors and publishers (e.g. Bettig, 1992). This seeming paradox is reconciled by the analyses of legal arguments that unveil the communicative interactions between the plaintiffs and the defendants, both of whom consisted of authors and copyright holders.

In an effort to understand the mechanisms by which copyright decisions are made, this book has conceptualized legal arguments made by the plaintiffs, the defendants, and the judges as a critical nexus that helps us explain the relationship between the decisions and other factors. In analyzing legal arguments, this study has employed various approaches that were suggested by scholars and critics. Critical scholars and historians have suggested focusing on the examination of the ways in which the copyright system is shaped by struggles among the stakeholders. Thus the characteristics of the actors, i.e., developers versus copyright holders, developers versus non-developers, and plaintiffs versus defendants, were employed as a main framework to examine the copyright arguments and decisions. Also, the frames of authorship, work, and use were found to be particularly useful in understanding the stakeholders' relationships and struggles that are manifested in their legal arguments, and in exploring the underlying values that are reflected and generated through the decision-making process regarding copyright protection of computer programs.

In the contemporary copyright discourse regarding computer programs, the idea of individual creation is constantly praised in numerous aspects. The obsession with "originality" in conceptions of copyright that Kaplan (1967) and other scholars have noted seems to be apparent in the copyright cases regarding computer programs as well. In earlier cases in which the question of the copyrightability of computer programs was addressed, originality was presented as the most important requirement for copyrightability. At the same time, the judges adopted the minimalistic view on the standard of originality, which only requires a potential author to make something "of his own" or "independently." The authorship concept is thus dissociated from the Romantic notion of "genius" and then reassociated with the lowest levels of creative activity. The construct of authorship has been mobilized yet remained central through the legal actors' constant efforts to legitimize their interests in computer programs. Since most of the plaintiffs were developers and copyright holders at the same time in earlier copyrightability cases, the concept of authorship praising the minimal amount of independent production was not so much a product of the struggle between the developers and the copyright holders as a product of the common interests of both parties. The rule that makes it easier to become an author thus rationalized extending copyright protection to a new kind of subject matter, computer programs.

Another important aspect of discourse in the early copyrightability cases was raised by the question as to what the copyrightable subject matter includes and whether computer programs can fall into that category. In order to make a decision regarding this new technology, judges analogized computer programs to a literary work or an artistic work, and videogames to an audiovisual work, both of which had been traditionally protected by copyright. As more and more judges and other legal actors followed this view, the computer program as a copyrightable subject matter (regardless of its form, function, and embodiment) was solidly established and typified as an important structural rule in copyright law, thus legitimately becoming a vehicle for a significant expansion of copyright protections to non-developers as well. On the other hand, when the judges focused their arguments on the nature of the work sometimes, they tended to limit copyright protection if they perceived computer programs as a utilitarian work, probably because it was perceived easier not to compensate the author when the work was objectified and detached from its author.

Although arguments focusing on the concept of work could be used for both broadening and limiting the scope of copyright, the concept of work alienated the work from its author and objectified the work, thus the leverage of publishers and other purchasers of authors' rights was increased. Critical scholars have suggested that it was through this use of the concept of work the copyright law of the printing press gave entrepreneurs a monopoly over the products with little regard to, or concern for, the authors who produce the product (see Patterson and Lindberg, 1991). Copyright arguments and decisions regarding computer software were continuously shaped by the interactions between these two seemingly contradictory concepts: the concept of authorship that was supported by common interests of developers and copyright holders, and the concept of work that seem to embrace the interests of non-developers rather than those of developers. These two concepts, however, did not replace or substitute each other. Nor did they remain the same constructs over time. The analysis of interactions between structural rules and actors' resources illustrates how these two concepts are mobilized in relation to each other through communicative activities of legal actors, and become constraints and enablements for future interactions of the legal actors.

The tension between the concept of work and that of authorship was keenly manifested in the cases that employed the work-for-hire doctrine, which regards the person, on whose behalf the work was made, as the author of the work, when a work is deemed to have been made-for-hire. Under this doctrine, the alienation of creative workers from the products of their labor is legally complete. But surprisingly, the notion of authorship with its concomitant value of originality is employed to support this doctrine. Because the prerequisite for the applicability of this doctrine is that the creator was an "employee" which is considered to be an opposite concept of "independent contractor," the creator who "independently developed" the program is out of the reach of this alienation and objectification of his or her work. Moreover, the employers' claims of authorship are rationalized in terms of "creative ideas," "supervision," and "inspirations," all of which are concurrent value of authorship. In this way, the emphasis given to the value of individual creativity is reinforced, and the authorship construct is extended to encompass the employer's creative ideas and inspirations.

The construct of authorship and that of work also comprise a critical part of the structural environment in which infringement decisions are made. The most simple and direct influence of these structural rules is found in the ways in which the legal actors relied on them in dealing with the issue of the validity of ownership of copyright and the question as to whether the copied portion was a copyrightable expression. These two issues comprise almost half of the arguments in infringement cases, and the plaintiffs, whether they were developers or non-developers, received a great amount of benefit by applying these traditional copyrightability rules. It is because these rules were typified and objectified in cases where the plaintiffs were usually developers and copyright holders at the same time, thus tended to grant copyright to the plaintiffs. As a result, the structural rules relating to independent production and to the computer program as a copyrightable subject matter were reproduced and reinforced in infringement cases.

It is only in the context of the substantial similarity issue where changes in structural rules occurred. As most of the arguments in the similarity issue compare the plaintiff's work and the defendant's work, thus centered around the nature of work, the concept of the authorship was severed from the plaintiff's work.

The structural rule regarding authorship that usually gave plaintiffs more advantage was thus not operating here. At the same time, as the arguments focused more on the defendant's work than the plaintiff's work, the structural rule regarding the computer programs as a copyrightable subject matter provided a similar application to the defendant's program. As a result, the defendants in the similarity issue gained more equal footing to compete with the plaintiffs with their works, and the structural rule focusing on the concept of work was transformed in a way that it encompasses the defendant's work as well as the plaintiff's work. In addition, as most of the defendants in the similarity issue developed their own programs, many of them were able to use their resources of being developers in shifting the focus of arguments from work to authorship by arguing that they have the "skills," "experience," "knowledge," and "talent" to develop their programs "independently." The concept of independent creation and expertise that had become objectified structural rules constrained legal actors' arguments but also enabled some actors who had traditionally been disadvantaged by the rules, when they employed their resources effectively, i.e., to be developers and be perceived as independent creators by the judges. This is striking evidence that a structural change is possible due to the duality of structure that becomes both the medium and the outcome of the interactions.

Another way in which the concept of authorship interacted with the concept of work was found in the judges' application of various tests to determine the similarity of the programs at issue. In determining similarities and differences between the two "works," judges criticized and diminished the lay observer test and encouraged the extrinsic test. Some judges even argued that a computer programmer was considered a lay observer (a reasonable person) in copyright cases. Consequently, most of the similarity cases were thus decided by expert testimony. When the different parties' testimonies contradicted each other, which was usually the case, the only device to evaluate the testimonies used in the courts was the expertise' background and knowledge. Therefore, even in the arguments that focused on the concept of work, the importance was given to the "expertise" and "skills" that are concurrent yet a slightly distorted value of authorship. Artistic creativity that had been emphasized in other areas of copyright, and independent creativity that had been emphasized in earlier cases of software copyright, was now transformed into "scientific expertise, knowledge, and skills." This transformation seems to reflect the tension between the acknowledgment of the unique aspect of computer programs and the need to apply the existing form of copyright law to the new subject matter. Through this transformation of the rule, the value of authorship remains to be emphasized, and extending the copyright law to computer programs is rationalized.

As the copyrightability of computer programs became objectified, and as many new cases began to involve both plaintiffs who are developers and who are non-developers and involve both defendants who are developers and non-developers, the question regarding the nature of the use of a program became significant. The issue of the use was mostly considered regarding the question as to whether the defendant's copying of the plaintiff's program constituted an infringement. Because no clear rules regarding the use of computer programs had been established yet, judges tended to turn into the existing structural rules that concern the authorship and the work.

This process again resulted in advantages to the plaintiffs, because the focus of the arguments tended to be on the plaintiff's work, even when the defendants were developers themselves. Some defendants were able to prevail in few cases in which the arguments remained focused on the nature of the defendant's use, which implicitly suggested that the use of the plaintiff's program did not make the defendant's work a product of "less independent" creation. In this way, the arguments regarding the use of a program were greatly influenced by the concept of authorship and that of work. Despite the fact that a new kind of issue was introduced, which can create a structural environment where the possibility of structural changes is great, and despite the fact that most of the defendants in these cases had the resource of being developers themselves, they were not able to make legal arguments in their favor. The reason for this was that the new rules that they mostly relied on were contextualized by the existing structural rules, especially the ones that traditionally disadvantaged the defendants. For example, had they focused their arguments on the defendant's authorship or the defendant's work, relating to which more favorable structural rules had been created in the similarity issue, their arguments would have been more effective than using new rules that had not been tested (such as adaptation and fair use) or the existing rules that were unfavorable to them (such as focus on the plaintiff's work or the plaintiff's authorship).

However, the processes regarding the use of the program seem not so much as a result of strategic activities as the unintended consequences of interactions between structural rules and resources. Both the plaintiffs and the defendants who were non-developers were constrained to focus their arguments on the issue of use rather than work or authorship given the existing structural environment. But the focus on the concept of use did not work against the plaintiffs who were non-developers because the related rules were in favor of them. On the contrary, the focus on the use became a real constraint on the defendants who were non-developers. As a result, different from any other issues of copyright cases, in the issue regarding the nature of use defendants were even more likely to lose the case when the plaintiffs were non-developers than when the plaintiffs were developers. This is thus an unintended yet real consequence of the interaction between the structural rules and the resources, where the apparent structural constraints turned out to be enablements for certain actors.

The implication of the arguments and decisions regarding the use of a program is significant. Structural rules that specifically concern the nature of the use are still scarce, and they tend not to evolve because they are often replaced by the rules regarding the authorship or the work. In this process, the structural rules regarding the authorship and the work are again reproduced and typified.

Concerns regarding the public interest and marketplace turned out to be hardly a basis of copyright decisions regarding computer programs. This is consistent with Jaszi (1991)'s argument that the public/private contradiction may not capture the true essence of the fundamental conflict of interests that underlie copyright, When the notions of public interest and market effect did become a basis, the concepts were distorted and the decisions tended to be made in favor of the plaintiffs rather than the defendants. For example, the public interest was often trivialized to mean the providing of a monetary reward to individual authors, and an extensive analysis of market consequence was rarely provided. Arguments that used these policy considerations tended to be placed in the context of, and be influenced by, other rules of authorship or work. As these considerations rarely operate as a decisive factor themselves, parties seem to have been reluctant to use these concerns as a rationale for their arguments. Therefore, workable rules related to policy considerations are yet to be created in future copyright arguments and to influence decisions regarding computer programs.

Thus, although many social debates have centered around the legitimate or the illegal use of computer programs, legal arguments in copyright law have not encompassed the notion of the use very well, and structural rules based on the concept of use of the program have not been established. In addition, although the concept of the use usually meant the defendant's use of the program in court cases, the concept in theory may be extended to encompass the use by people in general, that is, public use or the effects on the market. But the parties had been reluctant to use arguments related to the concept of the public interest or the concept of market consequences for many reasons. When those arguments do appear, courts often rejected or ignored arguments based on these concepts. Yet to be explored are whether any identifiable structural rules regarding the concept of the use would be established in copyright cases regarding computer programs, and if so, whether considerations regarding the public interest and the marketplace would be encompassed in the structural rules, and how the concepts of authorship and work would interact with the concept of use and possibly transform themselves in the process.

CHAPTER 9

Conclusion

I have examined how legal actors who have different interests and resources interact through their communicative activities and how these interactions using structural rules and resources shape the copyright law regarding computer programs. The structural rules mainly concerning the concept of authorship and work at first enabled the developers and copyright holders to make effective arguments to extend copyright protection on their behalf. When the cases began to involve more actors who are developers but not copyright holders and actors who are not developers but claim their rights in the programs, the struggle between the developers and non-developers was manifested in their arguments focusing on the concept of work and that of authorship. The constructs of authorship and the work have been mobilized through the actors' interactions, and in the process of constraining and enabling the actors the structural rules concerning the concept of authorship and work have been reproduced and sometimes transformed.

These particular dynamics have significance along two dimensions. The first regards the structural rules that have extended copyright protection to almost all the aspects of computer programs as long as they are shown to be independently produced. These rules can work as enablements when the actors use their resources of being developers effectively. At the same time, the authorship construct has mobilized and transformed itself throughout the copyright cases. Jaszi (1991) explains that the overall incoherence of the law's account of "authorship" may be best understood as reflecting a continuing struggle between the economic forces that would be best served by the further objectification of creative endeavor and the ideological persistence of creativity and individualism.

The second dimension regards the stakeholders of the copyright system of computer programs. Actors who develop their own programs, and thus who can claim themselves as "authors," possess the most important resource in making legal arguments. This is a consequence of the struggle (or cooperation) between authors and publishers in early copyright cases. On the other hand, in later cases non-developers who are usually copyright holders tried to alienate the work from its author in order to prevail. As the notion of the author tends to contextualize many arguments focusing on the work, this was not always successful. However, as demonstrated in the arguments regarding the concept of use, non-developers who are the plaintiffs may benefit from the structural rule that tends to favor the plaintiffs, which was a result of earlier cases that usually had developers-copyright holders as plaintiffs.

This book suggests several theoretical and practical implications. The first relates to the role of communication in legal decision-making process, and further to the role of communication in the process of structural change. Previous studies of law considered law to be independent and neutral, and even those that dealt with social structures and actors focused on economic and political factors. This book has endeavored to show the ways in which interactions among the actors with different political, economic, and social characteristics are manifested through communicative activities within the framework of structural rules. The only way that the legal actors were able to legitimize their interests and possibly transform the existing structural rules was through their communicative activities. The structural rules that emphasize authorship have been established, and the nature of the actor, i.e., if he was a developing entity, was found to be a single most important factor that influences the decisions made by the courts. However, only when the judicial actor could successfully present himself as a party that involved with developing activities, was the court more likely to accept his arguments than the other party's. When the actor was a developer but she focused her arguments on the nature of the work rather than her developing activity, the actor tended not to have any advantage over the other party. Therefore, it was the legitimacy gained by communicating the nature of the actor, rather than the nature of the actor itself, that made the difference in the ways the courts made decisions. Also, when the notion of work was severed from the notion of authorship, the defendants who were previously disadvantaged gained the opportunity to compete with the plaintiffs as a program versus a program. However, this opportunity was effectively used only when parties focused on their own developing activities in their arguments. This result has particular significance for the study of communication, in that the importance of the strategic use of structural rules and resources exercised in communication activities can be applied to other areas of communication that involve efforts to influence the authority and the outcome, let alone other conflicted areas of law.

The second implication concerns the assumptions and concepts related to the production and dissemination of information, which are reflected in the interactions among the judicial actors in this process. The legal decision-making process regarding information technology not only influences the ways in which information property is distributed and used, but also constructs meanings and values related to information and technologies. Arguments made by judicial actors not only reproduce the value system that emphasizes author and authorship in social relations that consist of authors, copyright holders, and users, but also contribute to the transformation of what authorship means and who is the author. The obsession with "originality" in conceptions of copyright that some scholars (Jaszi, 1991; Kaplan, 1967) have noted seems to be apparent in the copyright cases regarding computer programs as well. The standard of originality which had been based on the creativity and talent of a genius was minimized to independent production when applied to computer programs, and in the process, "skills," "knowledge," and "expertise" that are concurrent yet slightly distorted values constituted originality and authorship constructs. This process of meaning construction contributes to transforming our assumptions and ideas about information, technology, and knowledge.

The result of this book is somewhat contradictory to previous conclusions made by some scholars that the American copyright law protects publishers' or copyright holders' property rights while disregarding authors' rights. At least in the copyright case law regarding computer programs, it was found that the authors' and developers' rights were even more likely to be protected than those of publishers as copyright holders, and the authors' rights included moral aspects in terms of rewarding their originality and expertise as well as property rights that can be transferred to others. Therefore, it is suggested that an approach that distinguishes property rights and moral rights and compares the copyright laws of different countries based on this distinction has serious limitations. The U.S. copyright law that has been criticized as the most property-oriented law is actually operating based on the originality and expertise of developers rather than property value of each program. In addition, it seems that the notions regarding authors and property, such as economic rewards, are not separate concepts but are closely intertwined. Therefore, examining the interactive relationship between these concepts will yield useful understanding regarding different copyright systems. .

But this book is not a comparative study that tries to suggest in any way whose rights or what kind of rights the U.S. copyright protects more. Nor does it attempt to make a policy judgment regarding which way of implementing or interpreting copyright law is desirable. What it does show is how the value of author's independence and expertise became emphasized through the interaction between the copyright holders and developers. This emphasis is not explicitly apparent in the provisions of copyright law. Rather, it was found to be an intended and unintended result of the interactions between the actors using their rules and resources. This is the reason, as Giddens suggests, why an approach that considers the constraints of the structure and the resources of actors separately is limited, and also is the reason why focusing on the actors' interactions using structural rules and resources is needed to explore the structural reproduction and transformation.

Going back to policy implications, as some scholars have argued, this book has shown that copyright law tends to overlook users' rights and concerns as compared to those of developers and copyright holders. First of all, copyright cases regarding computer programs rarely involved users. This is in part attributed to the fact that litigation usually costs a large sum of money and effort. It shows that although the research presented in this book found that allocative resources in terms of revenues and the number of employees were not significantly related to the decisions, there could have been an indirect way in which economic resources related to judicial decisions. Exploring this relationship is beyond the scope of this book, thus future studies should be directed to examining the limitations and problems related to the fact that the main actors in copyright cases consist of copyright holders and developers, while the copyright case law would eventually be used as policy guidelines that apply to all the stakeholders including the producers, distributors, and users.

Furthermore, it is critical to note that the legal arguments in copyright cases related to computer programs do not include implications regarding the marketplace, industry, or the public interest, let alone individual users. The minimal discussion regarding the public interest is ironically based on the assumption that the public interest will be automatically served by rewarding the authors' creativity and efforts. It seems to reflect the norms and values embedded implicitly and explicitly in society, which reward scientific expertise and specialized knowledge without seriously questioning its legitimacy or effectiveness. More importantly, if power is exercised and reproduced by knowledge, it is not only by judicial holdings that influence the access to computer programs which are important sources of skills and expertise, but also by the process of acknowledging and constructing the concepts of authorship, knowledge, and expertise.

Epilogue

This study, for which data ended with cases held in 1993, concluded that the concept of use, despite the significance of users in copyright regime, has yet to be developed to play an important role in the legal arguments. Several years since then, it does not seem that clear structural rules based on the concept of use of the program have been established in the area of computer software copyright law. Fair use is a legal rule that is increasingly debated in most areas of copyright law, but still the four-factor considerations are taken into account in a similar way in software copyright cases. However, what may be considered a potential ground-breaking structural rule for not only software copyright issues but also for other copyright areas challenged by technological development emerged in a music-parody case, which will be discussed in detail later in this final chapter. Before doing so, however, it would be interesting to pay close attention to a relatively recent phenomenon known as reverse engineering, a method often used to achieve compatibility.

Reverse engineering is essentially a method by which computer programmers study an existing program in machine-readable code by breaking it down into human readable form to create a similar product, or one that can used in conjunction with the existing software (Behrens and Levary, 1997). Several years after two important cases involving reverse engineering, *Sega v. Accolade* (1992) and *Atari v. Nintendo* (1992) [which are also included in the analysis of this study], allowed reverse engineering in certain circumstances, debate and confusion still remain in the U.S. legal community as well as in software industry. Although current judicial sentiments toward compatibility can be interpreted as having a trend toward favoring copying necessary to achieve compatibility, those who disfavor it also exist at the same time (Teter, 1993). Many legal scholars seem to support the application of fair use doctrine to allow reverse engineering for the purpose of compatibility, acknowledging that achieving the compatibility is to further the constitutional mandate to promote progress (Georgenson, 1996; Behrens and Levary, 1997; Johnson, 1994, Ignatin, 1992). Even a compatibility exemption has been proposed to be added to the copyright law, allowing reverse engineering for the development of innovative, compatible programs (Ignatin, 1992). But some commentators have questioned whether the fair use doctrine is capable of addressing the issue of reverse engineering (Hager, 1994; Daughtry, 1994). In addition, even those who favor the application of fair use rule sometimes suggest different rationales to be applied in the future (Georgenson, 1996). The courts' analyses were often considered to be contrary to prior decisions, and thus unpersuasive, even when the outcomes of the analyses were believed to be consistent with the objectives of the copyright law. Thus the favorable sentiment toward the application of the fair use doctrine in this area stems more from the general acknowledgment of the need for the development of compatible programs that is essential to innovation in the computer industry rather than the agreement on the courts' analyses.

In that situation, the reverse engineering cases in which the fair use doctrine was applied have not established structural rules that could be adopted and followed in subsequent cases despite the significance of the issues regarding the concept of use and the widespread attention they obtained by the legal community. Williams (1996) suggested that *Campbell v. Acuff Rose Music* (1994) concerning a parody by 2 Live Crew, a rap group of the rock ballad "Oh Pretty Woman," if properly applied, could help resolve the uncertainty regarding the fair use doctrine and reverse engineering of software. The 2 Live Crew song "Pretty Woman" was intentionally based on the original rock song, and the lead vocalist and song writer Campbell's request for permission to use music and lyrics from the original was refused by Acuff-Rose, the record company who owned the copyright to the original song. Campbell nevertheless released his rap, but attributed the original song to its actual writers on their compact discs. Acuff-Rose sued for copyright infringement. The district court held that the 2 Live Crew song was a parody, that it took only what was necessary to create the parodic element, that Campbell's commercial purpose was no bar to a finding of fair use, and that it was extremely unlikely that 2 Live Crew's song could adversely affect the market for the original. The Sixth Circuit reversed and remanded, finding the lower court gave too little consideration to the commercial nature of the parody. In effect, the Court of Appeals held that there was a presumption that commercial use is not fair use. The Supreme Court reversed, holding that Campbell's parody could be fair use despite its commercial purpose. The Court focused not on market effects or on commercial purpose, but on the creative relationship between the infringed work and the infringing work. Justice Souter stated that "The central purpose of this investigation is ...; it asks, in other words, whether and to what extend the new work is 'transformative' (p. 1164)."

According to Williams (1996), courts adopting Campbell's rationale to the fair use analysis of reverse engineering cases would be able to persuasively explain why the commercial aspect of reverse engineering can be of less importance in certain circumstances and how, if the infringement has a transformative purpose, the resulting market harm is excusable. In this way, Williams argues, the outcome of the case may be the same, but the rationales of the analysis would be made explicit and copyright objective of advancing society's growth in the arts and sciences would be safeguarded. Thus, in other words, a structural rule that can provide guidelines with relation to the concept of use may also be established.

The possibility of this structural rule regarding the issue of use has greater implications for other types of digital works than computer software. The characteristics of digital technologies present considerable difficulty in applying the current copyright regime to cyberspace, and this difficulty does not stop with computer software programs but is even more compounded with respect to other contents expressed and disseminated in digital media, especially the Internet. The move from analog to digital technology enables the convergence of different forms of content such as video, sound, image, text, data, and computer code in a common system, which results in changes in the economics of content (Tapscott, 1996). Works in digital form can be easily replicated, transmitted, modified, manipulated, searched for, and linked. The new technological environment is radically altering the impact and implications of copyright law. It is particularly interesting to examine a recent case *Religious Technology v. Netcom* (1995) that dealt with the issue of fair use defense in the context of the Internet.

Religious Technology, the copyright holder of the works of the late founder of the Church Scientology, claimed that Netcom, a provider of Internet service whose client includes a bulletin board service (BBS) that operates Usenet service, was a contributory infringer of the copies of their works that are made and stored on its computer while servicing BBS. Through the analysis of four statutory factors, the court held that Netcom's posting of the plaintiff's works may not be found a fair use, in denying Netcom's motion for summary judgment. It is interesting to note that although the court stated that the analysis of the first three factors (the character of the use, the nature of the copyrighted work, and the amount of the portion used) weighed in favor of Netcom, it still held that Netcom's posting of the Religious Technology's works may not be considered a fair use, solely based on the fourth factor of the possible effect on the market. Placing more weight to one factor than others, particularly the fourth factor, is not unique in fair use analysis. However, the court's reasoning in the analysis of the fourth factor raises a concern regarding the applicability of the fair use defense on the Internet. A critical question in assessing the possible effect on the market is market substitution, whether consumers would not purchase the plaintiff's product because of the availability of the defendant's product. Netcom argued that the relevant question is whether the postings fulfill the demand of an individual who seeks to follow the religion's teachings, and not whether they suppress the desire of an individual who is affected by the criticism posted on the Usenet. But the court accepted the Religious Technology's argument that the Internet's extremely widespread distribution multiplies the effects of market substitution, and held that this factor weighs in favor of Religious Technology.

In this case, therefore, the potential effect on the market becomes the most important factor in determining whether posting a copyrighted work in the Internet is a violation of copyright, and the copyright holder could successfully use the Internet's widespread distribution system in arguing for the case of market substitution. Subsequently, the very characteristics of the Internet, its efficient and widely available electronic delivery system, will render any transmission of information on the Internet not be privileged as a fair use. In the same vein, the Clinton Administration's report on intellectual property rights, known as the White Paper (1995), aimed to eliminate fair-use rights whenever a use might be licensed, which has triggered criticism that the White Paper addresses the needs of commercial providers of copyrighted information while providing little support for the preservation of fair use and other public benefits (Mahon, 1996; Cate, 1996). Thus, while the fair use doctrine is designed to moderate the possibility of limiting use and production of works of authorship, the doctrine may not turn out to be useful in the context of the Internet. Again, the Campbell analysis asking whether the new work adds, in some significant way, to the universe of information available to society, rather than soley asking whether the purpotedly infringing work adversely affects the market for sales of the initial work, can be useful in the Internet as well (Benkler, 1996). If this rule of "transformativeness" is applied to works of authorship on the Internet, it can provide a helpful guideline about what kind of use of the existing copyright materials may constitute creative enough efforts to make new works of authorship, that is, "transformative."

It is yet to be seen to what extent this potential rule regarding the use of copyrighted works would be actually established as a structural rule that can influence the interactions between stakeholders. But some of the new trends in copyright such as shareware movement or so-called copy-left movement very seriously take this concept of use into account. These movements are not based on a singular position or rationale but present rather diverse alternative views on the current regime of copyright law. Before discussing these alternative views, it would be useful to address the current trends in copyright regimes with regard to the digital media. There have been domestic and international efforts to adapt and expand the law to the digital works. As copyright holders and many governments are concerned about the possibility of the Internet becoming a "global collection of copying machines" (Godwin, 1998), most national and international efforts to apply copyright regimes in the context of new technologies tend to be suggested in a way that results in strengthening copyright protection. In addition, among many features of the Internet, the most significant is the fact that it is inherently global. No other medium crosses national boundaries with such easiness. The global nature of the Internet triggers special efforts for establishing international standards of intellectual property protection in addition to reviewing and extending domestic laws. The first global attempt to adapt the world's copyright laws to digital works began in 1989 when the World Intellectual Property Organization (WIPO) decided to deal with how computers and networks affect copyrights. In December 1996, the Diplomatic Conference on Certain Copyright and Neighboring Rights Questions of the WIPO in Geneva adopted two international treaties: the Copyright Treaty and the Performances and Phonograms Treaty. Before then, linkage between trade and intellectual property was made, and the WTO (World Trade Organization) Treaty, signed by 117 signatories in April 1994, known as the Trade Related Aspects of Intellectual Property Rights (TRIPS), redefined and globalized intellectual property rights (Drahos, 1997).

Countries in which technologies are advanced and the Internet is widely used tend to pay more attention to applying and changing their domestic rules and in participating in international discussions. Developing countries seem to have been less inclined to take a leading role in this area, but are now facing pressures to change their domestic laws to conform to international standards or be equivalent to those of their trade partners. There are also internal pressures from certain industries and interest groups within the countries to adapt and modify their laws. But critics have argued that if these national and international efforts succeed, the result would be that all the information in cyberspace will be presumptively "owned" (Godwin, 1998). The broad application of copyright in cyberspace is likely to result in prohibiting the public access to information in the context of the Internet. This limitation on the access to and use of information is the primary concern of many critical scholars as well as the proponents of so called "copyleft" regime in cyberspace.

The access right has been presented by many scholars and activists as trumping over the value of private property interests or the usefulness of providing incentives to authors and inventors

(Chon, 1993). It is argued that the overall effect of enforcing copyright law in cyberspace is to restrict access to information in an unprecedented way, and prohibiting users from using and acting upon copyrighted works is dangerous from the perspective of social dialogue and political participation (Elkin-Koren, 1996; Cate, 1996). These arguments seem to be based on the assumption that the access to information is a fundamental, basic right that everyone needs to be ensured for his or her basic welfare. It is an argument that as we all need food, clothes, and a place to live, we also need essential information for survival and cultural enrichment. Thus not only authors and inventors but all persons have a stake in, and therefore a fundamental right of access to the information (Chon, 1993). Stemming from the perspective of the public interest, scholars making these arguments focus on social values such as democracy and social change. Based on the framework of private interest versus public interest, these arguments tend to view enhancing copyright protection as in favor of private interests, and limiting copyright protection as in favor of the public interest. Thus most of current discussions about copyright law on the Internet center around striking a proper balance between protecting copyrighted materials and protecting the public interest. But as we have seen in the analysis of legal arguments of this book, the public interest versus private rights framework tends not to provide informative results because the public interest is often trivialized to be achieved automatically by providing private rights in legal discourse. In addition, any legal and policy decisions based on this perspective are bound to making a choice between different values, thus resulting in making value judgment as to which value, either the public access to information or copyright holders' right, is more important than the other. Therefore, while some scholars would argue that democracy and the public interest should be the more important social objective, others would respond that although the public access and interest are indeed important social values, they are not directly related to copyright law.

This is why positioning the issue of access to and use of information in the context of copyright law should precede any further discussion. The general principle of copyright is that the remuneration to authors is a tool to establishing an incentive for authors to create, rather than the ultimate goal of the copyright law. Within this framework, the issue of access and use focuses more on the potential authors' access and use rather than the general public's or end users' use of copyrighted works. Incentives to authors should be provided to the extent to which the production of future works of authorship or of other kinds of products is not stifled. But there has been controversy regarding not only the appropriate amount of remuneration to ensure the incentive, but also the appropriate amount of incentives that should be pursued to establish. Related to this issue, economic analyses have been conducted on the optimal rate of copyright protection (Landes and Posner, 1989; Novos and Waldman, 1984). Attempting to measure theoretically the countervailing effects of increased copyright protection, namely the effect on the creation and the effect on the wide distribution and use, these scholars have found that the economically optimal level of protection is less than the level that maximizes the production of creative works, and that the level of copyright protection should be set low when the cost of expression varies elastically with the level of protection. Also, studies on illegal copying of intellectual property, such as books and computer software, have generally concluded that illegal copying is not as detrimental to the creator of the intellectual property as generally perceived (Liebowitz, 1985; Takeyama, 1994, 1997; Varian, 1997; Lunney, 1996). Although it seems to be generally believed that the more incentives there are, the better it is for progress, whether the current protection of an author's rights could defeat, rather than help, the future production of works of authorship has been a source of debate. In that sense, questioning whether a work of authorship "adds" significant value to the universe of information as in Campbell would be a very appropriate inquiry to determine the entitlement of copyright protection.

The characteristics of digital technology and computer networks change the value of information, which is based on its meaningfulness (Barlow, 1997). As the production and dissemination of information rapidly expand, points of view and authority can provide users useful guidance. Information on the Internet might be infinite and unbounded, but it is limited by the amount of human attention (Dyson, 1997). People's presence, time, and attention become valuable on the Internet. In the case of business information, value results from interpretation and analysis by people, which depends on the specific efforts and skill of those interpreting it (Dyson, 1997). Also, attending a concert and listening to a song on a tape may be quite difference experiences (Dyson, 1997). The value of information is thus generated by the activity and presence of a person rather than by the ownership of the content (Barlow, 1997). Building a relationship with a customer becomes more important rather than controlling the copies of the content (Dyson, 1997). The fact that services and real-time performance generate value presents an interesting shift in where the information economics will be based on: relationship rather than possession.

The relationship of sender and receiver of information, the depth of their interactivity, and the value of what is sent depend on the extent to which each individual receiver has the receptors such as shared terminology, attention, interest, language, paradigm, that are necessary to render what is received meaningful (Dyson, 1997). An important possibility is presented here: receiving information can often be as creative as producing it (Dyson, 1997). Having access to information and the ability to choose, process, edit and use it becomes more important. In cyberspace where many of the users of the information are creators and editors of information work at the same time, this is more so. The use of information is not only important for its own sake, but becomes a critical part of the inherent incentive system of copyright regime. In that sense, the notion of "transformative" use has particular significance in the context of digital media.

These new possibilities in cyberspace are not well encompassed by current copyright doctrines. This is not a surprising observation, if we reflect on the fact that copyright law evolved to address the special needs of print technology. Legal rules that are based on one kind of social reality may no longer be a coherent standard in the face of changes in the social reality. The ways of thinking about laws governing creativity, value, and progress may be guided by the changes in the culture and economics of works of authorship. Recognizing that the current copyright law is a product of print technology allows us to realize that the current debates and controversies regarding copyright protection in digital context are about establishing a new balance among everyone involved in the process including creators, performers, communicators, and users.

The changing circumstances also generate new dynamics among stakeholders in the national and international contexts. There have been forces in favor of stronger insurance for copyright holders to at least the same degree in cyberspace as in the physical world. But there still remains the opposition because the same degree of protection in cyberspace cannot coexist with a certain degree of access to digital information, which was being precariously achieved in the physical world. For example, while some developed countries want to use the WIPO to forge new law, many developing countries tended to see most of the proposed extensions of copyright law to cyberspace as being too much and too soon, partly because they could not yet understand all the potential ramifications of the proposals (Samuelson and Browning, 1997). In addition to the international treaties, many countries are facing explicit and implicit pressures from their trade partners who want equivalent kinds and degrees of intellectual property protection in their counterparts. Approaching intellectual property as a trade issue does have some merit, but it is usually at the expense of less developed countries. Moreover, viewing it as a trade issue may stifle the balance between economic issues and social/cultural issues, although both are legitimate considerations of intellectual property regime.

In this context, less developed countries have not traditionally been in favor of expanding and implementing intellectual property law in cyberspace, as well as in the physical world. Less developed countries tend to be information users rather than creators, which make them naturally less enthusiastic about strong insurance for creators by intellectual property law. However, as shown in the negotiation process for the WIPO treaties, the division of interests with regards to copyright protection is not so much between developed countries and developing countries (Samuelson and Browning, 1997). Often from the same country, big production companies lobbied for stronger protection, while telephone companies and Internet service providers supported moderate treaties that do not disregard their interests altogether. This suggests that the issue of intellectual property in the international context can no longer be thought of as an issue between information "haves" and "have-nots." Differences in economic resources among the countries cannot be completely ignored. However, the nations of the developing world do not oppose copyright protection per se, and they are subject to the same kind of internal lobbying as the developed countries. Content creators and performers want stronger protection, telecommunication companies do not want to share liability with pirates, and scientists, researchers and other users want enhanced access to information. Thus future discussions and negotiations are not so much to be placed according to the traditional line between the developed and developing worlds, between one region and another, between one nation and another. Rather, a new division emerges by new alliances of industries that cut across national boundaries and the traditional North-South line.

Fully understanding this new phenomenon as a new international structure of copyright will greatly help less developed countries not to fall behind in dealing with external and internal pressures to facilitate the fast-growing industry and adapt to the fast-changing society. Binding themselves to the traditional "haves" versus "have-nots" scheme and trying to employ the value of access right in international arguments will not work, even strategically. Copyright law, and all the related concepts and values such as the concept of ownership of written information or of "copying" as an act of piracy have not existed from the time started, but these are historical product of the invention of print technology and its wide use in publishing. Before print technology, writing a book and copying one were not distinguished, and copying a manuscript was far from an act to be prohibited but have considered an important goal (Katsh, 1989). Now with the electronic media, the dilemma arises not so much from increased copying that occurs, but from the fact that copying becomes a more accepted, fundamental, and even a necessary part of the creative process (Katsh, 1989). Thus the importance lies in understanding that what seems so natural, and so much of common sense is only a historical situation which has relative, not absolute, validity, and relevance. This understanding, combined with the awareness regarding new dynamics and the need for new balance, will equip those who might be disadvantaged in the current structural scheme to be able to play a leading role in participating in and possibly influencing the discussions that have tremendous economic and social ramifications in global context.

The development of computer and information technology has a greater implication regarding changes in the legal system. While legal frameworks shape the ways in which technology is developed and its applications are adopted in the society, technological developments and subsequent changes in the economic and cultural environment may also have important implications for the law—for what it is and how it works—by challenging assumptions that are relevant to the legal framework. This can be illustrated by carefully examining recent attempts to establish a global legal framework of copyright regarding digital works that applies across the world. Various difficulties related to international legal systems in general, such as the issue of the compulsory execution of international laws, jurisdictional problems, and possible conflicts between national and international laws have been widely recognized in the area of international law. The extremely limited effectiveness of government control in cyberspace has also been pointed out. For these matters, coexistence of very broad and loose global guidelines with specific local rules may be adopted as an alternative answer. But the important aspect that has not received adequate attention is the possible incompatibility between the traditional legal system in general and what is happening in cyberspace, or rather in information society of which cyberspace is a part.

In the context of cyberspace, voluntary efforts in the private sector have been suggested to be more effective rather than legal sanctions and formal regulatory measures. Thus normative and ethical methods and so-called soft laws have been searched for. The efforts to establish international legal or other formal frameworks regulating illegal or harmful materials on the Internet have failed in such international organizations as OECD due to practical reasons related to legal enforcement and to resistance of Netizens and other claiming freedom of expression. Currently many governments and organizations are working on finding alternative methods including self-regulation of service providers, technological solutions such as blocking and monitoring software, and educational measures directed to parents and teachers. But information laws such as copyright or obscenity are not only applied to cyberspace but also to the physical world. Any new regulatory attempts limited in cyberspace would bring about the issue of inconsistency. Thus the question is whether this phenomenon for self-regulation and soft-laws would be limited in the area of information or media laws or laws applied to cyberspace. The technological and social changes stemming from the development of information technology may influence not only cyberspace but also laws in the physical world, and change not only laws dealing with information issues but also the legal system in general.

Copyright law evolved in the context of the development of print technology. But not just copyright law or information-related legal areas but probably the current legal system itself, what is often called the "law," is so much of a product from a certain historical era, that it becomes less and less relevant as we are entering a new era (Katsh, 1989). This observation is not surprising given the fact that the foundation of law is the processing of information, and the goals and processes of the current law are based on the older methods of communication (Katsh, 1989). One example is that the favorable treatment of documents in writing as evidence compared to oral promises in most legal systems has its origin to the evolution of print technology (Katsh, 1989). And historically, those often called as alternative dispute resolution mechanisms have been the most commonly used mechanism sometime in the past, and the law now considered the most elaborate and refined has been an "alternative" method. As much as information laws and media laws regarding obscenity, pornography, copyright, privacy, internet domain names, and broadcasting influence the communication environment of our living, the legal system is affected by the changing modes of communication. Challenges occurring to the current copyright regimes are only a part of a broader and more significant process of legal change that occurs by the introduction of electronic media to the legal system based on print technology. In order to fully understand this process, legal changes should be systematically examined in relation to the changes in the mode of information and media of communication, through the oral speech, writing, print, and electronic media. For this endeavor, interdisciplinary approaches encompassing both perspectives of communication and law are particularly needed.

The distinction between what can be communicated and what cannot be communicated is constructed by the legal process and legal discourse. Also, the distinction between what should be governed and what should not be, and even what is law and what is not law, is constructed by the process of changes in the mode of communication. Thus law influences the communication environment and the mode of communication influences the law. At the same time, law "is" a process of communication and communication "is" a process of law in a broader sense that all strategic communication attempts to influence authority. Thus it is important to overcome not only the intellectual closure of law and communication studies as academic disciplines, but the closure of law and communication as analytic categories. Critical analyses of law and communication should not only explore the social construction of both law and communication but also the complex connection of the two. The discussion in this book suggests the inherent uncertainty, even indeterminacy concerning law and communication. It also suggests that it may be no longer possible to comfortably live and interact within the boundaries of the traditional and idealized concept of law as a set of legal rules or formal institutions and the traditional concept of communication as to what is allowed and what is not. Readjustments will be necessary in the future. But uncertainty opens up new possibilities. The process of inquiry and readjustment could be a welcome challenge to those who acknowledge that all concepts and categorizations are not natural but constructed.

Appendix I

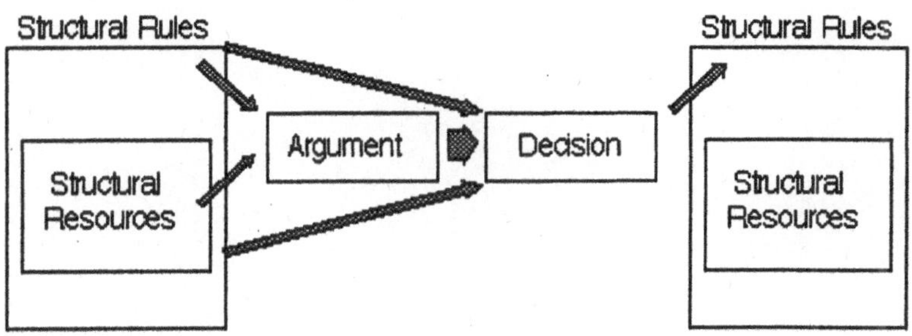

Figure 1. The Process of Structuration Through Communicative Actions

Appendix II

LIST OF SOFTWARE COPYRIGHT CASES

1. Accolade, Inc. v. Distinctive Software, Inc., Unlimited Software, Inc., Distinctive Management, Inc., Copy. L. Rep. (CCH) ¶26,612 (D.C.A. 1990).
2. Allen-Myland, Inc. v. International Business Machines Corporation, 746 F. Supp. 520 (D.P.A. 1990).
3. American Intelligent Machines v. Basic Computers, Inc., and Robert C. Hunt., Copy. L. Rep. (CCH) ¶25,322 (D.V.A. 1981).
4. Apple Computer, Inc. v. Formula International, Inc., 562 F. Supp. 775 (D.C.A. 1983).
5. Apple Computer, Inc. v. Formula International Inc., 725 F.2d 521 (9th Cir. 1984).
6. Apple Computer, Inc. v. Franklin Computer Corp., 545 F. Supp. 812 (D.P.A. 1982).
7. Apple Computer, Inc. v. Franklin Computer Corporation, 714 F.2d 1240 (3rd. Cir. 1983).
8. Apple Computer, Inc. v. Microsoft Corporation and Hewlett-Packard Company, 799 F. Supp. 1006 (D.C.A. 1991).
9. Apple Computer, Inc. v. Microsoft Corporation and Hewlett-Packard Company, 821 F. Supp. 161 (D.C.A. 1992).
10. Ashton-Tate Corporation v. Richard Ross, Bravo Technologies, Inc., 728 F. Supp. 597 (D.C.A. 1989).

11. Ashton-Tate Corporation v. Richard Ross, Bravo Technologies, Inc., 916 F.2d 516 (9th. Cir. 1990).
12. Atari, Inc. v. Amusement World, Inc., and Stephen D. Holniker, 547 F. Supp. 222 (D.M.A. 1981).
13. Atari, Inc. v. JS&A Group, Inc., Eastern Division., 597 F. Supp. 5 (D.I.L. 1983).
14. Atari Games Corp. and Tengen, Inc. v. Nintendo of America, Inc. and Nintendo Co., Ltd., 18 U.S.P.Q.2D (BNA) 1935 (D.C.A. 1991); Copy. L. Rep. (CCH) ¶26,703.
15. Atari Games Corp. and Tengen, Inc. v. Nintendo of America Inc. and Nintendo Co., Ltd., 975 F.2d 832 (Federal Cir. 1992); 24 U.S.P.Q.2D (BNA) 1015; Copy. L. Rep. (CCH) ¶26,978.
16. Atari, Inc. v. North American Philips Consumer Electronics Corp., Copy. L. D. ¶25,363 (D.I.L. 1981).
17. Atari, Inc. v. North American Philips Consumer Electronics Corp., 672 F. 2d 607 (7th Cir. 1982); 214 U.S.P.Q. 33.
18. Atari Games Corporation v. Ralph Oman, Register of Copyrights, 693 F. Supp. 1204 (D.D.C. 1988); 8 U.S.P.Q.2D (BNA) 1426; Copy. L. Rep. (CCH) ¶26,325.
19. Atari Games Corporation v. Ralph Oman, Register of Copyrights, 888 F.2d 878 (D.C. Cir. 1992); 12 U.S.P.Q.2D (BNA) 1791; Copy. L. Rep. (CCH) ¶26,490; 281 U.S. App. D.C. 181.
20. Atari, Inc. v. Ken Williams d/b/a On-Line Systems, Copy. L. Rep. (CCH) ¶25,412 (D.C.A. 1981); 217 U.S.P.Q. (BNA) 746.
21. Autoskills, Inc. v. National Educational Support Systems Inc., 793 F. Supp. 1557 (D.N.M. 1992); 24 U.S.P.Q.2D (BNA) 1107; Copy. L. Rep. (CCH) ¶26,948.
22. Avtec Systems, Inc. v. Jeffrey G. Peiffer, et. al., 805 F. Supp. 1312 (D.V.A. 1992); Copy. L.R. (CCH) ¶27,036.
23. Clifford Scott Aymes v. Jonathan J. Bonelli d/b/a Island Swimming Sales, Inc. and Island Recreational, 21 U.S.P.Q.2D (BNA) 1716 (D.N.Y. 1991); Copy. L. Rep. (CCH) ¶26,805.
24. Clifford Scott Aymes v. Jonathan Bonelli d/b/a Island Swimming Salies, Inc. and Island Recreational, 980 F. 2d 857 (2nd Cir. 1992).
25. BPI Systems, Inc. and BPI Services, Inc. v. William A. Leith, Transamerican Business System, Inc., and Tabs, Inc., 532 F. Supp. 208 (D.T.X. 1981); Copy. L. Rep. (CCH) ¶25,392.

26. BPI Systems, Inc. and BPI Services, Inc. v. William A. Leith, Transamerican Business System, Inc., and Tabs, Inc., 532 F. Supp. 208 (D.T.X. 1981); Copy. L. Rep. (CCH) ¶25,392.
27. Broderbund Software, Inc. and Pixellite Software v. Unison World, Inc., 648 F. Supp. 1127 (D.C.A. 1986); 231 U.S.P.Q. (BNA) 700.
28. Cable/Home Communication Corporation, M/A-Com, Inc., Home Box Office, Inc., and Showtime/The Movie Channel, Inc. v. Network Productions, Inc. and Shaun Kenny and Bob Cooper, Jr., et. al., 902 F.2d 829 (11th Cir. 1990); 15 U.S.P.Q.2D (BNA) 1001; Copy. L. Rep. (CCH) ¶26,588.
29. Cmax/Cleveland, Inc. d/b/a Computermax v. UCR, Inc., David T. Cherry, L & B Rents, Inc., South Carolina Retals, Inc. d.b.a Ace TV and James T. Archer, 804 F. Supp. 337 (D.G.A. 1992).
30. Computer Associates International, Inc. v. Altai, Inc., 775 F. Supp. 544 (D.N.Y. 1991); 20 U.S.P.Q.2D (BNA) 1641; Copy. L. Rep. (CCH) ¶26,783.
31. Computer Associates International, Inc. v. Altai, Inc., 775 F. Supp. 544 (D.N.Y. 1991); 20 U.S.P.Q.2D (BNA) 1641; Copy. L. Rep. (CCH) ¶26,783.
32 Computer Associates International, Inc. v. Altai, Inc., 982 F.2d 693; U.S.P.Q. 2d 1241 (2nd Cir. 1992).
33. Data Cash Systems, Inc. v. JS&A Group, Inc., Joseph Sugarman and Mary Stanke, 480 F. Supp. 1063 (D.I.L. 1979).
34. Data Cash Systems, Inc. v. JS&A Group, Inc., Joseph Sugarman and Mary Stanke, 628 F.2d 1038 (7th Cir. 1980); Copy. L. Rep. (CCH) ¶25,183; 208 U.S.P.Q. (BNA) 197.
35. Data East USA, Inc. v. Epyx, Inc., 862 F.2d 204 (9th Cir. 1988); 9 U.S.P.Q.2D (BNA) 1322; Copy. L. Rep. (CCH) ¶26,356.
36. Data General Corporation and Data General Service, Inc. v. Grunman Systems Support Corporation, Copy. L. Rep. (CCH) ¶26,399 (D.M.A. 1988).
37. Data Products, Inc. v. William C. Reppart, Jr., Joe Ellzey, Patrick Lee Morse, S T Paging, Inc., S T Broadcasting, Inc., and Breadbasket Enterprises, Inc., and Sunflower Telephone Company, Inc., S T Computer Resources, Inc., and S T Enterprises, Ltd., v. Claude Martin Pickett, 18 U.S.P.Q.2D (BNA) 1058 (D.K.S. 1990); Copy. L. Rep. (CCH) ¶26,723.

38. Datastorm Technologies, Inc. v. S-To-Go-Inc., 1989 U.S. Dist. LEXIS 18295 (D.T.X.).
39. Digital Communications Associates, Inc. v. Softklone Distributing Corporation, and Foretec Development Corporation, 659 F. Supp. 449 (D.G.A. 1987); 2 U.S.P.Q.2D (BNA) 1385; Copy. L. Rep. (CCH) ¶26,088.
40. Dynamic Solutions, Inc. v. Planning & Control, Inc., John Z. Censor d/b/a Censor & Company, Inc., and Censor & Company, 646 F. Supp. 1329 (D.N.Y. 1986); Copy. L. Rep. (CCH) ¶26,011.
41. Engineering Dynamics, Inc. v. Structural Software, Inc. and S. Rao Guntur, 785 F. Supp. 576 (D.L.O. 1991); 21 U.S.P.Q.2D (BNA) 1524; Copy. L. Rep. (CCH) ¶26,831.
42. Fonar Corporation, v. Deccaid Services, Inc., Equi Med Leasing, Inc., Medical Funding of America, Inc., David Smith, Morton Hackof, Stephen Steckler, Louis Treglia and Peter Kim, 787 F. Supp. 44 (D.N.Y. 1992); 1992 U.S. Dist. LEXIS 2771; Copy. L. Rep. (CCH) ¶26,927.
43. Foresight Resources Corporation v. Larry Pfortmiller, et. al., 719 F. Supp. 1006 (D.K.S. 1989); 1989 U.S. Dist. LEXIS 10486; 13 U.S.P.Q.2D (BNA) 1721; Copy. L. Rep. (CCH) ¶26,499.
44. Forry, Inc. v. Neundorfer, Inc., 1987 U.S. Dist. LEXIS 3320 (D.O.H.).
45. Anthony James Frybarger v. International Business Machines Corporation, Gebelli Software, Inc., and Nasir Gebelli, 812 F.2d 525 (9th Cir. 1987); 1987 U.S. App. LEXIS 3127; 2 U.S.P.Q.2D (BNA) 1135; Copy. L. Rep. (CCH) ¶26,073.
46. The Gates Rubber Company v. Bando American, Inc., Steven R. Piderit, Ron Newman, Deminse Hanano, and John Does, 798 F. Supp. 1499 (D.C.O 1992).
47. GCA Corporation v. Raymond Chance, Steven D. Foss, and Alan W. Kukas, individually and as a partnership d/b/a Site Services, 217 U.S.P.Q. (BNA) 718 (D.C.A. 1982).
48. GCA Corporation v. Raymond Chance, Steven D. Foss, and Alan W. Kukas, individually and as a partnership d/b/a Site Services, 217 U.S.P.Q. (BNA) 718 (D.C.A. 1982).
49. Richard E. Graham d/b/a Night Owl Computer Service v. Larry D. James, Copy. L. Rep. (CCH) ¶26,892 (D.N.Y. 1992).

50. Healthcare Affiliated Services, Inc. and Blue Cross of Western Pennsylvania v. Leslie C. Lippany, individually and doing business as Hospital Mycrosystems, Inc., 701 F. Supp. 1142 (D.P.A. 1988); Copy. L. Rep. (CCH) ¶26,393.
51. Hubco Data Products Corp. v. Management Assistance Inc., Copy. L. Rep. (CCH) ¶25,529 (D.I.D. 1983); 219 U.S.P.Q. (BNA) 450.
52. Integral Systems, Inc. v. Peoplesoft, Inc., 1991 U.S. Dist. LEXIS 20878 (D.C.A.).
53. ISC-Bunker Ramo Corporation v. Altech, Inc., 765 F. Supp. 1310 (D.I.L. 1990); Copy. L. Rep. (CCH) ¶26,795.
54. E. F. Johnson Co. v. Uniden Corporation of America, 623 F. Supp. 1485 (D.M.N. 1985); Copy. L. Rep. (CCH) ¶25,887; 228 U.S.P.Q. (BNA) 891.
55. Johnson Controls, Inc. v. Phoenix Control Systems, Inc., Rodney Larsen and Irene Larsen, husband and wife, John Schratz and Martha Schratz, husband and wife, 886 F.2d 1173 (9th Cir. 1989); 12 U.S.P.Q.2D (BNA) 1566; Copy. L. Rep. (CCH) ¶26,479.
56. Carolyn Kelstall-Whitney d/b/a Computerized Processing Unlimited v. Robert Charles Mahar, 1990 U.S. Dist. LEXIS 6186 (D.P.A.).
57. Kepner-Tregoe, Inc. v. Leadership Software, Inc. and Arthus G. Jago, 22 U.S.P.Q.2D (BNA) 1788 (D.T.X. 1992); Copy. L. Rep. (CCH) ¶26,946.
58. Lasercomb America, Inc. v. Holiday Steel Rule Die Corporation, Larry Holliday, and Job Reynolds, 656 F. Supp. 612 (D.N.C. 1987); 2 U.S.P.Q.2D (BNA) 1711; Copy. L. Rep. (CCH) ¶26,110.
59. Lasercomb America, Inc. v. Job Reynolds, Larry Holiday, and Holiday Steel Rule Die Corporation, 911 F.2d 970 (4th Cir. 1990); 15 U.S.P.Q.2D (BNA) 1846; Copy. L. Rep. (CCH) ¶26,619.
60. Lewis Galoob Toys, Inc. v. Nintendo of America, Inc. and Related and Consolidated Actions, 780 F. Supp. 1283 (D.C.A. 1991); 20 U.S.P.Q.2D (BNA) 1662; Copy. L. Rep. (CCH) ¶26,754.
61. Lewis Galoop Toys, Inc. v. Nintendo of America Inc., 964 F. 2d 965 (9th Cir. 1992); 22 U.S.P.Q. 2D 1857.

62. Lotus Development Corporation v. Borland International, Inc., 799 F. Supp. 203 (D.M.A. 1992), 831 F. Supp. 202 and 831 F. Supp. 223 combined (D.M.A. 1993).
63. Lotus Development Corporation v. Paperback Software, Ltd., 740 F. Supp. 37 (D.M.A. 1990); 15 U.S.P.Q.2D (BNA) 1577.
64. Manufacturers Technologies, Inc. v. Cams, Inc., Edward D. Cormier, Kenneth J. Laviana, and Norman St. Martin, 706 F. Supp. 984 (D.C.T. 1989); 10 U.S.P.Q.2D (BNA) 1321; Copy. L. Rep. (CCH) ¶26,423.
65. William M. Mercer, Inc. v. MacLean Associates, Inc., 18 U.S.P.Q.2D (BNA) 1807 (D.P.A. 1991).
66. MacLean Associates, Inc. v. W. M. Mercer-Meidinger-Hansen, 952 F.2d 769 (3rd Cir. 1991); 21 U.S.P.Q.2D (BNA) 1345; Copy. L. Rep. (CCH) ¶26,851.
67. Micro Consulting, Inc. v. Pedro Zubelda and Medical Electronic Data Exchange, Inc., 813 F. Supp. 1514 (D.O.K. 1990); Copy. L. Rep. (CCH) ¶27,105.
68. Micro-Sparc, Inc. v. Amtype Corporation, 592 F. Supp. 33 (D.M.A. 1984); Copy. L. Rep. (CCH) P25,706; 223 U.S.P.Q. (BNA) 1210.
69. Microsoft Corp. v. Very Competitive Computer Products Corp., 671 F. Supp. 1250, (D.C.A. 1987); Copyright L.Dec. (CCH) ¶26,123.
70. Midway Mfg. Co. v. Artic International, Inc., 547 F. Supp. 999 (D.I.L. 1982); Copy. L. Rep. (CCH) ¶25,448; 216 U.S.P.Q. (BNA) 413.
71. Midway Mfg. Co. v. Artic International, Inc., 704 F.2d 1009 (7th Cir. 1982); 9 Media L. Rep. 1605; 218 U.S.P.Q. (BNA) 791.
72. Midway Mfg. Co. v. Bandai-America, Inc., Baindai Company, Ltd., Bandai Overseas Corporation, Epoch Company, Ltd., Epoch Corporation, Toys R Us, Lionel Leisure, Inc., Best Products, Inc., Lash-Tamaron Distributors, Inc., and Coleco Industries, Inc. v. Bandai-America, inc., Bandai Company, Ltd., Bandai Overseas Corporation, Epoch Company, Ltd., and Epoch Corporation, 546 F. Supp. 125 (D.N.J. 1982); Copy. L. Rep. (CCH) ¶25,530; 216 U.S.P.Q. (BNA) 812.
73. Midway Mfg. Co. v. Dale Dirkschneider and Harold Peterson, individually and d/b/a A-1 Machines, Gerrit Kraayenbrink, individually and d/b/a Soo Valley Dist. Co., and Venture Line,

Inc., 543 F. Supp. 466 (D.N.B. 1981); Copy. L. Rep. (CCH) ¶25,469; 214 U.S.P.Q. (BNA) 417.

74. Midway Mfg. Co. v. Roger Strohon a/k/a Frederick Slayton, Kathy Strohon, Clidata Services, Inc., Gary Melnick, Update Kits, Inc., and Midwest Amusements Manufacturers and Distributors, 564 F. Supp. 741 (D.I.L. 1983); Copy. L. Rep. (CCH) ¶25,545; 219 U.S.P.Q. (BNA) 42.
75. M. Kramer Manufacturing Co., Inc. v. Hugh Andrews, et. al., Tim Caldwell, Drew's Distributing, Inc., Drew's Distributing Co., and Lynch Enterprises, Inc., 783 F.2d 421 (4th Cir. 1985); Copy. L. Rep. (CCH) ¶25,891; 228 U.S.P.Q. (BNA) 705.
76. National Car Rental System, Inc. v. Computer Associates International, Inc., 22 U.S.P.Q.2D (BNA) 1375 (D.M.N. 1992); Copy. L. Rep. (CCH) ¶26,862.
77. NEC Corporation and NEC Electronics, Inc. v. INTEL CORPORATION, 645 F. Supp. 590 (D.C.A. 1986); 1 U.S.P.Q.2D (BNA) 1492.
78. NEC Corporation and NEC Electronics, Inc. v. INTEL CORPORATION, 10 U.S.P.Q.2D (BNA) 1177 (D.C.A. 1989); Copy. L. Rep. (CCH) ¶26,379.
79. Nintendo of America, Inc. v. Bay Coin Distributors, Inc., Space Games for Profit, Inc., d/b/a Astro Games, Sandoi Kobler, and W. Kobler et. al., Copy. L. Rep. (CCH) ¶25,409 (D.N.Y. 1982).
80. Nintendo of America, Inc. v. Elcon Industries, Inc., et. al., 564 F. Supp. 937 (D.M.I. 1982); Copy. L. Rep. (CCH) ¶25,577.
81. Pearl Systems, Inc. v. Competition Electronics, Inc., 8 U.S.P.Q.2D (BNA) 1520 (D.F.L. 1988); Copy. L. Rep. (CCH) ¶26,338.
82. Plains Cotton Cooperative Association of Lubbock v. Goodpasture Computer Service, Inc., William James Godlove, Richard R. Fisher, Peter H. Cushman, and Clarence Michael Smith, 807 F.2d 1256 (5th Cir. 1987); 1 U.S.P.Q.2D (BNA) 1635; Copy. L. Rep. (CCH) ¶26,056.
83. PRC Realty Systems, Inc. v. National Association of Realtors, 766 F. Supp. 453 (D.V.A. 1991); 19 U.S.P.Q.2D (BNA) 1916; Copy. L. Rep. (CCH) ¶26,775.
84. Q-Co Industries, Inc. v. Sidney Hoffman, Dilip Som and Conputer Prompting Corp., 625 F. Supp. 608 (D.N.Y. 1985); 228 U.S.P.Q. (BNA) 554.

85. Qad, Inc., Karl Lopker, and Pam Lopker, v. ALN Associates, Inc., Sally Allen, Mike Allen, and Ronald Whiteford, 770 F. Supp. 1261 (D.I.L. 1991); 19 U.S.P.Q.2D (BNA) 1907; Copy. L. Rep. (CCH) ¶26,822.
86. Qad, Inc., Pamela Lopker and Karl Lopker, v. ALN Associates, Inc., Sally Allen, Mike Allen, and Ronald Whiteford, 974 F.2d 834 (7th Cir. 1992); 24 U.S.P.Q.2D (BNA) 1145; Copy. L. Rep. (CCH) ¶26,980.
87. Red Baron-Franklin Park, Inc. v. Taito Corp., 9 U.S.P.Q. 2D 1901 (D.V.A. 1988).
88. Red Baron-Franklin Park, Inc. v. Taito Corp., 883 F. 2d 275 (4th Cir. 1989); 11 U.S.P.Q. 2D 1548.
89. Relational Design & Technology, Inc. v. Data Team Corporation, Stuart Brock and Wesley Brock, 1993 U.S. Dist. LEXIS 7758 (D.K.S. 1993).
90. SAS Institute, Inc. v. S&H Computer Systems, Inc., 605 F. Supp. 816 (D.T.N. 1985); Copy. L. Rep. (CCH) ¶25,794; 225 U.S.P.Q. (BNA) 916.
91. Sega Enterprises, Ltd. v. Accolade, Inc., 785 F. Supp. 1392 (D.C.A. 1992); 23 U.S.P.Q.2D (BNA) 1440; Copy. L. Rep. (CCH) ¶26,895.
92. Sega Enterprises, Ltd. v. Accolade, Inc., 24 U.S.P.Q.2D (BNA) 1561 (9th Cir. 1993).
93. Service & Training, Inc. and Robert J. Montgomery v. Data General Corporation and Data General Services, 737 F. Supp. 334 (D.M.D. 1990); Copy. L. Rep. (CCH) ¶26,582.
94. Soft Computer Consultants, Inc. v. Shahram Lalehzarzadeh, Comtron, Inc., Biophil-Lindsay Laboratories, Inc., and Doctors Laboratory, Inc., Copy. L. Rep. (CCH) ¶26,403 (D.N.Y. 1988).
95. Softel, Inc. v. Dragon Medical and Scientific Communications, Inc., Dragon Group, Ltd. a/k/a Dragon Medical and Communications, Ltd., John R. Darsee, I. Eugene Hodge, and Nina Romanoff, 1992 U.S. Dist. LEXIS 9502 (D.N.Y.).
96. Softel, Inc. v. Dragon Medical and Scientific Communications, Inc., Dragon Group, Ltd. a/k/a Dragon Medical and Communications, Ltd., John R. Darsee, I. Eugene Hodge, and Nina Romanoff, 1992 U.S. Dist. LEXIS 9502 (D.N.Y.).

97. S.O.S., Inc. v. Payday, Inc., Computer Consulting Service, Bacchus Chu, and Eiichi Koyama, Payday, Inc. v. S.O.S., Inc., 1 U.S.P.Q. 2D (BNA) 1573 (D.C.A. 1986).
98. S.O.S., Inc. v. Payday, Inc., 886 F.2d 1081 (9th Cir. 1989); 12 U.S.P.Q.2D (BNA) 1241; Copy. L. Rep. (CCH) ¶26,469.
99. Stern Electronics, Inc. v. Harold Kaufman d/b/a Bay Coin, Omni Video Games, Inc., Ferncrest Distributors, Inc., Frank Gaglione and Kevin McIntyre, 523 F. Supp. 635 (D.N.Y. 1981); Copy. L. Rep. (CCH) ¶25,272; 213 U.S.P.Q. (BNA) 75.
100. Stern Electronics, Inc. v. Harold Kaufman d/b/a Bay Coin, et. al., and Omni Video Games, Inc., et. al., 669 F.2d 852 (2nd Cir. 1982); Copy. L. Rep. (CCH) ¶25,354; 213 U.S.P.Q. (BNA) 443.
101. Synercom Technology, Inc. v. University Computing Company and Engineering Dynamics, Inc., 462 F. Supp. 1003 (D.T.X. 1978); 199 U.S.P.Q. (BNA) 537.
102. Synercom Technology, Inc. v. University Computing Company and Engineering Dynamics, Inc., 462 F. Supp. 1003 (D.T.X. 1978); 199 U.S.P.Q. (BNA) 537.
103. Tandy Corporation v. Personal Micro Computers, Inc., Eaca International, Ltd., Eaca Electronics Corp. of America Compumart, Consumer Computers Mailholder, Simutek Computer Products, Robitaille & Sons Enterprise, Inc., d/b/a Tse Hardside, and Roger W. Robitaille, d/b/a the Software Exchange, 524 F. Supp. 171 (D.C.A. 1981); Copy. L. Rep. (CCH) ¶25,303; 214 U.S.P.Q. (BNA) 178.
104. TechniCAL, Inc. v. Allpax Products, Inc., Steve B. Hudson, Timothy Haley, Michael Blatiner and Randolph Waesche, 1990 U.S. Dist. LEXIS 3712 (D.L.O.).
105. Telemarketing Resources v. Symantec Corporation, John L. Friend, an individual and d/b/a Softworks Development, 12 U.S.P.Q.2D (BNA) 1991 (D.C.A. 1989); Copy. L. Rep. (CCH) ¶26,514.
106. Brown Bag Software, formerly Telemarketing Resources, Inc. v. Symantec Corp, John L. Friend, an individual and d/b/a Softworks Development, 960 F.2d 1465 (9th Cir. 1992); 22 U.S.P.Q.2D (BNA) 1429; Copy. L. Rep. (CCH) ¶26,896.
107. Vault Corporation v. Quaid Software Ltd., 655 F. Supp. 750 (D.L.O.); 2 U.S.P.Q.2D (BNA) 1407; Copy. L. Rep. (CCH) ¶26,103.

108. Vault Corporation v. Quaid Software Ltd., 847 F.2d 255 (5th Cir. 1988); 7 U.S.P.Q.2D (BNA) 1281.
109. Videotronics, Inc. v. Bend Electronics, Videotronics of Oregon, Inc. and Video Horizons, Inc., 586 F. Supp. 478 (D.N.V.); Copy. L. Rep. (CCH) ¶25,697; 223 U.S.P.Q. (BNA) 936.
110. Whelan Associates, Inc. v. Jaslow Dental Laboratory, Inc., et. al., 609 F. Supp. 1307 (D.P.A. 1985); Copy. L. Rep. (CCH) ¶25,785; 225 U.S.P.Q. (BNA) 156.
111. Whelan Associates, Inc. v. Jaslow Dental Laboratory, Inc., Dentcom, Inc., Edward Jaslow, Rand Jaslow, and Joseph M. Cerra, 797 F.2d 1222 (3rd Cir. 1986); Copy. L. Rep. (CCH) ¶25,978; 230 U.S.P.Q. (BNA) 481.
112. Williams Electronics, Inc. v. Artic International, Inc., and Sming Huang a/k/a Shih Ming Huang, Copy. L. Rep. (CCH) ¶25,503 (D.N.J. 1981)
113. Williams Electronics, Inc. v. Artic International, Inc., 685 F.2d 870 (3rd Cir. 1982); Copy. L. Rep. (CCH) ¶25,432; 215 U.S.P.Q. (BNA) 405.
114. Williams Electronics, Inc. v. Bally Manufacturing Corporation, 568 F. Supp. 1274 (D.I.L. 1983); 220 U.S.P.Q. (BNA) 1091.
115. Yamate USA Corporation v. Myron Sugarman, Atlantic & Pacific Amusement Corporation, 20 U.S.P.Q.2D (BNA) 1590 (D.N.J. 1991).

Appendix III

CODING SCHEMES FOR THE ANALYSIS OF ARGUMENTS

File Name: Short case name-court level-year
Name: Name of the case (X v. X)
Citation:
Date: YYMMDD
Court: District/appellate division State
Judge: Name (underline the writer of the opinion in appellate cases)
Characteristics : appointing President (party)
school graduated
age
Legal Topics: Authorship/Copyrightability/Infringement
Procedural Status: Summary judgment/Preliminary injunction/Final judgment
Parties: P : Name of the plaintiff .
Nature of the plaintiff (developer/copyright owner/both developer and copyright owner at the same time/retailer, etc.)
D : Name of the defendant
Nature of the defendant (developer/copyright owner/both developer and copyright owner at the same time/retailer, etc.)

Subject: The kind of computer programs in issue:
1. system programs / operating system programs / application programs
2. literal elements (source code / object code) / non-literal elements (structure, sequence, and/or organization, screen display and user interfaces, function or purpose)

Facts: Brief facts of the case and procedures

Focusing on : Who is the author, developer, copyright owner of the original program at issue?
If the program in issue is not one, what other programs, how they are developed?
Who sought what relief and claiming what?

Arguments per each Q (issues and theories):

1. Questions: The specific questions asked and tried to be answered "in" the arguments (answers)

2. Issues (small questions): underline disputed issue(s)

Copyrightability— Validity Certificate
Scope Originality
Authorship
Fixed in tangible medium
Literary work

Infringement— Ownership of copyright
—copyright certificate
—Copyrightability (validity and scope)
—Work made for hire
Copying
—Access + Substantial similarity
—Copyrightable expression (idea/expression)
—extrinsic (expert) and intrinsic (lay) tests
Krofft
—structure, sequence v. purpose
Whelan
—abstraction test (filtering, and comparison)
Nichols v. Universal
—utilitarian work
—adaptation (essential step/ archival)
—total concept and feel

Roth v. United

—iterative test

E.F. Johnson v. Uniden

If preliminary injunction case,

Probability of success on the merits
Irreparable harm
Balance of harm

Or,

The public interest
Irreparable harm + probability of success on the merits
Irreparable harm + serious issues and balance of harm

3. Judge's argument style (own argument only / own order but including parties' arguments as well / primarily following the party(s)'s argument order)

4. Code of Arguments:

Summarize the arguments in the court opinions in the order made by the judges. When the judges arguments were responding to the other actors' arguments, include the other actors arguments as well after P: and D:. Define one argument unit when the judge was dealing with one issue using a legal theory, a test, or supporting evidence. A sample of coding arguments is provided in the end of this coding sheet. The possible legal theories are presented below.

*Theories that are used to discuss each issue

Idea v. expression -- 17 U.S.C. §102 (b)
(merger/inseparability, scenes á faire, limited ways of expression)

Utilitarian (functional) work
Archive
Public domain (Publication)
Derivative work
Work made for hire

Fair use: 4 factors -
The purpose and character of use
The nature of the copyrighted work
The amount and substantiality of the portion used
Effect on the market (17 U.S.C. §107)

Personal use
First sale

Also define the main frame used by the each actor (authorship/nature of the work/nature of use of the program). An argument is coded as having a frame of the work when the argument is focused on the nature of the computer program, i.e., whether the program was a utilitarian work or an artistic work, whether the part of the program considered is an expression or idea, whether the two programs considered are similar or not. An argument is coded as having a frame of authorship when the argument is focused on the process of developing the program, i.e., which actor provided more input in developing the program, whether an-actor has a background and skill to possibly develop the program, etc. An argument is coded as having a frame of use when the argument is focused on the ways in which the program was used by another actor or the third party, i.e., whether an actor's use of the program developed by the other actor was legitimate. See page 87 of the text for examples of defining the frame of the arguments.

Also provide headings before the summary of the arguments in order to indicate the issue under which the argument is made.

P:

D:

J:

5. Define the Metaphors used by each actor:

Utilitarian work
Literary work
Audiovisual work
Artistic work

6. Did the arguments include the alleged infringer's effort to avoid copying?

Decisions: In summary judgment and preliminary injunction cases,

Motion granted or denied

In appeals case,

Affirmed or reversed

For or against deciding Infringement
Plaintiff or defendant wins
For or against copyright holder (if applicable)
For or against developer (if applicable)

*** A sample coding**

In Data Products v. William Rappart (Copyright Law Decisions ¶26,723), the opinion stated on page 24,225:

> Finally, the defendants argue that any modifications made to the TAS or cable TV program packages were valid under 17 U.S.C. §117. The argument is limited in scope: it would serve to protect the defendants only from infringement claims which are based on the modification of the programs for the use of Sunflower or its subsidiaries (Jetmore or Cablevision, Ltd.). It would not provide protection from the claims of infringement arising from the use of the programs by S T Enterprises or its subsidiaries. 17 U.S.C. §117 (1990 Supp.) provides in part:
>
> Notwithstanding the provisions of section 106, it is not an infringement for the owner of a copy of a computer program to make or authorize the making of another copy of adaptation of that computer program provided . . . (provision of 117 is presented here)
>
> DPI argues that §117 is inapplicable, since the modifications were not performed in the process of inputting the programs into the Sunflower computer, but were performed later. See, e.g., Micro-Sparc, Inc. v. Amtype Corp., 592 F. Supp. 33 (D.Mass. 1984). However, as Judge O'Conner recognized in Foresight Resources Corp. v. Pfortmiller, 719 F. Supp. 1006, 1009-10 (D.Kan. 1989), cases such as Micro-Sparc which apply 117 in a narrow manner are against the weight of recent authority and contrary to the intent of Congress. The better view is that (117 is designed to protect software purchasers who make modifications or enhancements to the software for their own use only. *Id.*, at 1010.
>
> But again, §117 has only a limited application in the present case. Under the statute, any modifications or enhancements to the DPI software would not constitute an infringement to the extent that they were used solely by Sunflower and its subsidiaries, Jetmore and Cablevision, Ltd. Any use of the software by S T Enterprises or its subsidiaries would not receive any protection from §117.

The above arguments are coded as:

1) infringement

D: Any modifications made were valid under 17 U.S.C. §117 (adaptation for utilitarian purpose and archival purpose).
—Frame: use
—Theory: adaptation

J: §117 has only limited application here because modification in this case is allowed to the software for their own use only, and D's other companies and subsidiaries (not only the ones who purchased the software at first) used the modification (*Foresight v. Pfortmiller, Micro-spare v. Amtype*).
—Frame: use
—Theory: adaptation

Appendix IV

Table 1: Cases in Different Circuits

Circuit Courts	Frequency of Cases
1	5
2	16
3	13
4	9
5	11
6	3
7	13
8	2
9	30
10	6
11	4
12	0
D.C.	2
Federal	1
1	115

Table 2: Cases by Legal Topics

Topic of the Case	Frequency of Cases
Copyrightability	6
Infringement	22
Copyrightability+Infringement	75
Ownership	12
Total	115

Table 3: Cases in Different Time Periods

Time Periods	Frequency of Cases
1978–80	4
1981–83	28
1984–87	19
1988–90	31
1991–93	33
Total	115

Table 4: Cases by Subject Matters

Subject Matter of the Case	Frequency of Cases
Operating system programs	17
Application program	65
Video game programs	33
Total	115

Table 5: Cases by the Nature of the Plaintiffs

Nature of the Plaintiffs	Frequency of Cases
Developers	7
Copyright holders	30
Developers/copyright holders	77
Unclear	1
Total	115

Table 6: Cases by the Nature of the Defendants

Nature of the Defendants	Frequency of Cases
Developers	68
Copyright holders	18
Retailers, etc.	21
Copyright Registar	2
Unclear	6
Total	115

Table 7: Cases by the Nature of the Case

Nature of the Case	Frequency of Cases
Developers against developer	59
Developer against non-developer	24
Non-developer against any	32
Total	115

Table 8: Cases by Decisions on the Scope of Copyright Protection

Decisions (Scope)	Frequency of Cases
Limiting copyright protection	43
Expanding copyright protection	69
Only the ownership issue	3
Total	115

Table 9: Cases by Decisions on the Copyrightability of the Subject Matter

Decisions (Copyrightability)	Frequency of Cases
Copyrigthable	26
Not copyrightable	3
Total	29

Table 10: Cases by Decisions on Infringement

Decisions (Infringement)	Frequency of Cases
Infringement occurred	65
Infringement did not occur	42
Total	107

Table 11: Frames Used in the Judges' Arguments

Frames		Frequency of Cases
Work	Plaintiff	100
	Defendant	62
Authorship	Plaintiff	27
	Defendant	17
Use	by Defendant	36
	by the Public	14
	Market consequences	7
Total		261

Table 12: Frames Used in Different Time Periods

	Frames		
Time	Work	Authorship	Use
1978–83	55 (80%)	5 (7%)	9 (13%)
1984–87	34 (76%)	7 (16%)	4 (9%)
1988–90	31 (46%)	14 (21%)	23 (34%)
1991–93	42 (53%)	16 (20%)	21 (27%)
Total	162 (62%)	42 (16%)	57 (22%)

Table: 13: Contexts of the Arguments in Differnet Time Periods

	Contexts					
Time Periods	Copyright*	Owner	Valid	Similar	Express	Infringe
1978–83	25 (36%)	2 (3%)	9 (13%)	11 (16%)	8 (12%)	14 (20%)
1984–87	18 (40%)	2 (4%)	1 (2%)	14 (31%)	3 (7%)	7 (16%)
1988–90	14 (21%)	5 (7%)	7 (10%)	16 (24%)	2 (3%)	24 (35%)
1991–93	1 (1%)	8 (10%)	4 (5%)	13 (17%)	26 (33%)	27 (34%)
Total	58 (22%)	17 (7%)	21 (8%)	54 (21%)	39 (15%)	72 (28%)

* Copyright: Copyrightability
Owner: Ownership disputes
Valid: Validity of copyright in infringement cases
Similar: Substantial similarity in infringement cases
Express: Idea versus expression in infringement cases
Infringe: Copyright as infringing use in infringement cases

Table 14: The Use of Frames according to the Context of the Arguments

	Frames						
	Work		Authorship			Use	
Contexts	P*	D	P	D	D	Public	Market
Copyright	50 (86%)	—	—	7 (12%)	—	—	1 (2%)
Owner	—	—	8 (47%)	9 (53%)	—	—	—
Valid	12 (58%)	1 (5%)	4 (19%)	2 (10%)	—	2 (10%)	—
Similar	1 (2%)	48 (89%)	—	5 (9%)	—	—	—
Express	32 (82%)	2 (5%)	4 (10%)	1 (3%)	—	—	—
Infringe	5 (7%)	11 (15%)	2 (3%)	—)	36 (50%)	12 (17%)	6 (8%)
Total	100 (38%)	62 (24%)	25 (10%)	17 (7%)	36 (14%)	14 (5%)	7 (3%)

* P: Plaintiff's work or authorship
D: Defendant's work or authorship or use
Public: Public intrest
Market: Market consequences or innovation

References

Acuff-Rose Music v. Campbell, 754 F. Supp. 1150 (M.D.Tenn. 1991).

Adler, Amy M. "Post-Modem Art and the Death of Obscenity Law," 99 *Yale Law Journal*: 1359-1378, 1990.

Aldrich, Howard E. *Organizations and Environments*. New Jersey: Prentice-Hall, 1979.

The American Bench—Judges of the Nation. 6th ed. Sacramento, CA: Foster-Long, Inc., 1991/92.

Barrow, John Perry. "The Economics of Ideas," WIRED 2.03, 1997.

Behrens, Brian C. & Reuven R. Levary. "Legal Aspects – Software Reverse Engineering and Copyright: Past, Present and Future," 31 *John Marshall Law Review*: 1-18, 1997.

Benkler, Yochai. *Rules of the Road for the Information Superhighway: Electronic Communication and the Law*. West Publishing, 1996.

Benko, Robert P. *Protecting Intellectual Property Rights: Issues and Controversies*. Washington, D.C.: American Enterprise Institute for Public Policy Research, 1987.

Benson, J. Kenneth. "The Organizational Network as Political Economy," 20 *Administrative Science Quarterly*: 229-49, 1975.

Berger, P. L., & T. Luckman. *The Social Construction of Reality*. New York: Doubleday & Company, Inc., 1966.

Bettig, Ronald V. *The Impact of New Communications Technology on Filmed-Entertainment Copyrights*. Ph.D. Dissertation. University of Illinois, 1989.

Bettig, Ronald V. "Critical Perspectives on the History and Philosophy of Copyright," 9 *Critical Studies in Mass Communication*: 131-155, 1992.

BNA's Directory of State & Federal Courts, Judges, & Clerks. 4th ed., Washington, D.C.: The Bureau of National Affairs, Inc., 1992.

Boyle, James. "The Politics of Reason: Critical Legal Theory and Local Social Thought," 133 *University of Pennsylvania Law Review*: 685-780, 1985.

Boyle, James. "A Theory of Law and Information: Copyright, Spleens, Blackmail, and Insider Trading," 80 *California Law Review*. 1413-1540, 1992.

Branscomb, Anne Wells. "Computer Software: Protecting the Crown Jewels of the Information Economy," in *Intellectual Property Rights in Science, Technology, and Economic Performance: International Comparisons*, edited by Francis W. Rushing and Carole Ganz Brown. Boulder: Westview Press, 1990.

Breyer, Stephen. "The Unease Case For Copyright: A Study on Copyright in Books, Photocopies, and Computer Programs," 84 *Harvard Law Review*: 281-299, 1970.

Campbell v. Acuff-Rose Musci, Inc., 972 F.2d 1429 (6th Cir. 1992).

Campbell v. Acuff-Rose Music, Inc., 510 U.S. 569, 114 S. Ct. 1164, 127 L.Ed.2d 500 (1994).

Casper, Jonathan. "The Supreme Court and National Policy Making," 70 *American Political Science Review*: 50-63. 1976.

Cate, Fred H. "Law in Cyberspace," 39 *Howard Law Journal*: 565-578, 1996.

Chesler, Mark A., Joseph Sanders, and Debra S. Kalmuss. *Social Science in Court: Mobilizing Experts in the School Desegregation Cases*. Madison: The University of Wisconsin Press, 1988.

Chon, Margaret. "Postmodern "Progress": Reconsidering the Copyright and Patent Power," 43 *DePaul Law Review* 97-146, 1993.

Cohen, Felix S. "Transcendental Nonsense and the Functional Approach," 35 *Columbia Law Review*: 809-849, 1935.

Cohen, Ira J. "Structuration Theory and Social Praxis," in *Social Theory Today*, edited by Anthony Giddens and Jonathan H. Turner. Stanford: Stanford University Press, 1987.

Conrey, John M., and William M. O'Barr. *Rules versus Relationships*. Chicago: The University of Chicago Press, 1990.

Dahl, Robert. "Decision-Making in a Democracy: The Supreme Court as National Policy Maker," 6 *Journal of Public Law*: 277-295, 1957.

Daughtrey, S. Carran. "Reverse Engineering of Software for Interoperability and Analysis," 47 *Vanderbilt Law Review*: 145-187, 1994.

Drahos, Peter. "Thinking Strategically about Intellectual Property Rights," *Telecommunication Policy*, Vol. 21, No. 3: 201-211, 1977.

Dyson, Esther. "Intellectual Property On the Net," Release 1.0, 1997.

Edelman, Murray. *Constructing the Political Spectacle*. Chicago: University of Chicago Press, 1988.

Eisenstein, Elizabeth. *The Printing Revolution in Early Modern Europe*. New York: Cambridge University Press, 1983.

Elkin-Koren, Niva. "Cyberlaw and Social Change: A Democratic Approach to Copyright Law in Cyberspace," 14 *Cardozo Art & Entertainment Law Journal;* 215-295, 1996.

Foucault, Michel. "What Is an Author?," in *Textual Strategies: Perspectives in Post-Structural Criticism*, edited by J. Harari. New York: Cornell University Press, 1979.

Foucault, Michel. *Power/Knowledge: Selected Interviews and Other Writings, 1972-1977*, edited by Collin Gordon. New York: Pantheon Books, 1980.

Fraser, Nancy. "The Uses and Abuses of French Discourse Theory for Feminist Politics," 9 *Theory, Culture and Society*: 51-71, 1992.

Gage, Thomas M. "Whelan Associates v. Jaslow Dental Laboratories: Copyright Protection for Computer Software Structure-What's the Purpose?" 1987 *Wisconsin Law Review*: 859-894, 1987.

Gamson, W.A. "A Constructionist Approach to Mass Media and Public Opinion," 11 *Symbolic Interaction*: 161-174, 1988.

Gamson, W.A. & Lasch, K.E. "The Political Culture of Social Welfare Policy," in *Evaluating the Welfare State: Social and Political Perspectives*, edited by Simon. E. Spiro & Ephraim. Yuchtman-Yaar (pp. 397-415). New York: Academic Press, 1983.

Geller, Paul Edward. "Must Copyright Be For Ever Caught Between Marketplace and Authorship Norms?," in *Of Authors and Origins*, edited by Brad Sherman and Alain Strowel (pp. 159-202). Clarendon Press: Oxford, 1994.

Georgenson, Karen E. "Reverse Engineering of Copyrighted Software: Fair Use Or Misuse?," *5 Albany Law Journal of Science and Technology*: 291-320, 1996.

Giddens, Anthony. *Central Problems in Social Theory: Action, Structure, and Contradiction in Social Analysis*. Berkeley: University of California Press, 1979.

Giddens, Anthony. *The Constitution of Society*. Berkeley and Los Angeles: University of California Press, 1984.

Ginsburg, Jane C. "A Tale of Two Copyrights: Literary Property in Revolutionary France and America," in *Of Authors and Origins*, edited by Brad Sherman and Alain Strowel (pp. 131-158). Clarendon Press: Oxford, 1994.

Gitlin, Todd. *The Whole World is Watching: Mass Media in the Making and Unmaking of the News Left*. Berkeley: University of California Press, 1980.

Glick. Henry R. and Craig F. Emmert. "Stability and Change: Characteristics of State Supreme Court Judges," 70 *Judicature*: 107-112, 1986.

Godwin, Mike. *Cyber Rights*. New York: Times Books, 1998.

Goffman, Erving. *Frame Analysis: An Essay on the Organization of Experience*. Boston: Northwestern University Press, 1974.

Goldberg, Morton David. *Copyright Protection for Computer Software: A Summary of Authorities, with an Emphasis on Current Judicial Developments*. Washington, D.C.: Prentice Hall Law and Business and The U.S. Copyright Office, 1992.

Goldstein, Paul. *Copyright's Highway: The Law and Lore of Copyright from Gutenberg to the Celestial Jukebox*. Hill and Wang: New York, 1994.

Gordon, Robert W. "New Developments in Legal theory," in *Politics and Law*, edited by David Kairys. New York: Pantheon Books, 1982.

Gordon, Robert W. "Critical Legal Histories," 36 *Stanford Law Review*: 1-2, 1984.

Harger, Christopher W. "Apples & Orages: Reverse Engineering as a Fair Use After Atari v. Nintendo and Sega v. Accolade," 20 *Rutgers Computer Technology Lawe Journal*: 259-327, 1994.

Hall, Stuart. "Encoding/Decoding." in *Culture, Media, Language: Working Papers in Cultural Studies*, edited by Stuart Hall, D. Hebson, A Lowe, and P. Willis. London: Hutchinson, 1980.

Hall, Stuart. "The Rediscovery of 'Ideology': Return of the Repressed in Media Studies," in *Culture, Society, and the Media*, edited by Michael Gurevitch et. al. London & New York: Methen, 1982.

Ignatin, Gary R. "Let the Hackers Hack: Allowing the Reverse Engineering of Copyrighted Computer Programs to Achieve Compatibility," 140 *University of Pennsylvania Law Review*: 1999-2050, 1992.

Information Infrastructure Task Force, *Intellectual Property and the National Information Infrastructure: The Report of the Working Group on Intellectual Property Rights*, Sep. 1995.

Jaszi, Peter. "Toward a Theory of Copyright: The Metamorphoses of 'Authorship'," 1991 *Duke Law Journal*: 455-502, 1991.

Jaszi, Peter. "On the Author Effect: Contemporary Copyright and Collective Creativity," in *The Construction of Authorship*, edited by Martha Woodmansee and Peter Jaszi. Duke University Press: Durham and London, 1994.

Johnson, Virginia A. "Byte After Byte, The Courts Nibble Away at Copyright Protection of Software," 10 *Georgia State University Law Review*: 543-587, 1994.

Kairys, David. "Introduction," in *Politics and Law*, edited by David Kairys. New York: Pantheon Books, 1982.

Kaplan, Benjamin. *An Unhurried View of Copyright*. New York: Columbia University Press, 1967.

Katsh, M. Ethan. *The Electronic Media and the Transformation of Law*. New York: Oxford University Press, 1989.

Knoke, David, and James R. Wood. *Organized for Action: Commitment in Voluntary Associations*. New Jersey: Rutgers University Press, 1981.

Landes, W. and R. Posner. "An Economic Analysis of Copyright Law," 18 *Journal of Legal Studies*: 325-363, 1989.

Liebowitz, J. "Copying and Indirect Appropriability: Photocopying of Journals," *Journal of Political Economy* 93: 945-957, 1985.

Lauman, Edward O., and David Knoke. *The Organizational State: Social Choice in National Policy Domains*. Madison: The University of Wisconsin Press, 1987.

Locke, John. *Two Treatises of Government*. New York: Hafner Press, 1947.

McManus, John. "How Objective is Local Television News?," 18 *Mass Comm Review*: 21-30, 1991.

Mahon, James. "A Commentary on Proposals for Copyright Protection on the National Information Infrastructure," 22 *Rutgers Computer & Technology Law Journal*: 233-266, 1996.

Majone, G. *Evidence, Argument and Persuasion in the Policy Process*. New Haven: Yale University Press, 1989.

Miliband, Ralph. *The State in Capitalist Society: An Analysis of the Western System of Power*. Chicago: University of Chicago Press, 1969.

Miliband, Ralph. "The Capitalist State: Reply to Nicos Poulantzas," 59 *New Left Review*: 53-59. 1970.

Nagel, Stuart. "Political Party Affiliation and Judges' Decisions," 55 *American Political Science Review*: 843-850, 1961.

Novos, I., & M. Waldman. "The Effects of Increased Copyright Protection: An Analytic Approach," 92 *Journal of Political Economy*: 236-246, 1984.

Office of Technology Assessment, Congress of the United States. *Intellectual Property Rights in an Age of Electronics and Information.* 1986.

Office of Technology Assessment, Congress of the United States. *Critical Connections: Communication for the Future.* 1990.

Office of Technology Assessment, Congress of the United States. *Finding a Balance: Computer Software, Intellectual Property and the Challenge of Technological Change.* 1992.

Olsen, Frances. "Feminism and Critical Legal Theory: An American Perspective," 18 *International Journal of the Sociology of Law*: 199-215, 1990.

Pfeffer, Jeffrey. "Size and Composition of Corporate Boards of Directors: The Organization and its Environment," 17 *Administrative Science Quarterly*: 218-228, 1972.

Parsons, Patrick R. "Defining Cable Television: Structuring and Public Policy," 39 *Journal of Communication*: 10-26, 1989.

Parsons, Talcott. Societies: *Evolutionary and Comparative Perspectives.* New Jersey: Prentice-Hall, 1966.

Patterson, L. Ray, and Stanley W. Lindberg. *The Nature of Copyright: A Law of Users' Rights.* Athens and London: The University of Georgia Press, 1991.

Ploman, Edward W., and L. Clark Hamilton. *Copyright: Intellectual Property in the Information Age.* London, Boston and Henley: Routledge & Kegan Paul, 1980.

Poulantzas, Nicos. "The Problem of the Capitalist State," 58 *New Left Review*: 67-78, 1969.

Religious Technology v. Netcom, 907 F. Supp. 1361 (1995).

Samuelson, Pamela, and John Browning. "Netizen," WIRED 5.03, 1997.

Samuelson, Pamela, Randell Davis, Mitchell D. Kapor, and J. H. Reichman. "A Manifesto Concerning the Legal Protection of Computer Programs," 94 *Columbia Law Review*: 2308-2431, 1994.

Santos, Boaventura De Sousa. "Law: A Map of Misreading: Toward a Postmodern Conception of Law," 14 *Journal of Law and Society*: 279-302, 1987.

Sherman, Brad, and Alain Strowel (eds.). *Of Authors and Origins*. Clarendon Press: Oxford, 1994.

Snow, David A., and Robert Benford. "Ideology, Frame Resonance, and Participant Mobilization," *International Social Movement Research*, Vol. 1:197-217, 1988.

Streeter, Thomas. "Beyond Freedom of Speech and the Public Interest: The Relevance of Critical Legal Studies to Communications Policy," 40 *Journal of Communication*: 43-63, 1990.

Streeter, Thomas. "The Cable Fable Revisited: Discourse, Policy, and the Making of Cable Television," 4 *Critical Studies in Mass Communication*: 174-200, 1987.

Takeyama, L. "The Welfare Implications of Unauthorized Reproduction of Intellectual Property in the Presence of Demand Network Externalities," 42 *Journal of Industrial Economics*: 155-166, 1994.

Takeyama, L. "The Intertemporal Consequences of Unauthorized Reproduction of Intellectual Property," 15 *Journal of Law and Economics*: 511-522, 1997.

Tapscott, Don. *The Digital Economy*. New York: McGraw Hill, 1996.

Teter, Tomothy S. "Merger and the Machines: An Analysis of the Pro-Compatibility Trend in Computer Software Copyright Cases," 45 *Stanford Law Review*: 1061-1098, 1993.

Tuchman, G. *Making News: A Study in the Construction of Reality*. New York: Free Press, 1978.

Ulmer, Sidney. "The Political Party Variable in the Michigan Supreme Court," 11 *Journal of Public Law*: 352-362, 1962.

Unger, Roberto Mangaberia. *The Critical Legal Studies Movement*. Cambridge and London: Harvard University Press, 1983.

van Dijk, Teun. A. *News as Discourse*. New Jersey: Lawrence Publishers, 1990.

Varian, H. "Buying, Sharing and Renting Information Goods," *unpublished manuscript*, 1997.

Williams, John A. "Can Reverse Engineering of Software Ever Be Fair Use? Application of Campbell's 'Transformative Use' Concept," 71 *Washington Law Review*: 255-283, 1996.

Woodmansee, Martha. "On the Author Effect: Recovering Collectivity," in *The Construction of Authorship*, edited by Martha Woodmansee and Peter Jaszi. Durham and London: Duke University Press, 1994.

Woodmansee, Martha, and Peter Jaszi (eds.). *The Construction of Authorship*. Durham and London: Duke University Press, 1994.

Wren, Christopher G., and Jill Robinson Wren. *The Legal Research Manual: A Game Plan for Legal Research and Analysis*. Madison: A-R Editions, Inc., 1983.

Index